Linux Shell
Scripting with Bash

Linux Shell Scripting with Bash

Ken O. Burtch

Sams Publishing, 800 East 96th Street, Indianapolis, Indiana 46240

Linux Shell Scripting with Bash

International Standard Book Number: 0-672-32642-6

Library of Congress Catalog Card Number: 2003112582

Printed in the United States of America

First Printing: February 2004

07   6   5

Trademarks

Warning and Disclaimer

Bulk Sales

Sams Publishing offers excellent discounts on this book when ordered in quantity for bulk purchases or special sales. For more information, please contact

U.S. Corporate and Government Sales
1-800-382-3419
corpsales@pearsontechgroup.com

For sales outside of the U.S., please contact

International Sales
international@pearsoned.com

Acquisitions Editor
Scott Meyers

Managing Editor
Charlotte Clapp

Project Editor
Elizabeth Finney

Copy Editor
Kezia Endsley

Indexer
Ken Johnson

Proofreader
Leslie Joseph

Technical Editor
John Traenkenschuh

Publishing Coordinator
Vanessa Evans

Multimedia Developer
Dan Scherf

Designer
Gary Adair

Page Layout
Brad Chinn
Susan Geiselman

❖

To F. Ray Skilton

Professor and Author

Who taught me more about computers over tea

than I ever learned in a lecture hall.

❖

Contents at a Glance

Table of Contents

About the Author

Ken Burtch graduated with a Computer Science first class honors degree from Brock University in St. Catharines, Canada, and did his Masters work at Queen's University in Kingston, Canada. He has been using Linux since version 0.97, at a time before Linux was popular. He is the founder of PegaSoft Canada (`http://www.pegasoft.ca`), an association that promotes Linux advocacy, education, and development in southern Ontario. He has worked with a number of companies, including Mackenzie Financial Corporation, one of Canada's largest mutual fund companies. Ken is an active member of the Writers' Circle of Durham Region and his award-winning short story, "Distance," was recently published in the "Signatures" anthology (ISBN 0973210001).

Acknowledgments

You're reading the acknowledgements? Excellent!

Technical books today can go from first word to press in as little as four months. This project took more than two years to complete, painstakingly researched and carefully developed. If this book seems different from other titles on your bookshelf, there's good reason for it and a lot of good people behind it.

In the summer of 1999, I talked with Michael Slaughter at Addison-Wesley publishing about writing a series of Linux books. Because Linux begins with Bash, Bash would be the topic of my first book. So if you've been dying for a good Bash book, thank Michael.

Lawrence Law, a Unix programmer who's worked both sides of the Pacific, offered practical tips for keeping the book fresh and interesting, while debating the existence of God and competent IT management.

Chris Browne, Linux author and speaker, took time out from maintaining the .org and .info domains to give much needed advice on getting published. A big thanks for fitting me in between TLUG and Postgres.

Chris Johnson took time away from chess tournaments and writing Bash algorithms to question all aspects of my research. I haven't seen him since we discussed this book, but I imagine he'll show up to a PegaSoft meeting to collect a signed copy soon enough.

When Addison-Wesley was taken over by Prentice Hall, the manuscript bounced around until it fell into the inbox of Katie Mohr at Sams Publishing. If you're glad this book is in your hands, buy her a coffee. She was the one who pitched it to the People Who Make the Choice.

If you're thinking "cool" and "I need this book on my shelf," you're not the first. That honor goes to the early reviewers of the manuscript, the ones who persuaded the powers that be that this book was gold. I don't have your names, but I read your comments.

Scott Meyers, Senior Development Editor, has left the manuscript primarily as he received it. If you like the book, email Scott and tell him he made the right choice not to mess with a Good Thing.

I never figured out exactly what Elizabeth Finney, the Production Editor, does. But her title has "production" in it, so she must be very important. Probably a wealthy supermodel who graduated from Harvard and is a presidential advisor. Say, Liz, if you're interested in balding Linux geeks, give me a call.

Because I'm from Canada, Kezia Endsley, the copy editor, was responsible for squashing every extraneous "u," hacking every "which" to "that," and making sure that zed's were all pummeled to zee's. So little escaped her eye that I think I'll have her look over my income tax next year.

John Traenkenschuh, the Tech Editor and Chief Guru, ran every single example in this book to make sure no last-minute bugs made it into print. Are you still wondering, John, why Linus is Finnish but "Linux" is pronounced with a Swedish accent? There are more things in heaven and Earth, John, than are dreamt of in your philosophy.

And thanks to you, the reader, for taking the time to find out why this book is different. If you want to see more books of this caliber, contact Sams Publishing and let them know what you think.

—Ken O. Burtch
November 2003

We Want to Hear from You!

As the reader of this book, *you* are our most important critic and commentator. We value your opinion and want to know what we're doing right, what we could do better, what areas you'd like to see us publish in, and any other words of wisdom you're willing to pass our way.

You can email or write me directly to let me know what you did or didn't like about this book—as well as what we can do to make our books stronger.

Please note that I cannot help you with technical problems related to the topic of this book, and that due to the high volume of mail I receive, I might not be able to reply to every message.

When you write, please be sure to include this book's title and author as well as your name and phone or email address. I will carefully review your comments and share them with the author and editors who worked on the book.

Email: opensource@samspublishing.com
Mail: Mark Taber
         Associate Publisher
         Sams Publishing
         800 East 96th Street
         Indianapolis, IN 46240 USA

Reader Services

For more information about this book or others from Sams Publishing, visit our Web site at www.samspublishing.com. Type the ISBN (excluding hyphens) or the title of the book in the Search box to find the book you're looking for.

Introduction
COSC 101

Most senior students who supervised introductory computer science labs at Brock University back when I was there kicked their feet up on the front desk with a calculus book cracked open and growled when their homework was interrupted by a question. As anyone will tell you, I never fit the mold of the typical student. In my first lab, I put together a short booklet covering all the questions I had when I took my first lab in COSC 101; namely what was that funny prompt drawn in flickering green on the ailing terminals and how the heck can you use it to give yourself a cool nickname like VAX Dude in the DEC VMS process?

I inadvertently left a pile of my booklets behind and the next day one of the other supervisors stomped up to me and angrily waved one in my face. Her class wanted to know why she hadn't covered any of the material in the booklet. Doing an introductory lesson in shell usage in the first lab would have cut into her homework time, and I had better make sure it did not happen again. It didn't, and my lab students gained about a three-week advantage over the others in view of the fact they didn't have to learn the development environment piecemeal between assignments.

Many books, and many teachers, try to separate computer languages from the environment in which they run. That's like talking about cooking an egg without indicating whether the egg will be cooked in a microwave oven, fried in a frying pan, or boiled in a pot of water. The environment affects what you can do and how you can do it. This is also true with shells.

So don't let a disgruntled supervisor prevent you from getting your feet grounded in the fundamentals. Like my first-year lab booklet, this chapter provides background information on where the *Bourne Again Shell* came from and why it was developed. Shell programming has its own unique mindset and a quick review is never a waste of time.

Notation Used in This Book

The following standard notations have been adopted for this book for introducing new terms, describing command syntax, and so forth.

- *Italics* emphases points in the text and new terms
- A `non-proportional font` represents sample Bash scripts, commands, switches, filenames, and directories

- Bash is an acronym but is written without all capitals for readability
- Control-K represents a key combination created by holding down the Ctrl key and then pressing the K key before releasing the Ctrl key
- The Return key refers to the carriage return key, marked Return or Enter depending on your keyboard
- A `non-proportional italic` font indicates a value to be substituted with the appropriate text. For example, in `-o file`, the word `file` should be substituted with the appropriate file for the switch.

The Origin of Bash

A *shell* is a program that runs operating system commands. Using a conventional desktop, the user selects an item with the mouse and then applies an action to it, such as highlighting an icon and choosing to copy it. In a shell, the person types instructions (or actions) followed by the targets and any special options. This counterintuitive interface can confuse new users who are used to conventional desktops.

The first Unix shell was the developed by Steven R. Bourne in 1974 for the Seventh Edition of Unix. Called the Bourne shell (or *sh*) in honor of its creator, it set the standard for Unix shells, including the default dollar sign ($) prompt common to most shells.

Users frequently had to type the same commands over and over again. Writing a program to repeat their commands required a high-level language like C. Instead, it was useful to compose a list of commands for the shell to execute, as if the shell was following a well-rehearsed script. With the addition of features to make simple decisions and loops, these *shell scripts* could run commands and determine whether they succeeded or failed, taking appropriate action, without resorting to a different language. When commands are combined in new ways in a script, a script conceptually becomes a new command. Scripts can customize and extend operating systems.

Designed to be as small and as open as possible, any feature that did not have to be built into the shell wasn't. Even arithmetic was performed by other programs outside of the shell. This slowed the shell, but speed was not an important factor when the shell spent most of its time waiting on other programs or on the user. To the shell's advantage, if a user needed new or better capabilities, the user could write additional scripts to provide those additional capabilities.

Many rival shells began to appear, offering improvements in speed and capabilities. Two of the most common successors were *csh*, a shell loosely based on the C language, and the Korn shell (*ksh*), an improved Bourne shell developed by David G. Korn. Shell designers incorporated commands into the shell for better speed and portability and to make the shells easier to work with. Successful features were freely copied between shells as they matured.

An enhanced version of the Bourne shell was developed as part of the GNU project used by the Linux operating system. The shell was called Bash (for the pun "Bourne

Again Shell"). This shell was compatible with the original shell created by Steven R. Bourne, but included many enhancements. It was also compliant with the POSIX standard for shells.

Bash is the standard shell provided with most Linux distributions, including Red Hat, SuSE, Mandrake, Slackware, and UnitedLinux.

When Is a Program a Shell Script?

A script is similar to a program but there is no formal definition for what constitutes a script. It is a type of simple program, and scripts and programs share many features in common. Linux programmers with few special requirements never advance beyond writing shell scripts.

As shells matured, they gained many features that you might not expect to find in a program designed to schedule commands. Most shells, including Bash, can perform bit manipulation, string processing, and TCP/IP connections. They have typed variables, built-in commands, and user-defined functions. The distinction between shells and programming languages has become blurred.

In general, there are two key differences between shell scripts and more complex programs. First, shells are designed to handle short, simple tasks. They lack the rigid structure and semantic checking of a high-level language. Shell scripts can be written quickly because they assume the programmer knows what he or she is doing, and for short scripts, this is usually true. Second, shells always execute their scripts slowly. Although most shells perform some kind of pre-processing to speed up execution, they still interpret and carry out one line at time. High-level languages are faster because they almost always translate a program into machine language to gain the best performance.

When tackling any programming problem, it's essential to choose the right tool for the job. Developing large projects as shell scripts will mean your project will run slowly and be difficult to maintain. Developing scripts in a high-level language will lead to a longer and more costly development time.

The Necessity of Structured Shell Programming

Shell scripts remain a staple of the business world. With high development costs, it is not practical to develop everything in a high-level language. Many business processes are simply a matter of following a series of steps, after which the results are labeled and archived. This is the very type of activity scripts are made to handle.

Over time, shells have collected new features, often by copying the capabilities of other shells. In his book, *The Humane Interface,* Apple Macintosh interface designer Jef Raskin once spoke with a pilot regarding the design of the plane's autopilot. The device was designed with five ways to enter coordinates. The reason for this design was to reduce training costs by emulating other autopilots. However, a pilot pointed out that the operator of the aircraft is responsible for knowing how to operate every piece of equipment, and that meant he had to know how to adjust the autopilot in each of the five ways.

Many shells, including Bash, have developed a mixture of features with specialized or arcane applications. Like the autopilot, it is not always clear how these features should be used nor which features are provided primarily for compatibility. Too often, poorly designed scripts are all-but illegible to another programmer, or even to the same programmer a few months after a script was hastily assembled.

This presents a problem for serious business scripts. The cost of developing a high-level language solution is high, but a disorganized shell script can be expensive to maintain over time. As the needs of the business change, and the shell script is modified by successive generations of programmers, the problem escalates.

As a rule of thumb, business programs never go away. At one place I recently worked, what started off as a simple shell script used to print reports gradually evolved into a Web-based reporting system complete with personal customizations and secure access. The original programmer had no idea what his script would become.

Because of the essential openness and complex syntax of Bash, it's to the benefit of any serious project to adapt some kind of standard. Bash is very forgiving, but the costs are not. For example, there are many ways to add 2 + 2 in Bash. Like the autopilot anecdote, it's not practical to expect the programmers who maintain the scripts to have to deal with this kind of redundancy.

Likewise, shell word quoting is sometimes optional, sometimes required, depending on the context. A command that works with one form of quotation can suddenly stop working when different data appears in the quotes.

Issues like shell word quoting, specialized capabilities, or portability features, when abused, can lead to increased maintenance and long-term development costs.

Installing Bash

Bash is the standard shell on most Linux distributions. However, there are other Linux shells available and there's no requirement that Bash should be present on any particular distribution.

The Bash shell is open source software released under the GNU Pubic License (GPL). If you need to install Bash, the C language source code is freely available from the Free Software Foundation at `http://www.gnu.org` or through one of its download mirrors.

The Bash installation procedure can vary over time. Complete instructions are found in the README file that accompanies the sources. However, the installation is largely automated. The basic procedure is as follows:

1. Run the `configure` program to determine your operating system and verify the features necessary to compile Bash.

2. Run `make` to build Bash.

3. Run `make tests`. This will run diagnostic tests to ensure Bash was built properly.

4. Run `make install` to install Bash under the `/usr/local/` subdirectory.

Assuming your PATH variable is set correctly, you can start Bash by typing bash at the shell prompt.

If you do not have superuser privileges on your computer, you can still compile and install Bash under your personal account. Use the –prefix option with configure to specify the directory to install Bash in. For example, –prefix=$HOME or –prefix=$HOME/bash might be good choices.

Bash and Other Scripting Tools

Ksh, Perl, and Python are similar, but not identical, to Bash.

The *Korn shell* (*ksh*) is an enhanced version of the Bourne shell. A public domain version exists called *pdksh*. Korn shell is a popular shell on many commercial Unix systems. Most, but not all, of the Korn shell's features work under Bash. Both shells can do bitwise arithmetic, for example. Some features have different names. The Korn shell built-in print command is a rough equivalent to the Bash printf command, and the Korn shell whence command is equivalent to the type command. A complete list of differences and porting issues is available in the Bash FAQ at http://www.faqs.org/faqs/unix-faq/shell/bash/.

Perl (Practical Extraction and Report Language) is, as its name suggests, a scripting language for generating reports. It combines the features of a shell language, the sed command, and the awk command to create a single tool. It is not a shell and Perl scripts are not compatible with Bash.

Python (named after the "Monty Python" comedy troupe) is an interpreted language designed for small projects needing rapid development. It is not a shell, but like Bash, it contains many features designed for interactive sessions. Python scripts are not compatible with Bash.

1

The Linux Environment

IN THE EARLY DAYS OF COMPUTERS, instructions and data were often divided into two separate storage areas. Modern computers follow what is called a "von Neumann architecture," a design proposed by the Hungarian-born computer scientist John von Neumann. These machines have one storage area for both data and instructions. Effectively, instructions and data were treated the same, making computer simpler to build and use.

Unix-based operating systems, including Linux, extend this principle to long-term storage. Linux organizes information on a disk as a collection of files. Every file, whether a program or data, is treated the same, making the operating system very simple to build as well as flexible to use. Commands that work on a certain kind of file tend to have a similar effect on other kinds of files as well, thus reducing the number of commands a programmer needs to learn.

This chapter presents an overview of the Linux operating system, including how it is organized and its common conventions. If you are new to Linux, you are not expected to understand all the terms presented here. After this foundation, future chapters demonstrate these principles using practical examples.

The Origin of Linux

The Linux operating system was created as a hobby by a young student, Linus Torvalds, at the University of Helsinki in Finland. Linus, interested in the Unix clone operating system Minix, wanted to create an expanded version of Minix with more capabilities. He began his work in 1991 when he released version 0.02 and invited programmers to participate in his project. Version 1.0 was released in 1994.

Linux uses GNU General Public License (GPL) and its source code is freely available to everyone. Linux *distributions*, CD-ROMs with the Linux kernel and other software ready for installation, do not have to be free, but the Linux source code must remain available. Making source code available is known as distributing *open source*.

The word "Linux" is properly pronounced using a Swedish accent, making it difficult to say in North America. It is most often pronounced with a short "i" and with the first syllable stressed, as in LIH–nicks, but it is sometimes pronounced LYE–nicks (the angli-cized "Linus' Unix") or LEE–nucks.

Strictly speaking, Linux refers to the operating system kernel that starts and manages other programs and provides access to system resources. The various open source shells, compilers, standard libraries, and commands are a part of another project called GNU. The GNU project was started by the Free Software Foundation (FSF) as an attempt to create a free version of Unix. The main Linux C compiler, gcc, is a part of the GNU project.

There is also a GNU kernel project, but the Linux kernel has largely superseded this effort.

X Windows is also not strictly a part of Linux. Xfree86, the open source version of X Windows, was adapted to the Linux operating system and was released under a different license.

Files and File Systems

Each Linux disk (or other long-term block storage device) contains a collection of files organized according to a policy or set of rules called a *file system*. Each disk can be divid-ed into *partitions* (or "slices"), whereby every partition has its own file system. Linux is not restricted to a single file system for all disks: the user can use disks created by other operating systems as if they were native Linux disks.

The standard file system is the second extended file system, or *ext2*. This is the second revision of the Minix file system with support for large disk sizes and filenames. ext2 permits partitions up to 4TB (terabytes), files up to 2GB (gigabytes), and 255-character filenames. Newer distributions use *ext3*, a version of ext2 with special features for error recovery.

Support for other file systems might be available depending on your distribution and installation options. They might include Microsoft Windows NT, Apple HFS, or journal-ing file systems.

The ext2 file system uses caching to increase performance. If an ext2 disk is not properly shut down, files can be corrupted or lost. It is vitally important that a Linux computer is shut down properly or is protected by some kind of uninterruptible power supply.

To save space, ext2 files that contain large amounts of zeros (called *sparse files*) are not actually stored on a disk. Certain shell commands provide options for creating and han-dling sparse files.

Each file is identified by a name, and the allowed names are determined by the file system. For practicality, the names seldom exceed 32 characters and usually consist of lowercase characters, underscores, minus signs, and periods. Spaces and punctuation sym-bols, for example, are permitted, but can cause problems in shell scripts that do not expect them.

Filenames do not require a suffix to identify their contents, but they are often used to avoid confusion about what data is contained in files. Some common suffix codes include:

- .sh—A Bash shell script
- .txt—A generic text file
- .log—A log file
- .html—A HTML Web page
- .tgz (or .tar.gz)—Compressed file archive

Commands usually have no suffix.

Directories

Shell scripts, text files, and executable commands and other normal files are collectively referred to as *regular files*. They contain data that can be read or instructions that can be executed. There are also files that are not regular, such as directories or named pipes; they contain unique data or have special behaviors when they are accessed.

Files are organized into *directories*, or listings of files. Like all other files in Linux, a directory is also treated as a file. Each directory can, in turn, contain subdirectories, creating hierarchical listings.

Directories are organized into a single monolithic tree. The top-most directory is called the *root directory*. Unlike some other operating systems that have separately labeled disks, Linux treats any disk drives as subdirectories within the main directory structure. From a user's point of view, it's impossible to tell which disk a particular directory belongs to: Everything appears as if it belongs to a single disk.

A *pathname* is a string that identifies the location of a particular file, the sequences of directories to move through to find it. The root directory is denoted by a forward slash (/) character, and so /payroll.dat represents a file named payroll.dat, located in the top-most directory. Using more directory names and forward slashes can specify additional directories.

When users log in, they are placed in a personal directory called their *home directory*. By convention, Linux home directories are located under the directory /home. The pathname /home/jgulbis/payroll.dat indicates a file named payroll.dat in the home directory of the user jgulbis. The home directory is represented by a tilde (~) in Bash.

The *current directory* (or *working directory*) is denoted by a period (.). When a pathname doesn't start with a leading slash, Bash assumes it's a path relative to the current directory. ./payroll.dat and payroll.dat both refer to a file named payroll.txt in the current directory. When running programs, this might not be true. This exception is discussed in the next chapter.

The *parent directory* is represented by a double period (..). The double period can be used at any place in a path to move towards the root of the directory tree, effectively canceling the previously mentioned directory in a path. However, it makes the most sense to use the double period as the first directory in a path. If your current directory is /home/jgulbis, the pathname ../kburtch/payroll.dat is the same as the pathname /home/kburtch/payroll.dat. The double period represents the parent directory of /home/jgulbis, the /home directory.

Pathnames without a beginning slash are called *relative paths* because they specify the location of a file in comparison to the current directory. Relative paths are useful for representing files in your current directory or subdirectories of your current directory.

Pathnames with a beginning slash are called *absolute paths*. Absolute paths describe the location of a file in relationship to the root directory. No matter where your current directory is, absolute paths always identify the file precisely. Absolute paths are useful when locating common files that are always stored in the same place.

There are no set rules governing where files are located, and their placement is chosen by your Linux distribution. Early variations of Unix stored standard programs in /bin, home directories in /usr, and programs specific to a computer in /usr/bin. As the number and type of programs grew, the number and function of the common directories changed.

Most Linux distributions include the following directories:

- /dev—Contains device drivers
- /bin and /usr/bin—Contains standard Linux commands
- /lib and /usr/lib—Contains standard Linux libraries
- /var—Contains configuration and log files
- /etc—Contains default configuration files
- /usr/local/bin—Contains commands not a part of the distribution, added by your administrator
- /opt—Contains commercial software
- /tmp—Stores temporary files
- /sbin and /usr/sbin—Contains system administration commands (/sbin stands for "safe" bin)

Inodes and Links

Normally, each file is listed in a single directory. Linux can create additional listings for a single file. These shortcuts are called *links* and can refer to any kind of file.

Links come in two varieties. A *hard link* is a reference to another file in the current directory or a different directory. Whenever some action is performed to the hard link, it is actually done to the file the hard link refers to. Hard links are accessed quickly because they do not have to be *dereferenced*, but Linux limits where a hard link can be placed. As long as a file is being referred to by at least one directory entry, it won't be deleted. For example, if a file has one hard link, both the link and the original file have to be deleted to remove the file.

The second and more common link is the *symbolic link*. This link is a file that contains the pathname of another file. Unlike hard links, symbolic links have no restrictions on where they can be used. They are slower and some commands affect the link file itself instead of the file the link points to. Symbolic links are not "hard" because they have to be dereferenced: When Linux opens the symbolic link file, it reads the correct pathname and opens that file instead. When the file being referred to is deleted, the symbolic link file becomes a *dangling link* to a non-existent file.

Using links means that two different pathnames can indicate the same file. To identify a particular file, Linux assigns a number to each file. This number is called the *inode* (or "index node") and is unique to any storage device. If two pathnames refer to a file with the same inode, one of the paths is a hard link.

In the ext2 file system, there is a limited number of inodes, which in turn places an upper limit to the number of files that can be stored on a disk. The number of inodes compared to the amount of disk space is called the *inode density*. The density is specified when a disk or partition is initialized. Most Linux distributions use an inode density of 4K, or one node per every 4096 bytes of disk space.

Pipe and Socket Files

Pipe files are a special kind of file shared between two programs. The file acts as a buffer for sharing information. One program writes to the pipe file and the other reads from the pipe. When the pipe file reaches a certain size, Linux halts the writing program until the reading program can "catch up."

A similar kind of file is called a Unix domain *socket file*. A socket file acts like a pipe but works using network sockets. However, this kind of file is not easily used in shell scripts and it won't be covered in this book.

Device Files

The last common kind of nonregular file is a *device file*. Keeping with the file-oriented design of Linux, devices are represented by files. Device files allow direct communication to a particular device attached to a computer. There are actually two kinds of device files, but shell programmers are mainly interested in the type called *character device files*.

All devices files are located in the /dev directory. Even though many files are listed in /dev, not all of these devices might actually be present. Rather, /dev contains a list of devices that can be attached to your computer because the Linux kernel was configured to recognize them if they were attached.

Most of these files are not accessible to regular users, but there are a few that are open to general use. One important device file available to all users is /dev/null. This file represents an imaginary "black hole" device attached to your computer that consumes anything sent to it. This is useful for discarding unwanted responses from a shell command. /dev/null can also be read, but the file is always empty.

Another device file is /dev/zero. This file contains an endless stream of zeros, and can be used to create new files that are filled entirely with zeros.

There are a variety of other devices that might appear in /dev, depending on your distribution and computer hardware. Common device files include:

- `/dev/tty`—The terminal window (or console) your program is running under
- `/dev/dsp`—The interface that plays AU sound files on your sound card
- `/dev/fd0`—The first floppy drive
- `/dev/hda1`—The first IDE drive partition
- `/dev/sda1`—The first SCSI drive partition

The name `tty`, for historical reasons, is a short form of "teletypewriter," a printer and keyboard connected to a computer by a cable.

With this overview of the Linux philosophy, you are ready to begin using Linux through the Bash shell.

2

Operating the Shell

ONE DAY MY FATHER WAS WORKING on the electrical wiring on his pontoon boat. He worked for several hours without success. No matter what he tried, he couldn't get his running lights to work. Frustrated, he turned the light switch off... and the lights came on.

This chapter is a brief overview of how to use the shell in an interactive session at the Bash command prompt. Like my father and his wiring problem, understanding how commands work at the fundamental, interactive level is important before digging into the intricacies of scripts. That is, unless you like unexpected surprises.

Bash Keywords

A *keyword* is a word or symbol that has a special meaning to a computer language. The following symbols and words have special meanings to Bash when they are unquoted and the first word of a command.

!	esac	select	}
case	fi	then	[[
do	for	until	]]
done	function	while	
elif	if	time	
else	in	{	

Unlike most computer languages, Bash allows keywords to be used as variable names even though this can make scripts difficult to read. To keep scripts understandable, keywords should not be used for variable names.

Command Basics

The commands that can be typed at the Bash shell prompt are usually Linux programs stored externally on your file system. Some commands are built into the shell for speed, standardization, or because they can function properly only when they are built-in.

No matter what their source, commands fall into a number of informal categories. *Utilities* are general-purpose commands useful in many applications, such as returning the date or counting the number of lines in a file.

Filters are commands that take the results of one command and modify them in some way, such as removing unwanted lines or substituting one word for another. Many commands act as filters under the right circumstances.

To execute a command, type it at the Bash command prompt. The prompt is usually a $, but often Linux distributions customize it to something else. S.u.S.E., for example, uses a > command prompt.

The `date` command prints the current date and time on the screen.

```
$ date
Wed Apr  4 10:44:52 EDT 2001
```

All files, including shell commands, are case-sensitive. By convention, all shell commands are in lowercase.

```
$ DATE
bash: DATE: command not found
```

Arguments are additional information supplied to a command to change its behavior. The `date` command takes a format argument to change the appearance of the date and time.

```
$ date '+%H:%M'
10:44
```

Switches (also called "options" or "flags") are characters proceeded by a minus sign that enable command features. To see the date in Coordinated Universal Time (UTC, formerly called GMT), use the `-u` switch.

```
$ date -u
Wed Apr  4 14:46:41 UTC 2001
```

Because the terms "options" and "flags" are used in so many contexts, they are referred to as switches in this book.

Switches and arguments are collectively called *parameters*. Some commands allow any number of parameters or have parameters that can be arranged in complex ways.

The GNU and Linux convention is for longer, more readable options to be proceeded by a double minus sign. The longer equivalent to the `-u` switch is `--universal`.

```
$ date --universal
Wed Apr  4 14:46:41 UTC 2001
```

The long switches remind the reader exactly what the switch does. This makes future debugging of shell scripts much easier because there is no standard convention for the short switches across Linux commands. Most Linux commands recognize the long switches `--help`, `--verbose`, and `--version`.

Comments can be added to the end of any command or they can be typed on a line by themselves. Comments are denoted with a number sign (#).

```
$ date --universal # show the date in UTC format
```

Built-in Bash commands and most other GNU software treat -- as a special switch that indicates the end of a list of switches. This can be used when one of the arguments starts with a minus sign.

Command-Line Editing

There are special key combinations to edit what you type or to repeat previous commands.

Bash has two editing modes. These modes emulate the keys used in two popular Linux text editors. *Vi mode* mimics the vi and vim editors. *Emacs mode* works like emacs, nano or pico.

The current editing mode can be checked with the shopt command. shopt -o emacs is on if you are in emacs mode. shopt -o vi is on if you are in vi mode. Only one mode can be on at a time.

```
$ shopt -o emacs
emacs           on
$ shopt -o vi
vi              off
```

Regardless of the mode, the arrow keys move the cursor and step through the most recently executed command:

- *Left arrow*—Moves back one character to the left. No characters are erased.
- *Right arrow*—Moves forward one character to the right.
- *Up arrow*—Moves to the previous command in the command history.
- *Down arrow*—Moves to the next command in the command history (if any).

Using the left and right arrows, the cursor moves to any position in the command. In the middle of a line, new text is inserted into the line without overwriting any old typing.

Emacs mode is the default mode on all the major Linux distributions. The most common emacs keys are as follows:

- **control-b**—Moves back one character to the left. No characters are erased.
- **control-f**—Moves forward one character to the right.
- **control-p**—Moves to the previous command in the command history.
- **control-n**—Moves to the next command in the command history (if any).
- **Tab key**—Finds a matching filename and completes it if there is one exact match.

The filename completion feature attempts to find a matching filename beginning with the final word on the line. If a matching filename is found, the rest of the filename is typed in by Bash. For example,

```
$ dat
```

is completed when the Tab key is pressed to

```
$ date
```

if date is the only command that can be found starting with the characters dat. The vi mode key combinations are as follows:

- **Esc**—Enters/exits editing mode.
- **h**—Moves back one character to the left. No characters are erased.
- **l**—Moves forward one character to the right.
- **k**—Moves to the previous command in the command history.
- **j**—Moves to the next command in the command history (if any).
- **Esc twice**—Finds a matching filename and completes it if there is one exact match.

A complete list of key combinations (or *bindings*) is listed in the Bash man page in the Readline section. The default key combinations can be changed, listed, or reassigned using the bind command. To avoid confusion, it is best to work with the defaults unless you have a specific application in mind.

Other editing keys are controlled by the older Linux stty (*set teletype*) command. Running stty shows the common command keys as well as other information about your session. Use the -a (*all*) switch for all settings.

```
$ stty
speed 9600 baud; evenp hupcl
intr = ^C; erase = ^?; kill = ^X;
eol2 = ^@; swtch = ^@;
susp = ^Z; dsusp = ^Y;
werase = ^W; lnext = ^@;
-inpck -istrip icrnl -ixany ixoff onlcr
-iexten echo echoe echok
-echoctl -echoke
```

Many of these settings are used only when you're working with serial port devices and can be ignored otherwise. The other settings are control key combinations marked with a caret (^) symbol. Keys with ^@ (or ASCII 0) are not defined. The keys are as follows:

- **erase** (usually ^?, which is the backspace key on IBM-style keyboards)—Moves left and erases one character.
- **intr** (usually ^c)—Interrupts/stops the current program or cancels the current line.
- **kill** (usually ^x)—Erases the current line.

- **rprnt** (usually ^R)—Redraws the current line.
- **stop** (usually ^S)—Pauses the program so you can read the results on the screen.
- **start** (usually ^Q)—Resumes the program.
- **susp** (usually ^Z)—Suspends the current program.
- **werase** (usually ^W)—Erases the last word typed.

To change the suspend character to control-v, type

```
$ stty susp '^v'
```

Changing key combinations can be very difficult. For example, if you are running an *X Windows server* (the software that runs on a client computer) on a Microsoft Windows computer to access a Linux computer, key combinations can be affected by the following:

- Microsoft Windows
- The X server software
- The Linux window manager
- The stty settings

Each acts like layers of an onion and they must all be in agreement. For example, shift-insert, often used to paste text, might be handled by your X Window server before your Linux computer or your shell have a chance to see it.

Variable Assignments and Displaying Messages

Variables can be created and assigned text using an equals sign. Surround the text with double quotes.

```
$ FILENAME="info.txt"
```

The value of variables can be printed using the printf command. printf has two arguments: a formatting code, and the variable to display. For simple variables, the formatting code is "%s\n" and the variable name should appear in double quotes with a dollar sign in front of the name

```
$ printf "%s\n" "$FILENAME"
info.txt
```

printf can also display simple messages. Put the message in the place of the formatting code.

```
$ printf "Bash is a great shell.\n"
Bash is a great shell.
```

printf and variables play an important role in shell scripting and they are described in greater detail in the chapters to come.

The results of a command can be assigned to a variable using backquotes.

```
$ DATE=`date`
$ printf "%s\n" "$DATE"
Wed Feb 13 15:36:41 EST 2002
```

The date shown is the date when the variable DATE is assigned its value. The value of the variable remains the same until a new value is assigned.

```
$ printf "%s\n" "$DATE"
Wed Feb 13 15:36:41 EST 2002
$ DATE=`date`
$ printf "%s\n" "$DATE"
Wed Feb 13 15:36:48 EST 2002
```

Multiple Commands

Multiple commands can be combined on a single line. How they are executed depends on what symbols separate them.

If each command is separated by a semicolon, the commands are executed consecutively, one after another.

```
$ printf "%s\n" "This is executed" ; printf "%s\n" "And so is this"
This is executed
And so is this
```

If each command is separated by a double ampersand (&&), the commands are executed until one of them fails or until all the commands are executed.

```
$ date && printf "%s\n" "The date command was successful"
Wed Aug 15 14:36:32 EDT 2001
The date command was successful
```

If each command is separated by a double vertical bar (||), the commands are executed as long as each one fails until all the commands are executed.

```
$ date 'duck!' || printf "%s\n" "The date command failed"
date: bad conversion
The date command failed
```

Semicolons, double ampersands, and double vertical bars can be freely mixed in a single line.

```
$ date 'format-this!' || printf "%s\n" "The date command failed" && \
printf "%s\n" "But the printf didn't!"
date: bad conversion
The date command failed
But the printf didn't!
```

These are primarily intended as command-line shortcuts: When mixed with redirection operators such as >, a long command chain is difficult to read and you should avoid it in scripts.

Command History

Bash keeps a list of the most recently typed commands. This list is the *command history*.

The easiest way to browse the command history is with the Up and Down arrow keys. The history can also be searched with an exclamation mark (!). This denotes the start of a command name to be completed by Bash. Bash executes the most recent command that matches. For example,

```
$ date
Wed Apr  4 11:55:58 EDT 2001
$ !d
Wed Apr  4 11:55:58 EDT 2001
```

If there is no matching command, Bash replies with an `event not found` error message.

```
$ !x
bash: !x: event not found
```

A double ! repeats the last command.

```
$ date
Thu Jul  5 14:03:25 EDT 2001
$ !!
date
Thu Jul  5 14:03:28 EDT 2001
```

There are many variations of the ! command to provide shortcuts in specific situations.

A negative number indicates the relative line number. That is, it indicates the number of commands to move back in the history to find the one to execute. !! is the same as !-1.

```
$ date
Thu Jul  5 14:04:54 EDT 2001
$ printf "%s\n" $PWD
/home/kburtch/
$ !-2
date
Thu Jul  5 14:05:15 EDT 2001
```

The !# repeats the content of the current command line. (Don't confuse this with #! in shell scripts.) Use this to run a set of commands twice.

```
$ date ; sleep 5 ; !#
date ; sleep 5 ; date ; sleep 5 ;
Fri Jan 18 15:26:54 EST 2002
Fri Jan 18 15:26:59 EST 2002
```

Bash keeps the command history in a file called `.bash_history` unless a variable called `HISTFILE` is defined. Each time you quit a Bash session, Bash saves the history of your session to the history file. If the `histappend` shell option is on, the history is appended to the old history up to the maximum allowed size of the history file. Each time you start a Bash session, the history is loaded again from the file.

Another shell option, `histverify`, enables you to edit the command after it's retrieved instead of executing it immediately.

Bash has a built-in command, `history`, which gives full control over the command history. The `history` command with no parameters lists the command history. If you don't want to see the entire history, specify the number of command lines to show.

```
$ history 10
 1026   set -o emacs
 1027   stty
 1028   man stty
 1029   stty -a
 1030   date edhhh
 1031   date edhhh
 1032   date
 1033   date
 1034   !
 1035   history 10
```

You can test which command will be matched during a history completion using the -p switch.

```
$ history -p !d
history -p date
date
```

A particular command line can be referred to by the line number.

```
$ !1133
date
Thu Jul  5 14:09:05 EDT 2001
```

`history -d` deletes an entry in the history.

```
$ history -d 1029
$ history 10
 1027   stty
 1028   man stty
 1029   date edhhh
 1030   date edhhh
 1031   date
 1032   date
 1033   !
 1034   history 10
 1035   history -d 1029
 1036   history 10
```

The -s switch adds new history entries. -w (*write*) and -r (*read*) save or load the history from a file, respectively. The -a (*append*) switch appends the current session history to the history file. This is done automatically when you quit the shell. The -n switch loads the complete history from the history file. history -c (*clear*) deletes the entire history.

The command history can be searched with !? for the most recent command containing the text. If there is additional typing after the !? search, the command fragment will be delineated with a trailing ?.

```
$ date
Thu Jul  5 14:12:33 EDT 2001
$ !?ate
date
Thu Jul  5 14:12:38 EDT 2001
$ !?da? '+%Y'
date '+%Y'
2001
```

The quick substitution history command, ^, runs the last command again, replacing one string with another.

```
$ date '+%Y'
2001
$ ^%Y^%m^
date '+%m'
07
```

The Bash history can be turned off by unsetting the -o history shell option. The cmdhist option saves multiple line commands in the history. The lithist option breaks up commands separated by semicolons into separate lines.

Directory Commands

The built-in pwd (*present working directory*) command returns the name of your current directory.

```
$ pwd
/home/kburtch
```

Although you might not think such a simple command needs options, pwd has a couple of switches. The -P (*physical*) switchshows the actual directory, whereas the default -L (*logical*) switch shows the directory, including any symbolic links. For example, if /home was a link to a directory called /user_drive/homes, the switches work as follows:

```
$ pwd -P
/user_drive/homes/kburtch
$ pwd -L
/home/kburtch
```

The built-in cd (*change directory*) command changes your current directory. As discussed in Chapter 1, "The Linux Environment," the special directory .. represents the parent directory, whereas . represents the current directory.

```
$ pwd
/home/kburtch
$ cd .
$ pwd
/home/kburtch
$ cd ..
$ pwd
/home
$ cd kburtch
$ pwd
/home/kburtch
```

Each time you change the directory, Bash updates the variable PWD containing the path to your current working directory. Bash also maintains a second variable called OLD-PWD that contains the last directory you were in.

Using the *minus sign* (-) with cd, you can switch between the current directory and the last directory. This is a useful shortcut if you are doing work in two different directories.

```
$ pwd
/home/kburtch
$ cd ..
$ pwd
/home
$ cd -
$ pwd
/home/kburtch
$ cd -
$ pwd
/home
```

The tilde (~) represents your current directory. Use it to move to a directory relative to your home directory. To move to a directory called mail in your home directory, type

```
$ cd ~/mail
```

Although . and .. work in all Linux programs, ~ and - are features of Bash and only work with Bash and Bash scripts.

cd by itself returns you to your home directory, the same as cd ~.

If a CDPATH variable exists, it is assumed to contain a list of directories similar to the PATH variable. This is a throwback to the days when a user was only able to use one shell session on his terminal and is now considered a security risk. Its use should be avoided.

Specialized Navigation and History

Because most users can open multiple shell sessions, there is little need for complex movement between directories. `cd` - switches between two directories, which is suitable for most circumstances. However, if you are restricted to a single shell session and want Bash to remember more directories, there are three built-in commands that maintain a list of directories.

The built-in `dirs` command shows the list of saved directories. The current directory is always the first item in the list.

```
$ dirs
~
```

The built-in `pushd` (*push directory*) command adds (or pushes) directories onto the list and changes the current directory to the new directory.

```
$ pushd /home/kburtch/invoices
~/invoices ~
$ pushd /home/kburtch/work
~/work ~/invoices ~
$ pwd
/home/kburtch/work
```

There are now three directories in the list.

The `-n` (*no change*) switch will put a directory into the list without changing directories. `-N` (*rotate Nth*) moves the nth directory from the left (or, with +N, from the right) to the top of the list.

The `dirs -l` switch displays the directory names without any short forms.

```
$ dirs -l
/home/kburtch/work /home/kburtch/invoices /home/kburtch
```

The `-v` switch displays the list as a single column, and `-p` shows the same information without the list position. The `-c` switch clears the list. The `-N` (*view Nth*) shows the nth directory from the left (or, with +N, from the right).

```
$ dirs +1
~
```

The built-in `popd` (*pop directory*) command is the opposite of the `pushd`. `popd` discards the first directory and moves to the next directory in the list.

```
$ popd
~/invoices ~
$ pwd
/home/kburtch/invoices
```

The switches for `popd` are similar to `pushd`: `-n` to pop without moving, and `-N` to delete the Nth entry from the left (or, with +N, the right).

The Colon Command

The simplest shell command is the colon (:). This is the *colon command* (sometimes called a "no-op" or "null command") and does nothing. What's the use of a command that does nothing? There are some places in shell programs where a statement is required. In those cases, you can use : to indicate nothing special should be done.

At the command prompt, : has no effect.

```
$ :
$
```

The colon command can have parameters and file redirections. This can have strange effects, such as running the date command using backquotes, giving the results to the null command that quietly discards them.

```
$ : `date`
$
```

This has the same effect as redirecting the output of date to the /dev/null file.

```
$ date > /dev/null
```

Backquotes and redirection are discussed in an upcoming chapter.

Reference Section

date Command Switches

- --date=s (or -d s)—Displays time described by s.
- --file=f (or -f f)—Displays times listed in file f.
- --iso-8601=t (or -I t)—Displays an ISO-8601 standard time.
- --reference=f (or -r f)—Displays last modification date of file.
- --rfc-822 (or -R)—Uses RFC-822 format.
- --universal (or --utc or -u)—Uses Coordinated Universal Time.

stty Command Switches

- --all (or -a)—Displays all stty settings.
- --save (or -g)—Displays settings so they can be used as parameters to stty.
- --file=d (or -F d)—Opens tty device d instead of stdin.

`history` Command Switches

- `-a`—Appends to history file.
- `-c`—Clears history.
- `-d`—Deletes history entry.
- `-n`—Loads from history file.
- `-p`—Performs history lookup/substitution.
- `-r`—Reads history from a file.
- `-s`—Adds new history entries.

`pwd` Command Switches

- `-P`—Physical directory
- `-L`—Logical directory

`dirs` Command Switches

- `-c`—Clears all entries
- `-l`—Shows a long listing (no tildes)
- `-p`—Lists the entries
- `-v`—Shows a verbose listing

3

Files, Users, and Shell Customization

Whesn a friend of mine got a new Unix computer, the console display didn't look quite right. When we tried to view files, the operating system didn't know how big the screen was. It displayed the entire file instead of a screen at a time.

My Unix was a bit rusty at the time, but I remembered that there was a `stty` command to change attributes of the display. Looking at the help listing for `stty`, I noticed a person could set the `rows` and the `line`. Thinking that `line` must be the number of lines on the display, I typed `stty line 24`. The computer stopped responding, forcing us to reboot it.

We phoned up a Unix professional who had the same operating system. He said, "That should have worked. Let me try it." There was a brief pause. "I locked up my computer, too."

It turned out that `stty line 24` set the serial port for the display, changing it to port 24 when there was no device connected to port 24. With the wide variety of options available to Unix-based operating systems like Linux, it can sometimes be difficult to predict what a command actually does. This chapter expands on the last chapter, covering more basic commands and their many, sometimes confusing, options.

Listing Files

The `ls` (*list*) command shows the contents of the current directory. Although `ls` is a familiar command available on all Unix-like operating system, Linux uses the `ls` command from the GNU `fileutils` project and has many special switches and features.

```
$ ls
archive    check-orders.sh orders.txt
```

`ls` has switches that affect how the files are listed, including the level of detail, the sorting order, and the number of columns. Most Linux distributions set up certain

defaults for `ls` command. Red Hat, for example, has the `-q` and `-F` switches on by
default. From the point of view of script writing, it's not safe to use the `ls` command in
a script without specifying the appropriate switches because you can't be sure which
defaults a particular distribution uses.

`ls` hides files that begin with a period. This is the Linux convention for configuration
files, history files, and other files that a user isn't normally interested in. To see these files,
use the `-A` (*all*) switch. Use `-a` (*absolutely all*) to show the implicit . and . . files as well.

```
$ ls -A
.bash_history  .bash_logout  .bash_profile  .bashrc  archive
check-orders.sh  orders.txt
```

The filenames can be printed in color to show the kind of file they are. The colors
are defined in a file `/etc/DIR_COLORS`. You can customize the colors using a
`.dir_colors` file in your own directory. The format of the file is described in the
`/etc/DIR_COLORS` file.

To display the files without color and with symbols instead, use the `--color` and
`--classify` (or `-F`) switches. (On most Linux distributions, this feature is turned on
using aliases.)

```
$ ls --color=never --classify
archive/  check-orders.sh*  orders.txt
```

The `--classify` symbols are directories (`/`), programs (`*`), symbolic links (`@`), pipes (`|`),
and Unix domain socket files (`=`). These symbols are not a part of the name: They are
hints as to the type of file. In this example, `archive` is a directory and `check-orders.sh`
is a program.

Another very important switch is `--hide-control-chars` (or `-q`). Linux filenames
can contain any character, even control characters. It is possible to create a filename with
hidden characters in the name. In these cases, you can't rename or delete the file unless
you know what the hidden characters are. Contrary to what the name implies, the
`--hide-control-chars` switch displays any unprintable characters in the filename as
question marks, making their locations visible.

```
$ rm orders.txt
rm: orders.txt non-existent
$ ls --color=never --classify --hide-control-chars
archive/  check-orders.sh*  orde?rs.txt
```

A complete list of switches appears at the end of this chapter.

`printf` **Command**

The built-in `printf` (*print formatted*) command prints a message to the screen. You will
use this command a lot in shell scripts.

`printf` is very similar to the C standard I/O `printf()` function, but they are not
identical. In particular, single- and double-quoted strings are treated differently in shell
scripts than in C programs.

The first parameter is a format string describing how the items being printed will be represented. For example, the special formatting code "%d" represents an integer number, and the code "%f" represents a floating-point number.

```
$ printf "%d\n" 5
5
$ printf "%f\n" 5
5.000000
```

Include a format code for each item you want to print. Each format code is replaced with the appropriate value when printed. Any characters in the format string that are not part of a formatting instruction are treated as printable characters.

```
$ printf "There are %d customers with purchases over %d.\n" 50 20000
There are 50 customers with purchases over 20000.
```

printf is sometimes used to redirect a variable or some unchanging input to a command. For example, suppose all you want to do is pipe a variable to a command. Instead of using printf, Bash provides a shortcut <<< redirection operator. <<< redirects a string into a command as if it were piped using printf.

The tr command can convert text to uppercase. This example shows an error message being converted to uppercase with both printf and <<<.

```
$ printf "%s\n" "$ERRMSG" | tr [:lower:] [:upper:]
WARNING: THE FILES FROM THE OHIO OFFICE HAVEN'T ARRIVED.
$ tr [:lower:] [:upper:] <<< "$ERRMSG"
WARNING: THE FILES FROM THE OHIO OFFICE HAVEN'T ARRIVED.
```

The format codes include the following.

- %a—Represent a floating-point number in hexadecimal format, using lowercase letters
- %A—Represent a floating point number in hexadecimal format, using uppercase letters
- %b—Expand backslash sequences
- %c—Represent a single character
- %d—Display a signed number
- %e—Display a floating-point number, shown in exponential (also called "scientific") notation
- %f (or %F)—Display a floating-point number without exponential notation
- %g—(*General*) Let Bash choose %e or %f, depending on the value
- %i—Same as %d
- %o—Display an octal number
- %q—Quote a string so it can be read properly by a shell script

- %s—Display an unquoted string
- %u—Display an unsigned number
- %x—Display an unsigned hexadecimal number, using lowercase letters
- %X—Display an unsigned hexadecimal number, using uppercase letters
- %%—Display a percent sign

If a number is too large, Bash reports an out-of-range error.

```
$ printf "%d\n" 123456789123456789012
bash: printf: warning: 123456789123456789012: Numerical result out of range
```

For compatibility with C's printf, Bash also recognizes the following flags, but treats them the same as %d:

- %j—A C intmax_t or uintmax_t integer
- %t—A C ptrdiff_t integer
- %z—A C size_t or ssize_t integer

Also for C compatibility, you can preface the format codes with a l or L to indicate a long number.

The %q format is important in shell script programming and it is discussed in the quoting section, in the Chapter 5, "Variables."

To create reports with neat columns, numbers can proceed many of the formatting codes to indicate the width of a column. For example, "%10d" prints a signed number in a column 10 characters wide.

```
$ printf "%10d\n" 11
        11
```

Likewise, a negative number left-justifies the columns.

```
$ printf "%-10d %-10d\n" 11 12
11         12
```

A number with a decimal point represents a column width and a minimum number of digits (or decimal places with floating-point values). For example, "%10.5f" indicates a floating-point number in a 10-character column with a minimum of five decimal places.

```
$ printf "%10.5f\n" 17.2
  17.20000
```

Finally, an apostrophe (')displays the number with thousands groupings based on the current country locale.

The \n in the format string is an example of a backslash code for representing unprintable characters. \n indicates a new line should be started. There are special backslash formatting codes for the representation of unprintable characters.

- \b—Backspace
- \f—Form feed (that is, eject a page on a printer)
- \n—Start a new line
- \r—Carriage return
- \t—Tab
- \v—Vertical tab
- \'—Single quote character (for compatibility with C)
- \\—Backslash
- \0n—n is an octal number representing an 8-bit ASCII character

```
$ printf "Two separate\nlines\n"
Two separate
lines
```

Any 8-bit byte or ASCII character can be represented by \0 or \ and its octal value.

```
$ printf "ASCII 65 (octal 101) is the character \0101\n"
ASCII 65 (octal 101) is the character A
```

printf recognizes numbers beginning with a zero as octal notation, and numbers beginning with 0x as hexadecimal notation. As a result, printf can convert numbers between these different notations.

```
$ printf "%d\n" 010
8
$ printf "%d\n " 0xF
15
$ printf "0x%X\n " 15
0xF
$ printf "0%o\n " 8
010
```

Most Linux distributions also have a separate printf command to be compliant with the POSIX standard.

Getting Help

The Bash shell comes with a built-in help command to describe the various built-in Bash commands. The -s switch displays a summary for the command you specify.

```
$ help -s printf
printf: printf format [arguments]
```

Help only describes Bash commands. To get help on Linux commands, you need to use the man (*manual*) command.

```
$ man date
```

Linux divides its manual pages into a number of logical volumes. `man` displays any matching entries from any volume. Volume 1 contains the commands you can execute from the shell. To restrict your search to shell commands, use `man 1`.

```
$ man 1 date
```

If there are pages in more than one manual volume, only the page from the first volume that matches your search is displayed. To find matching pages across all manual volumes, use the `-a` (*all*) switch.

The `-k` switch searches the Linux manual for a particular keyword and lists all man pages referring to that keyword.

```
$ man 1 -k alias
```

The command `help type` gives you different information than `man 1 type`. The `help type` command tells you about Bash's built-in `type` command, whereas the `man 1 type` command tells you about the Linux `type` command. If you are not sure whether a command is a Bash command, always try the `help` command before using the `man` command.

Fixing the Display

There will be times when a Bash session becomes unusable. Certain character sequences can lock your display, hide what you type, or change the characters being shown into strange symbols. This can happen, for example, when you're trying to display a binary file.

The `reset` command attempts to restore a Bash session to a safe, sane state.

If reset fails, you might also need to use `stty sane` to restore the session to a normal state.

The `clear` command clears the display and returns the cursor to the upper-left corner.

Working with Files

There are several Linux commands for removing, copying, and moving files.

`mkdir` (*make directory*) creates a new directory. Use `mkdir` to organize your files.

```
$ mkdir prototypes
$ ls -l
total 4
drwxr-xr-x   2 ken      users        4096 Jan 24 12:50 prototypes
```

There are two switches for `mkdir`:

- `--mode=m` (`-m`)—Sets the permission mode (as in `chmod`)
- `--parents` (`-p`)—Makes all necessary directories even if they don't currently exist

```
$ mkdir --parents --mode=550 read_only/backup/january
$ ls -l
```

```
total 4
drwxr-xr-x   2 ken       users        4096 Jan 24 12:50 backup
drwxr-xr-x   3 ken       users        4096 Jan 24 12:51 read_only
$ ls -l read_only/backup
total 4
dr-xr-x---   2 ken       users        4096 Jan 24 12:51 january
```

The values for mode are discussed with the chmod command in Chapter 15, "Shell Security." However, when --parents is used, the --mode affects only the final directory in the list.

rmdir (*remove directory*) deletes a directory. The directory must be empty before it can be removed. There are two switches:

- --ignore-fail-on-non-empty—Doesn't report an error when it can't delete a directory with files still in it
- --parents (-p)—Removes all parent directories as well as the subdirectory

```
$ rmdir read_only
rmdir: read_only: Directory not empty
$ rmdir --parents read_only/backup/january/
```

The rm (*remove*) command permanently deletes files. If the file is a symbolic or hard link, it removes the link but leaves the file intact.

```
$ rm old_notes.txt
$ ls old_notes.txt
ls: old_notes.txt: No such file or directory
```

There are several switches for rm:

- --directory (-d)—Removes a directory
- --force (-f)—Never prompts the user and ignores missing files
- --interactive (-i)—Always prompts the user
- --recursive (-r or -R)—Removes contents of all subdirectories

Using the --recursive and --force switches simultaneously removes all the specified files, including all subdirectories, without warning. Make sure you are deleting the correct files.

Some Linux distributions have the --interactive switch on by default so that rm requires that you confirm when you want to delete a particular file.

```
$ rm --interactive old_notes.txt
rm: remove 'old_notes.txt'? y
$
```

Normally rm won't delete a directory, but the --recursive switch deletes any directories encountered.

The cp (*copy*) command copies files from any location to another. If the final file listed is a directory, copy copies the other files into that directory.

There are many switches for `copy`—the complete list is in the reference section at the end of this chapter. Some common switches are as follows:

- `--force` (`-f`)—Never prompts the user; always overwrites
- `--interactive` (`-i`)—Always prompts user
- `--link` (`-l`)—Creates a hard link instead of copying
- `--parents` (`-P`)—Appends the source path to destination directory
- `--recursive` (`-R`)—Copies any subdirectories
- `--symbolic-link` (`-s`)—Creates a symbolic link instead of copying
- `--update` (`-u`)—Overwrites old files or copies missing files

```
$ cp notes.txt old_notes.txt # copying
$ mkdir backup
$ cp old_notes.txt backup
$ ls backup
old_notes.txt
```

Like `rm`, some Linux distributions have `--interactive` on by default, warning when a file will be overwritten.

```
$ cp --interactive project_notes.txt old_notes
cp: overwrite 'old_notes/project_notes.txt'? n
$
```

The `mv` (*move*) command moves and renames files. This is the same as making a copy of the file and deleting the original. Move also effectively renames a file by moving it to a new name in the same directory.

```
$ mv notes.txt project_notes.txt # renaming
```

The most common `mv` switches are similar to `cp`:

- `--backup` (`-b`)—Makes a backup of any existing file before overwriting by adding a ~ to the name
- `--force` (`-f`)—Never prompts the user; always overwrites
- `--interactive` (`-i`)—Always prompts the user before overwriting
- `--update` (`-u`)—Overwrites old files or copies missing files

There is no `--recursive` switch. When `move` moves a directory, it moves the directory and all its contents automatically.

The `namei` (*name inode*) command lists all the components in a path, including any symbolic links.

```
$ namei files
f: files
 l files -> /home/ken/bash/scripts
 d /
```

```
d home
d ken
d bash
d scripts
```

In this case, the file named `files` is a symbolic link. Each of the files in the link path is a directory, marked with a `d`. Other file designations include `l` for symbolic link, `s` for socket, `b` for block device, `c` for character device, `-` for regular file, and `?` for an error accessing a file in the path.

Complete file permissions, such as seen with `ls -l`, can be shown with the `-m` (*mode*) switch.

Working with People

There are several commands for checking to see who is on the computer and what they are doing.

The `finger` command shows who is on the computer and provides additional information, including how long their session has been idle, and their contact information.

```
$ finger
Login       Name                TTY Idle    When     Bldg.        Phone
dhu     Dick Hu             *p6  4:25 Thu 14:12  4th Floor    ext 2214
mchung  Michael Chung       *con 5:07 Fri 09:57  OS Support   ext 1101
bgill   Biringer Gill       *p7   15  Fri 13:32
```

Some versions of Linux no longer include `finger` because of security concerns over `finger`'s `.plan` files. Read the `finger` manual page for more information.

There are several other commands with similar functions. The `users` command shows a list of login names.

```
$ users
bgill dhu mchung
```

The `who` command shows who is on the computer, which connection they are using, and when they signed on.

```
$ who
dhu         ttyp6         Mar 29 14:12
mchung      console       Apr  6 09:57
bgill       ttyp7         Apr  6 13:32
```

The `w` command provides even more information, including system statistics and what the users are currently running.

```
$ w
  3:18pm  up 9 days, 20:33,  3 users,  load average: 0.64, 0.66, 0.64
User        tty           login@ idle   JCPU   PCPU  what
dhu         ttyp6         2:12pm 4:28   8:01   8:01  csh
mchung      console       9:57am 5:10                sh
bgill       ttyp7         1:32pm  19                 bash
```

Shell Aliases

An *alias* is a short form of a command. The built-in `alias` command creates simple abbreviations for the current Bash session.

To create an alias, use the `alias` command to assign a command and its switches a name.

```
$ alias lf='ls -qFl'
$ lf
-rw-r-----   1 kburtch     devgroup       10809 Apr  6 11:00 assets.txt
-rw-r-----   1 kburtch     devgroup        4713 Mar  9 2000 mailing_list.txt
```

Typing the `alias` command by itself, or with the `-p` switch, lists the current aliases.

```
$ alias
alias lf='ls -qFl'
```

Bash interprets an alias only once, allowing the aliasing of a command with its own name.

```
$ alias ls='ls -qF'  # Bash isn't confused
```

Normally, only the first word of a command is checked for an alias. As a special exception, if the last character in the alias string is a blank, Bash checks the next word in the command to see whether it is also an alias.

There is no method for giving arguments to an alias. If arguments are needed, define a more powerful shell function instead.

The built-in `unalias` command removes an alias. Use the `-a` switch to remove them all.

Most Linux distributions have aliases defined for common commands. `dir`, for example, is often an alias for `ls`. Some distributions define an alias for commands such as `rm -i` to force user prompting, which is not required by default. This can be a problem for some users such as experienced Unix programmers who are used to working with these features disabled. Use `unalias` to remove any aliases that you don't want to use.

Aliases mixed with shell functions can be confusing because aliases are expanded only when a line from a script is read. If aliases are used in a shell function, they are expanded when the shell function is defined, not when it is executed. For this reason, it is safer to avoid aliases altogether in shell scripts. However, they can be turned on in scripts using the `shopt -s expand_aliases` command.

The Bash Hash Table

When a command is executed without naming a path, the shell searches for the command (in the directories listed in the PATH variable). When the Bash finds the command, it remembers where it is, storing the location in a *hash table*. Thereafter, Bash checks the table for the location of the command instead of searching for the command again, making commands run faster. However, if the command moves after Bash has recorded its location, the shell won't be able to find the command.

The built-in `hash` command maintains the hash table. Without any switches, hash lists the memorized commands, where they are, and the number of times the command has been executed during this session.

```
$ hash
hits    command
   1    /bin/ls
   1    /bin/uname
   1    /usr/bin/tput
   1    /bin/stty
   1    /usr/bin/uptime
   1    /usr/bin/man
```

When a command is specified, Bash searches for the new location of the command. For example, if you create your own `ls` command in your current directory, and the PATH variable gives precedence to files in your current directory, the `hash ls` command finds your `ls` command first, replacing `/bin/ls` with `./ls`.

```
$ hash ls
$ hash
hits    command
   1    /bin/touch
   0    ./ls
   1    /bin/chmod
```

The -p (*path*) switch explicitly sets a path for a command. The -d (*delete*) switch deletes a specific entry, and -r (*remove*) clears the hash table, removing all commands. The -t (*table*) option lists the pathnames for specific commands, and -l (*list*) lists the commands in a format that allows them to be reused by the `hash` command.

```
$ hash -t ls less
ls      /bin/ls
less    /usr/bin/less
```

Customizing Your Prompt

The default Bash interactive prompt is a dollar sign ($), although some distributions use a different symbol. Most Linux distributions redefine the prompt to include additional information, such as your current login and computer, which is useful when you're moving between accounts and computers.

If a variable named PS1 (*prompt string 1*) is defined, Bash will use the value of this variable for your main prompt. If you include variable names in the string, Bash will substitute the value of the variables into your prompt.

```
$ declare -x PS1="Bash $ "
Bash $ pwd
/home/kburtch/archive
Bash $
```

The following declares a three-line prompt with a blank line, the current directory, the old current directory, login name, computer name, and a bold **$**.

```
$ declare -x PS1="
\$PWD (\$OLDPWD)
\$LOGNAME@'uname -n'\['tput bold'\] \$ \['tput rmso'\]"


/home/kburtch/archive (/home/kburtch/work)
kburtch@linux_box $
```

The \[and \] should surround the display formatting characters returned by tput. Otherwise, Bash assumes that all the prompt characters are printable and will not wrap long input lines properly.

Bash has a PS2 (*prompt string 2*) variable, which is the prompt for incomplete command lines such as when you use a multiline quotation. By default, this prompt is a greater-than sign (>).

Bash recognizes the following escape sequences in a prompt.

- \a—A beep (the ASCII bell character)
- \A—24 time in HH:MM format
- \d—The date in "weekday-month-date" format
- \D{*s*}—Runs the C statftime function with format string *s*
- \e—The ASCII escape character
- \h—The hostname
- \H—The complete hostname, including the domain
- \j—The number of jobs in the job table
- \l—The tty device
- \n—A new line
- \r—A carriage return
- \s—The name of the shell
- \t—The 24 hour time
- \T—The 12 hour time
- \@—The time in AM/PM format
- \u—The username
- \v—The Bash version
- \V—The Bash release
- \w—The current working directory
- \W—The basename of the current working directory
- \!—The position of the command in the history list
- \#—The sequential command number for the session

- \$—Default prompt (# for the superuser, otherwise $)
- \nnn—ASCII character in octal format
- \\—A backslash
- \[—Begins a sequence of nonprintable characters
- \]—Ends a sequence of nonprintable characters

Variables are discussed more in Chapter 5. You can disable variable substitution by turning off the `promptvars` shell option.

Long Command Lines

Long command lines are automatically scrolled by Bash: When your cursor reaches the right-hand side of the window, Bash continues the command on the next line.

If you want to break up a command so that it fits on more than one line, use a back-slash (\) as the last character on the line. Bash will print the continuation prompt, usually a >, to indicate that this is a continuation of the previous line.

```
$ printf "%s\n" "This is a very long printf.  How long is it?\
> It's so long that I continued it on the next line."
This is a very long printf.  How long is it? It's so long that I continued it on
the next line.
```

Customizing Command-Line Editing

The `bind` command enables you to change the editing keys, editing options, as well as create keyboard macros. Changes affect only the current editing mode.

The -p or -P switches display the various command-line *editing functions*—the key combinations that will activate them. The -P switch displays the information in an easy-to-read format.

```
$ shopt -o emacs
emacs           on
$ bind -P | head -5

abort can be found on "\C-g", "\C-x\C-g", "\e\C-g".
accept-line can be found on "\C-j", "\C-m".
alias-expand-line is not bound to any keys
arrow-key-prefix is not bound to any keys
$ shopt -s -o vi
$ bind -P | head -5

abort is not bound to any keys
accept-line can be found on "\C-j", "\C-m".
alias-expand-line is not bound to any keys
arrow-key-prefix is not bound to any keys
```

A particular edit mode can be chosen with the –m (*keymap*) switch.

```
$ bind -P -m vi | head -5
```

```
abort can be found on "\C-g".
accept-line can be found on "\C-j", "\C-m".
alias-expand-line is not bound to any keys
arrow-key-prefix is not bound to any keys
```

Special keys are indicated by backslash codes. These codes are based on the ones used by the emacs text editor.

- \\—A backslash
- \"—A double quote
- \'—A single quote
- \a—An alert (bell)
- \b—A backspace
- \c—The Control key
- \d—Delete
- \e—The Escape key
- \f—A form feed
- \M—The emacs meta key
- \n—A new line (line feed)
- \r—A carriage return
- \t—A horizontal tab
- \v—A vertical tab
- *nnn*—ASCII code in octal format
- \x*nnn*—ASCII code in the hexadecimal format

For example, control-g is represented by the sequence \c-g.

The -l (*list*) switch lists all possible keyboard functions.

```
$ bind -l | head -5
abort
accept-line
alias-expand-line
arrow-key-prefix
backward-char
```

To view a particular function, use the -q (*query*) switch.

```
$ shopt -s -o emacs
$ bind -q abort
abort can be invoked via "\C-g", "\C-x\C-g", "\e\C-g".
```

A binding can be removed using -u (*unbind*). If there is more than one binding, the first one is removed.

```
$ bind -u abort
$ bind -q abort
abort can be invoked via "\C-x\C-g", "\e\C-g"
```

Alternatively, the -r (*remove*) removes a binding by its key sequence.

```
$ bind -r "\e\C-g"
$ bind -q abort
abort can be invoked via "\C-x\C-g".
```

New bindings can be added using the key sequence, a colon, and the name of the editing function. For example, the backward-kill-line function erases everything from the beginning of the line to the cursor position. In vi mode, backward-kill-line isn't normally bound to any keys so it can't be used.

```
$ shopt -s -o vi
$ bind -q backward-kill-line
backward-kill-line is not bound to any keys.
```

However, bind can assign backward-kill-line to a new key combination.

```
$ bind "\C-w:backward-kill-line"
$ bind -q backward-kill-line
backward-kill-line can be invoked via "\C-w".
```

Now control-w erases to the start of the line.

Besides keys that activate specific edit functions, there are also a number of options (or *variables*). The -v or -V switches show the keyboard options. -V is easier to read.

```
$ bind -v | head -5
set blink-matching-paren on
set completion-ignore-case off
set convert-meta on
set disable-completion off
set enable-keypad off
$ bind -V | head -5
blink-matching-paren is set to 'on'
completion-ignore-case is set to 'off'
convert-meta is set to 'on'
disable-completion is set to 'off'
enable-keypad is set to 'off'
```

These options can be turned on and off.

```
$ bind "set enable-keypad on"
$ bind -V | head -5
blink-matching-paren is set to 'on'
completion-ignore-case is set to 'off'
```

```
convert-meta is set to 'on'
disable-completion is set to 'off'
enable-keypad is set to 'on'
```

A complete listing of all functions and options is available on the Readline manual page.

The `bind` command can also define *keyboard macros*. These are short sequences of keys that are automatically expanded to a longer, common sequence to reduce the amount of typing. The -s or -S switches list all currently defined macros. The -v switch is more "human readable."

The format for creating a macro is the same as the one used to assign functions, except that \″ must appear around the expanded text.

```
$ bind -S
$ bind "\C-w:\" >/dev/null\""
$ bind -S
\C-w outputs  >/dev/null
```

Control-w will now insert >dev/null into the current line.

Your Session Profile

When you log into a computer and start a new Bash session, you might need to type several commands to customize your session. Perhaps you want to change the editing mode from emacs to vi, create new key bindings, or change your command-line prompt. Rather than typing these commands, Bash will run these commands for you each time you log on if they are saved in a special file. This file is called a *profile file* because it contains the commands to tailor the session to your particular requirements.

The original Bourne shell ran two profile files whenever a user logged on. First, a file called /etc/profile was the general profile file executed for all users. Second, if a file named .profile appeared in the user's home directory, this contained additional commands for each user. Bash mimics this behavior when it is started as sh instead of bash.

Bash extended the principle to run several profile files depending on the circumstances. In addition, Linux distributions often customize the general profile files to run additional commands stored in other scripts.

Bash differentiates between a login session and other instances. Bash runs as a *login shell* when a user or program first logs in or when a login is simulated with Bash's --login (or -l) switch. A login shell is not necessarily one that presents a user with a prompt. It only indicates that Bash is the top program in the current session, and when Bash completes its run, the login session will be over.

The login_shell shell option is turned on when you are in a login shell. This option can be used to verify that you are in a login shell.

```
$ shopt login_shell
login_shell     on
```

Bash runs as an interactive shell when it is started without a script or when the -i switch is used. An interactive shell presents the user with a command prompt. An interactive shell is not necessarily a login shell. A user can start a non-login interactive shell by typing `bash` at a Bash prompt, thus starting a new copy of Bash.

Whether the Bash session is interactive or a login shell determines which profile files are used. This way, Bash separates commands specifically for customizing an interactive session from the more general-purpose commands.

The `/etc/profile` file contains the setup commands and environment changes common to all users. A general profile file might look something like this:

```
#!/etc/profile
# No core files by default
ulimit -S -c 0 > /dev/null 2>&1
# HOSTNAME is the result of running the hostname command
declare -x HOSTNAME=`/bin/hostname`
# No more than 1000 lines of Bash command history
declare -x HISTSIZE=1000
# If PostgreSQL is installed, add the Postgres commands
# to the user's PATH
If test -r /usr/bin/pgsql/bin ; then
    declare -x PATH="$PATH"":/usr/bin/pgsql/bin"
fi
# end of general profile
```

Only the superuser can edit this file. When Bash is used as a login shell, it executes the first file it finds named `~/.bash_profile`, `~/.bash_login`, or `~/.profile`. When a session completes, Bash runs `~/.bash_logout`, if it exists.

For example, SuSE Linux uses `~/.profile` for the user's profile file. (You can check this by listing the files in your home directory.) By editing this file, you can add commands that will always execute when you log in.

```
# My profile

shopt -s -o emacs    # I prefer emacs mode to vi mode
date                 # display the date when I log on
```

Test the changes by simulating a login with the `--login` switch.

```
$ bash --login
Wed Feb  6 15:20:35 EST 2002
$ shopt -o emacs
emacs          on
$ logout
```

Running a new Bash interactive session without logging in will not run the profile file.

```
$ bash
$ logout
bash: logout: not login shell: use 'exit'
$ exit
```

Scripts will not normally execute the login profile scripts. Bash will load a profile for scripts if the BASH_ENV environment variable contains a pathname to a file to execute. However, you should avoid using BASH_ENV. Setting the common environment for a set of scripts is usually done with the source command, which is discussed in Chapter 14, "Functions and Script Execution." BASH_ENV has no effect on interactive sessions.

You can stop the running of the login profile files by using the --noprofile switch.

Bash runs a different set of files for interactive sessions that are not also login sessions. Bash looks for a customization script called ~/.bashrc (Bash resources) and executes it instead of the login profile files. Aliased functions are only allowed in the resource files. A different resource file can be specified with the --init-file or --rcfile switch. A typical resource file might contain the following:

```
# /etc/bashrc
# Don't let others write to the user's files
umask 002
# Alias ls to provide default switches
alias ls='ls -qF'
```

Some distributions add lines to your login profile to run the commands in ~/.bashrc as well. This is not a feature of Bash, but a change made by your Linux distribution. You can add the following lines to the ~/.bashrc file to test its behavior:

```
# My bashrc Resource File Customizations
printf "%s\n" ".bashrc has run"
```

Test it from the command prompt by starting new sessions. In this case, SuSE Linux always runs the resource file.

```
$ bash --login
.bashrc has run
$ logout
$ bash
.bashrc has run
$ exit
```

As a result, you cannot be certain of the behavior of the resource file without checking your distribution.

Resource files can be suppressed with the --norc switch.

Your distribution can run other files as well during login:

- Red Hat and Mandrake Linux separates your customizations, putting functions and aliases in ~/.bashrc and other customization in ~/.bash_profile. Their .bash_profile script will automatically run a .bashrc file as well, if it is present.

- SuSE Linux separates your customizations, putting functions and aliases in ~/.bashrc and other customization in ~/.profile. Their .profile script will automatically run a .bashrc file as well, if it is present.

- SCO Linux (also called Caldera Linux) uses ~/.profile, which calls ~/.bashrc. It then runs the profile script from ~/etc/config.d/shells to configure the system defaults. When ~/.bashrc runs, it calls /etc/config.d/shells/bashrc to set up the non-interactive defaults. User's personal customizations should be stored in ~/.profile-private and ~/.bashrc-private, respectively.

Likewise, the general profile files can be customized:

- Red Hat and Mandrake split customizations into /etc/bashrc and /etc/profile to mimic the behavior of a user's profile files. Further system scripts automatically executed are for specifically installed packages stored in /etc/profile.d.

- SuSE Linux automatically set the contents of many files in the /etc directory, including /etc/profile. As a result, personal changes must stored in a separate file called /etc/profile.local or they can be lost when the system is reconfigured or upgraded. Other system scripts automatically executed are /etc/SuSEconfig and scripts for installed software packages stored in /etc/profile.d. SuSE also includes an /etc/profile.dos script to define customizations for users coming from MS-DOS. This is enabled by SuSE configuration software, but it can also be executed from your /etc/profile.local file.

- SCO Linux only puts minimum setup information common to any Bourne-based shells in /etc/profile. Common Bash settings should be configured in /etc/config.d/shells/profile and /etc/config.d/shells/bashrc.

Reference Section

ls **Command Switches**

- --all (or -a)—Shows all files, including . and ..
- --almost-all (or -A)—Shows all files except . and ..
- --block-size=n—Shows the size of files as n-byte blocks
- --classify (or -F)—Appends a symbol to a filename to indicate its type
- --color=t—Uses color for filenames, t equals never, always, or auto.
- --dereference (or -L)—Shows items referenced by symbolic links
- --directory (or -d)—Shows information about a directory instead of showing its contents
- --dired (or -D)—Output for emacs dired mode
- --escape (or -b)—Prints octal escape sequences for unprintable characters
- --file-type (or -p)—Same as --classify
- --format=across (or -x)—Sorts by lines instead of columns
- --format=commas (or -m)—Shows filenames as a list separated by commas
- --format=long (or -l)—Shows detailed (long) listings

- `--format=single-column` (or `-1`)—Shows results as one file per line
- `--format=verbose`—Same as the long format
- `--format=vertical` (or `-C`)—Lists entries by columns
- `--full-time`—Shows full date and time
- `--hide-control-chars` (or `-q`)—Displays a ? for unprintable characters in file-names
- `--human-readable` (or `-h`)—Shows sizes in kilobytes, megabytes, and so on, instead of raw bytes
- `--ignore=p` (or `-I`)—Ignores files matching the pattern p
- `--ignore-backups` (or `-B`)—Does not list files ending with ~
- `--indicator-style=classify`—Same as `--classify`
- `--indicator-style=none`—Don't classify files
- `--indicator-style=file-type`—Same as `--file-type`
- `--inode` (or `-i`)—Prints the inode number for the file
- `--kilobytes` (or `-k`)—Same as block size 1024
- `-f`—Does not sort, enable `-aU`, disable `-lst`
- `--literal` (or `-N`)—Shows unprintable characters in names as-is (unlike `-q`)
- `--no-group` (or `-G`)—Hides the group that owns the file
- `--numeric-uid-gid` (or `-n`)—Shows UIDs and GIDs as numbers not names
- `-o`—Shows long listings without the file group ownership information
- `--quote-name` (or `-Q`)—Encloses filenames in double quotes
- `--quoting-style=literal`—Same as `--literal`
- `--quoting-style=locale`—Uses locale's quoting style around individual file-names
- `--quoting-style=shell`—Uses shell quoting when necessary around individual filenames
- `--quoting-style=shell-always`—Always uses shell quoting around individual filenames
- `--quoting-style=c`—Uses C string quoting around individual filenames
- `--quoting-style=escape`—Escapes special characters with backslashes
- `--reverse` (or `-r`)—Reverses the sorting order
- `--recursive` (or `-R`)—Lists the contents of all subdirectories
- `--si` (or `-h`)—Similar to `--human-readable`, but uses powers of 1000 instead of 1024
- `--size` (or `-s`)—Prints the size in blocks
- `--sort=size` (or `-S`)—Sorts by file size

- `--sort=extension` (or `-X`)—Sorts by filename suffix
- `--sort=none` (or `-U`)—Sorts by the order the files are physically stored in their directory
- `--sort=time` (or `-t`)—Sorts by time. By default, `--time=ctime`
- `--sort=version` (or `-v`)—Sorts alphabetically, taking into account GNU version number conventions
- `--time=atime` (or `-u`)—Sorts by access time
- `--time=access`—Same as `atime`
- `--time=use`—Same as `ctime`
- `--time=ctime` (or `-c`)—Shows change time; sorts by change time if `-t`
- `--time=status`—Same as `ctime`
- `--tabsize=n` (or `-T`)—Assumes Tab stops are every n characters instead of eight characters
- `--width=n` (or `-w`)—Assumes screen is n characters wide instead of what it actually is

`printf` **Formatting Codes**

- `%b`—Expands backslash sequences
- `%c`—Displays a single character
- `%d`—Displays a signed number
- `%e`—Displays a floating-point number, exponential (also called scientific) notation
- `%f`—Displays a floating-point number
- `%g`—Uses `%f` or `%e` depending on the value
- `%i`—Same as `%d`
- `%o`—Displays an octal number
- `%q`—Quotes the string so it can be read properly by a shell script
- `%s`—Displays an unquoted string
- `%u`—Displays an unsigned number
- `%x`—Displays an unsigned hexadecimal number, using lowercase letters
- `%X`—Displays an unsigned hexadecimal number, using uppercase letters
- `%%`—Displays a percent sign

`printf` **Backslash Codes**

- `\b`—Backspace
- `\f`—Form feed (that is, eject a page on a printer)

- \n—Start a new line
- \r—Carriage return
- \t—Tab
- \v—Vertical tab
- \'—Single quote character (for compatibility with C)
- \\—Backslash
- \0n—n is an octal number representing an 8-bit ASCII character

rm **Command Switches**

- --directory (or -d)—Removes the directory
- --force (or -f)—Never prompts the user and ignores missing files
- --interactive (or -i)—Always prompts the user
- --recursive (or -r or -R)—remove contents of all subdirectories

cp **Command Switches**

- --archive (or -a)—Same as -dpR
- --backup (or -b)—Makes a backup of any existing file before overwriting by adding a ~ to the name
- --backup=none/off—Never makes numbered backups
- --backup=numbered/t—Always makes numbered backups
- --backup=existing/nul—Makes numbered backups if they already exist; otherwise make tilde backups
- --backup=simple/never—Always makes tilde backups
- --no-dereference (or -d)—Preserves links
- --force (or -f)—Never prompts the user; always overwrites
- --interactive (or -i)—Always prompts the user
- --link (or -l)—Creates a hard link instead of copying
- --preserve (or -p)—Preserves file attributes and ownership if possible
- --parents (or -P)—Appends the source path to the destination directory
- --recursive (or -R)—Copies any subdirectories
- -r—Similar to --recursive, but doesn't include special handling of pipes and other files that cannot be copied properly
- --sparse=w—Truncates sparse files (w=never), creates them in full (w=always), or truncates at the command's discretion (w=auto, default).

- `--strip-trailing-slashes`—Removes trailing slashes from the pathnames of the files to copy
- `--symbolic-link` (or `-s`)—Creates a symbolic link instead of copying
- `--suffix=`*s* (or `-S s`)—Replaces pathname suffix with new suffix *s*
- `--target-directory=`*d*—Copies files to directory *d*
- `--update` (or `-u`)—Overwrites old files or copies missing files
- `--one-file-system` (or `-x`)—Stays on the current file system

mv **Command Switches**

- `--backup` (or `-b`)—Makes a backup of any existing file before overwriting by adding a ~ to the name
- `--backup=none/off`—Never makes numbered backups
- `--backup=numbered/t`—Always makes numbered backups
- `--backup=existing/nul`—Make numbered backups if they already exist; otherwise make tilde backups
- `--backup=simple/never`—Always make tilde backups
- `--force` (or `-f`)—Never prompts the user; always overwrites
- `--interactive` (or `-i`)—Always prompts the user
- `--strip-trailing-slashes`—Removes trailing slashes from the pathnames of the files to copy
- `--suffix=`*s* (or `-S`)—Replaces pathname suffix with new suffix *s*
- `--target-directory=`*d*—Copies files to directory *d*
- `--update` (or `-u`)—Overwrites old files or copies missing files

## 4

Script Basics

I WAS FIRST INTRODUCED TO COMPUTERS when my high school purchased a shiny new TRS-80, Model I. The computer was installed in the library, free for anybody to use. I remember following the dog-eared manual and typing in my first BASIC program.

```
10 PRINT "KEN WAS HERE";
20 GOTO 10
```

When I ran the program, I was in for a surprise. Not only did the computer faithfully carry out my instructions over and over, but also the words scrolling up the screen formed a shifting pattern. When the screen became full, it scrolled to make room for more messages. If I changed the length of the message to a number that evenly divided into 64 (the TRS-80 had 64 character lines), the messages marched up the screen in neat columns. There was unexpected magic in my name.

The joy of programming is the joy of creating something new by giving "to airy nothing a local habitation and a name." Even bugs, in their quaint way, are unexpected signposts on the long road of creativity that offer choices depending on how you decide to deal with them. One choice leads to another, and no two programs of any size are the same. They are truly the offspring of a creative process as much as any painting, song, or poem.

In Bash, the journey starts with a programmer's first script. This chapter introduces the basic techniques of shell scripting—creating an organized script, redirecting standard file descriptors, and working with different kinds of commands.

Creating a Script

By convention, Bash shell scripts have names ending with .sh. Listing 4.1 shows a script called hello.sh, a very short script that writes a message on the screen.

Listing 4.1 `hello.sh`

```
# hello.sh
# This is my first shell script

printf "Hello!  Bash is wonderful."
exit 0
```

Lines beginning with number signs (#) are comments. They are notes to the reader and do not affect the execution of a script. Everything between the number sign and the end of the line is effectively ignored by Bash.

Comments should always be informative, describing what the script is trying to accomplish, not a blow-by-blow recount of what each command is doing. I've seen too many scripts with only a single comment at the top reading "Abandon Hope All Ye Who Enter Here". In a business environment, clear and informative comments help to troubleshoot and debug obscure problems.

The `exit` command, followed by a zero, informs the program running your shell script that the script ran successfully.

You can run your script by starting a new shell:

```
$ bash hello.sh
```

If there are no mistakes, Bash responds with this message:

```
Hello!  Bash is wonderful.!
```

Creating a Well-Behaved Script

Suppose your job is to write a shell script to run the `sync` command when there are no users on the system. The following commands are adequate to do the job.

```
USERS=`who | wc -l`
if [ $USERS -eq 0 ] ; then
    sync
fi
```

This works suitably well at the Bash prompt. But consider the following questions:

- How does Linux know that this is a Bash script?
- If there is more than one `who` command on the computer, which one executes?
- How does the script inform the program that runs it if it succeeds or fails?
- What happens if the `sync` command was accidentally deleted or if the system administrator altered the permissions?

Bash is a very flexible language: It needs to be if it is going to be used interactively. But in script writing, this flexibility can lead to security loopholes and unexpected behavior. For a shell script to be "well-behaved," it has to do more than simply execute the same commands typed at the Bash dollar prompt.

A well-structured Bash script can be divided into five sections:

- The header
- Global declarations
- Sanity checks
- The main script
- Cleanup

Each of these sections plays an important role in the design of a script. Next, you take a look at the previous example and see how you can improve it by examining each of the sections.

The Header

The header defines what kind of script this is, who wrote it, what version it is, and what assumptions or shell options Bash uses.

The very first line of a script is the *header line*. This line begins with #! at the top of the script, flush with the left margin. This character combination identifies the kind of script. Linux uses this information to start the right program to run the script. For Bash scripts, this line is the absolute pathname indicating where the Bash interpreter resides. On most Linux distributions, the first header line is as follows

```
#!/bin/bash
```

If you don't know the location of the Bash shell, use the Linux whereis command to find it:

```
$ whereis bash
bash: /bin/bash
```

The beginning of a typical script looks like this

```
#!/bin/bash
#
# Flush disks if nobody is on the computer
#
# Ken O. Burtch
# CVS: $Header$

shopt -s -o nounset
```

The Bash header line is followed by comments describing the purpose of the script and who wrote it. The cvs line is explained in Chapter 8, "Debugging and Version Control." The shopt -s -o nounset command detects some spelling mistakes by reporting undefined variables.

Global Declarations

All declarations that apply to the entirety of the script should occur at the top of the script, beneath the header. By placing *global declarations* in one place, you make it easy for someone to refer to them while reading the script

```
# Global Declarations

declare -rx SCRIPT=${0##*/}            # SCRIPT is the name of this script

declare -rx who="/usr/bin/who"         # the who command - man 1 who
declare -rx sync="/bin/sync"           # the sync command - man 1 sync
declare -rx wc="/usr/bin/wc"           # the wc command - man 1 wc
```

Sanity Checks

The next section, *sanity checks*, protects the script from unexpected changes in the computer. Normally, when a command runs at the command prompt, Bash searches several directories for the command you want to run. If it can't find the command, perhaps because of a spelling mistake, Bash reports an error. This kind of behavior is good for working interactively with Bash because it saves time and any mistakes are easily corrected with a few keystrokes.

Scripts, on the other hand, run without any human supervision. Before a script executes any statements, it needs to verify that all the necessary files are accessible. All required commands should be executable and stored in the expected locations. These checks are sometimes called *sanity checks* because they do not let the script begin its main task unless the computer is in a known, or "sane," state. This is especially important with operating systems such as Linux that are highly customizable: What is true on one computer might not be true on another.

Another way of putting it is that Bash relies on runtime error checking. Most errors are only caught when the faulty statement executes. Checking for dangerous situations early in the script prevents the script from failing in the middle of a task, otherwise making it difficult to determine where the script left off and what needs to be done to continue.

Sometimes system administrators unintentionally delete or change the accessibility of a file, making it unavailable to a script. Other times, changes in the environment can change which commands are executed. Malicious computer users have also been known to tamper with a person's login profile so that the commands you think you are running are not the ones you are actually using.

In the case of the sample script, you need to verify that the commands you need are where they're supposed to be and are available to the script.

```
# Sanity checks

if test -z "$BASH" ; then
```

```
    printf "$SCRIPT:$LINENO: please run this script with the BASH shell\n" >&2
    exit 192
fi
if test ! -x "$who" ; then
    printf "$SCRIPT:$LINENO: the command $who is not available — \
aborting\n " >&2
    exit 192
fi
if test ! -x "$sync" ; then
    printf "$SCRIPT:$LINENO: the command $sync is not available — \
aborting\n " >&2
    exit 192
fi
if test ! -x "$wc" ; then
    printf "$SCRIPT:$LINENO: the command $wc is not available — \
aborting\n " >&2
    exit 192
fi
```

The Main Script

When you have verified that the system is sane, the script can proceed to do its work.

```
# Flush disks if nobody is on the computer

USERS=`who | wc -l`
if [ $USERS -eq 0 ] ; then
    sync
fi
```

Cleanup

Finally, the script needs to clean up after itself. Any temporary files should be deleted, and the script returns a status code to the person or program running the script. In this case, there are no files to clean up. More complex scripts might use a variable to keep track of that status code returned by a failed command.

By placing the cleanup section at the end of the program, there is one unique place to perform your housekeeping tasks, as opposed to duplicating them throughout the script.

```
exit 0  # all is well
```

The completed script looks like Listing 4.2.

Listing 4.2 `flush.sh`

```bash
#!/bin/bash
#
# Flush disks if nobody is on the computer
#
# Ken O. Burtch
# CVS: $Header$

shopt -s -o nounset

# Global Declarations

declare -rx SCRIPT=${0##*/}          # SCRIPT is the name of this script

declare -rx who="/usr/bin/who"       # the who command - man 1 who
declare -rx sync="/bin/sync"         # the sync command - man 1 sync
declare -rx wc="/usr/bin/wc"         # the wc command - man 1 wc

# Sanity checks

if test -z "$BASH" ; then
   printf "$SCRIPT:$LINENO: please run this script with the BASH shell\n" >&2
   exit 192
fi
if test ! -x "$who" ; then
   printf "$SCRIPT:$LINENO: the command $who is not available - aborting\n" >&2
   exit 192
fi
if test ! -x "$sync" ; then
   printf "$SCRIPT:$LINENO: the command $sync is not available — \
aborting\n " >&2
   exit 192
fi
if test ! -x "$wc" ; then
   printf "$SCRIPT:$LINENO: the command $wc is not available — aborting\n " >&2
   exit 192
fi

# Flush disks if nobody is on the computer

USERS=`$who | $wc -l`
if [ $USERS -eq 0 ] ; then
   $sync
fi

# Cleanup

exit 0  # all is well
```

This script is much longer than the four-line script that introduced this section. In general, the longer the main script, the less overhead imposed by the lines in a well-behaved script. This new script is much more secure and reliable than a script containing only the main script.

Stopping a Script

The `logout` command, which ends an interactive login session, cannot be used to stop a script. (After all, a script is not a login session.) Instead, Bash provides two built-in commands for terminating a script.

As seen previously, the `exit` command unconditionally stops a script. `exit` can include a status code to return to the caller of the script. A status code of `0` indicates no error. If the status code is omitted, the status of the last command executed by the script is returned. As a result, it's always best to supply an exit status.

```
exit 0 # all is well
```

A script automatically stops when it reaches its end as if there was an implicit `exit` typed there, but the exit status is the status of the last command executed.

The `suspend` command likewise unconditionally stops a script. However, unlike `exit`, execution is suspended until the script is signaled to wake up and resume the next statement after the `suspend` command.

```
suspend # wait until notified otherwise
```

This command is discussed in more detail later in Chapter 10, "Job Control and Signals."

There is also a Linux utility called `sleep`. Sleep suspends the script for a specific number of seconds after which it wakes up and resumes the next statement after the `sleep` command.

```
sleep 5 # wait for 5 seconds
```

`Sleep` is useful for placing pauses in the script, enabling the user to read what's been displayed so far. `Sleep` isn't suitable for synchronizing events, however, because how long a particular program runs on the computer often depends on the system load, number of users, hardware upgrades, and other factors outside of the script's control.

Reading Keyboard Input

The built-in `read` command stops the script and waits for the user to type something from the keyboard. The text typed is assigned to the variable that accompanies the `read` command.

```
printf "Archive files for how many days? "
read ARCHIVE_DAYS
```

In this example, the variable ARCHIVE_DAYS contains the number of days typed by the user.

There are a number of options for read. First, -p (*prompt*) is a shorthand feature that combines the printf and read statements. read displays a short message before waiting for the user to respond.

```
read -p "Archive files for how many days? " ARCHIVE_DAYS
```

The -r (*raw input*) option disables the backslash escaping of special characters. Normally, read understands escape sequences such as \n when they're typed by the user. Using raw input, read treats the backspace the same as any other character typed on the keyboard. You need to use -r only when you need to handle the backslash character yourself.

```
read -p "Enter a Microsoft Windows pathname (backslashes allowed): " -r MS_PATH
```

The -e option works only interactively, not in shell scripts. It enables you to use Bash's history features to select the line to return. For example, you can use the Up and Down Arrow keys to move through recently typed commands.

A timeout can be set up using the -t (*timeout*) switch. If nothing is typed by the end of the timeout period, the shell continues with the next command and the value of the variable is unchanged. If the user starts typing after the timeout period ends, anything typed is lost. The timeout is measured in seconds.

```
read -t 5 FILENAME # wait up to 5 seconds to read a filename
```

If there is a variable called TMOUT, Bash times out after the number of seconds in the variable even if -t is not used.

A limit can be placed on the number of characters to read using the -n (*number of characters*) switch. If the maximum number of characters is reached, the shell continues with the next command without waiting for the Enter/Return key to be pressed.

```
read -n 10 FILENAME # read no more than 10 characters
```

If you don't supply a variable, read puts the typed text into a variable named REPLY. Well-structured scripts should avoid this default behavior to make it clear to a script reader where the value of REPLY is coming from.

Read also has some special purpose options that are discussed later in Chapter 13, "Console Scripting." While reading from the keyboard, read normally returns a status code of 0.

Basic Redirection

You can divert messages from commands like printf to files or other commands. Bash refers to this as *redirection*. There are a large number of redirection operators.

The > operator redirects the messages of a command to a file. The redirection operator is followed by the name of the file the messages should be written to. For example, to write the message "The processing is complete" to a file named results.txt, you use

```
printf "The processing is complete" > results.txt
```

The > operator always overwrites the named file. If a series of printf messages are redirected to the same file, only the last message appears.

To add messages to a file without overwriting the earlier ones, Bash has an append operator, >>. This operator redirects messages to the end of a file.

```
printf "The processing is complete" > results.txt
printf "There were no errors" >> results.txt
```

The results.txt file contains these two lines:

```
The processing is complete
There were no errors
```

In the same way, input can be redirected to a command from a file. The input redirection symbol is <. For example, the wc (*word count*) utility gathers statistics about a file. To count the number of lines in a file, use

```
wc —lines < purchase_orders.txt
```

wc —lines treats the contents of purchase_orders.txt as if it were typed in from the keyboard.

Instead of files, the results of a command can be redirected as input to another command. This process is called *piping* and uses the vertical bar (or *pipe*) operator |.

```
who | wc —lines  # count the number of users
```

Any number of commands can be strung together with vertical bar symbols. A group of such commands is called a *pipeline*.

If one command ends prematurely in a series of pipe commands, for example, because you interrupted a command with a control-c, Bash displays the message "Broken Pipe" on the screen.

The lines following a command can also be read and processed by the command. The operator << treats the lines following it in a script as if they were typed from the keyboard. The operator needs to be followed by a marker that denotes the end of the lines.

```
wc —lines << END_OF_LIST
   Jones, Allen
   Grates, William
   Oregano, Percy
END_OF_LIST
```

In this example, Bash treats the three lines between the END_OF_LIST markers as if they were being typed from the keyboard or read from a file embedded in the script. The line count returned by wc is 3.

The data in the `<<` list is known as a *here file* (or a *here document*) because the word HERE was often used in Bourne shell scripts as the marker word.

Newer versions of Bash have another here file redirection operator, `<<<`, which redirects a single line of text. There is an example in the section in Chapter 2, "Operating the Shell."

Standard Output, Error, and Input

Linux assumes that all output is going to some kind of file. To Linux, the screen is a file called `/dev/tty`.

```
printf "Sales are up" > /dev/tty    # display on the screen
```

When messages aren't redirected in your program, the messages don't go directly to the screen. Instead, the output goes through a special file called *standard output*. By default, standard output represents the screen. Everything sent through standard output is redirected to the screen. Bash uses the symbol `&1` to refer to standard output, and you can explicitly redirect messages to it.

```
printf "Sales are up" > results.txt   # sent to a file on disk
printf "Sales are up" > /dev/tty      # send explicitly to the screen
printf "Sales are up"                 # sent to screen via standard output
printf "Sales are up >&1             # same as the last one
printf "Sales are up >/dev/stdout    # same as the last one
```

`/dev/stdout` is another name for the standard output file. The last three examples are identical. Make sure `&1` is directly beside the redirect symbol, with no intervening spaces.

Standard output does not have to refer to the screen. For example, consider the following script called `listorders.sh`:

```
#!/bin/bash
#
# This script shows a long listing of the contents of the orders subdirectory.
shopt -s -o nounset

ls -l incoming/orders
exit 0
```

Suppose you run this script and redirect the contents to a file.

```
$ bash listorders.sh > listing.txt
```

Inside the script, standard output no longer refers to the screen. Instead, standard output refers to the file you've redirected the output to, in this case `listing.txt`.

```
ls -l incoming/orders              # listing saved in listing.txt
ls -l incoming/orders 1>&1         # listing saved in listing.txt
ls -l incoming/orders > /dev/tty   # listing displayed on screen
```

Using standard output is a way to send all the output from a script and any commands in it to a new destination.

A script doesn't usually need to know where the messages are going: There's always the possibility they were redirected. However, when errors occur and when warning messages are printed to the user, you don't want these messages to get redirected along with everything else.

Linux defines a second file especially for messages intended for the user called *standard error*. This file represents the destination for all error messages. The symbol for standard error is &2. /dev/stderr can also be used. The default destination, like standard output, is the screen. For example,

```
printf "$SCRIPT:$LINENO: No files available for processing" >&2
```

This command appears to work the same as a `printf` without the `>&2` redirection, but there is an important difference. It displays an error message to the screen, no matter where standard output has been previously redirected.

Because standard error, like standard output, is a kind of renaming of another destination, standard error can likewise be redirected. The redirection symbols for standard error are the same as standard output except they begin with the number 2.

```
$ bash listorders.sh 2> listorders_errors.txt
```

In this example, all the error messages from the `listorders.sh` script are saved in the file `listorders_errors.txt`.

If the `ls` command wrote the error messages directly to the screen with /dev/tty, there would be no way to redirect the messages to a separate file.

Linux treats all input as if it was being read from a file. This special file is called *standard input*, and uses the symbol &0. /dev/stdin can also be used for standard input. When commands are joined together with the | symbol, the standard input of the second command becomes the standard output of the first command.

Redirections can be combined for a single command. Order is important as each redirection is handled left-to-right. To redirect both standard output and standard error to a single file, the following command works.

```
$ bash listorders.sh > listorders_errors.txt >&2
```

However, reversing the order of the redirections does not work because it redirects standard error to the old standard output and then redirects standard output to the file `listorders_errors.txt`.

Because redirecting both standard input and standard error is so common, Bash provides a short form `&>` that redirects both.

```
$ bash listorders.sh &> listorders_errors.txt
```

Built-In Versus Linux Commands

The original Bourne shell was designed in a way that anything that was not an essential part of the shell was implemented as some program outside of the shell itself. Even arithmetic, for example, had to be performed by an outside program. This design made the Bourne shell very flexible, but it also introduced a couple of drawbacks. First, it was slow because programs were constantly loading and restarting to perform even the simplest of tasks. Second, it made shell scripts difficult to port because there were no guarantees that a command on one operating system was implemented the same way on another; such commands might not even have been available.

To deal with these problems, Bash has many of its fundamental commands built-in. But for basic compatibility with the older Bourne shell, Linux still implements its own version of Bash's commands. For instance, test is a built-in command in Bash, but Linux also provides its own program /usr/bin/test for shells that don't provide a built-in version of test.

If you don't know whether a command is built-in, the Bash type command will tell you. If the command is a Linux command, it shows the path of the command (like the Linux whereis command).

```
$ type cd
cd is a shell builtin
$ type id
id is /usr/bin/id
```

The -t (*type*) switch displays the type of command. The -p (*path*) switch returns just the hash table value for this command, as opposed to the first occurrence in the PATH variable, suppressing other information. The -a (*all*) flag lists all variations of a command.

```
$ type -a pwd
pwd is a shell builtin
pwd is /bin/pwd.
```

There are two switches that limit the scope of a search. The -f switch does not check any Bash functions that are declared. The -P switch goes further, checking for the path to a Linux command and ignoring any Bash commands, functions, or aliases.

The builtin command explicitly runs a built-in command. The command runs even if there's an alias with the same name.

```
builtin pwd
```

Likewise, command explicitly runs a Linux command, even if there's a built-in command or alias with the same name.

```
command pwd
```

With -v or -V, command lists information about the command such as its pathname. If -p is used, command searches the standard Linux bin libraries for the command; this is useful if you've changed the PATH variable.

A complete list of built-in shell commands appears in Appendix B.

Although `builtin` and `command` are useful in testing and porting older scripts to Bash, well-structured scripts should not rely on them because they indicate ambiguity in a script's design.

The built-in `enable` command temporarily hides the shell built-in commands and re-enables them later. The -n switch disables the command.

```
$ enable test
$ type test
test is a shell builtin
$ enable -n test
$ type test
test is /usr/bin/test
```

The -d switch disables the built-in command and releases any memory it was using. It can be reloaded with the -f switch, whereby the filename containing the built-in must be specified.

With -p, all enabled shell built-ins are printed. You can combine -p with -n to list the disabled built-ins, or use -a to show them all. The -s switch restricts the listing to POSIX special built-ins.

```
$ enable -pn
enable -n test
```

In well-structured scripts, `enable` should be used in your global declaration section. Using `enable` throughout a script makes it difficult to remember whether a particular command is a built-in command.

The Set and Shopt Commands

Bash contains many optional features that can be enabled or disabled. These options pertain to how Bash responds interactively with the user, how it behaves in shell scripts, and how compatible Bash is with other shells and standards.

Bash options can be enabled or disabled by commands or as a command switch when Bash is started. For example, to start a Bash session and disallow the use of undefined variables, use this:

```
$ bash -o nounset
```

In a script or at the Bash dollar prompt, you can disallow the use of undefined variables by using this:

```
$ shopt -s -o nounset
```

Historically, the `set` command was used to turn options on and off. As the number of options grew, `set` became more difficult to use because options are represented by single letter codes. As a result, Bash provides the `shopt` (*shell option*) command to turn options on and off by name instead of a letter. You can set certain options only by letter. Others are available only under the `shopt` command. This makes finding and setting a particular option a confusing task.

`shopt -s` (*set*) turns on a particular shell option. `shopt -u` (*unset*) turns off an option. Without an `-s` or `-u`, `shopt` toggles the current setting.

```
$ shopt -u -o nounset
```

`shopt` by itself or with `-p` prints a list of options and shows whether they are on, excluding the `-o` options. To see these options, you need to set `-o`. A list of the letter codes is stored in the shell variable `$-`.

Most of these switches are useful in special circumstances. For example, with UUCP networking, the exclamation mark (!) is used in email addresses, but Bash uses the ! for history processing. History processing can be disabled using this:

```
$ shopt -u -o histexpand
```

With history disabled, UUCP email addresses can be used in the interactive command line. Afterwards, history processing can be turned back on again.

Reference Section

`command` Command Switches

- `-p`—Searches the standard Linux binary libraries for the command
- `-v`—Describes the command
- `-V`—Describes the command in detail

`enable` Command Switches

- `-a`—Displays all built-in commands and whether they are enabled
- `-d`—Disables and deletes the built-in command
- `-f` *file*—Enables and loads the built-in command
- `-n`—Disables the built-in command
- `-p`—Prints a list of built-in commands
- `-s`—Restricts results to special POSIX built-ins

`read` Command Switches

- `-a` *array*—Reads text into this array
- `-d` *d*—Stops reading at character *d* instead of a new line

- -e—Uses interactive editing
- -n *num*—Reads num characters instead of the entire line
- -p *prompt*—Displays a prompt
- -r—Displays raw input
- -s—Hides the characters typed
- -t *sec*—Times out after *sec* seconds

suspend **Command Switches**

- -f—Suspends even if this is a login shell

Variables

THE RESULTS OF COMMANDS CAN be written to a file or saved in variables. Because variables are saved in memory, they tend to be faster to examine than files. Bash doesn't put an upper limit on the size of a variable: They are large enough to contain anything you will ever need to hold.

Using variables is essential to shell script programming. This chapter is an in-depth look at variables and how they are used in the shell, from basic variables to expanding variables with the `eval` command.

Variable Basics

Variables are declared using the Bash `declare` command. To declare a variable named COST, use this:

```
$ declare COST
```

Use the built-in `typeset` statement for compatibility with the Korn shell. If you are using Bash, use `declare` instead. `declare` has all the features of the older typeset command.

Choosing good variable names is important. One time, when I was grading a first-year computer science assignment, a student used 26 variables named A to Z. There was no explanation about what the variables represented and it took me half an hour to determine whether the program actually worked. (Surprisingly, it did.)

Names should also be consistent. In the mutual fund industry, for example, "portfolios," "accounts," and "funds" often mean the same thing. It is better to use one of these three names throughout your script. If three different terms are used, the reader might assume there are subtle differences in meaning between them.

Because Bash does minimum checking of variable names, even with the `nounset` option turned on, another common mistake is using a variable that looks the same. In my first year in university, I ran into an old friend who was frustrated because his Fortran program wasn't working. When I examined it closely, I saw that he had declared a variable called HIGH, but in the body of his program he spelled the variable HI. When the program printed the value of HIGH, it was zero because it was never actually assigned a value. The same kind of situation can occur in Bash scripts.

Variable names begin with a leading alphabetic or underscore character followed by additional alphanumeric characters or underscores.

Although variables can be in upper- or lowercase, tradition dictates variables are named in uppercase so as not to be confused with shell commands, which are almost always in lowercase. TOTAL, ORDERS_EUROPE, and _W3C are all legitimate variable names. There are no *reserved words*, which are words that are reserved for a specific purpose in the shell.

Variables are assigned new values with an equals sign (=). To assign an empty string to a variable, don't supply any value.

```
$ COST=
```

Otherwise, include some text to be assigned.

```
$ COST=0
```

Although printf %d prints a zero for both a value of zero and an empty string, Bash considers the two values to be different. A variable with no value is not the same as a variable with a value of zero.

Values can also be assigned with the let statement described in Chapter 6.

Bash differentiates between a variable's name and the value the variable represents. To refer to the value of a variable, you must precede the name with a dollar sign ($).

```
$ printf "%s" $COST
0
```

The dollar sign means "substitute." The shell replaces $COST with the value COST represents. In this case, the value of COST is zero. After substituting the value of COST, the command becomes:

```
$ printf "%d" 0
```

Bash executes this command and displays a zero.

Values can be assigned an initial value when the variable is first declared.

```
$ declare COST=5
$ printf "%d" $COST
5
```

Because declare is a command, variables are created only when the declare command is executed. They remain in existence until the script ends or until the variable is destroyed with the built-in unset command.

```
$ unset COST
```

The unset command is a command-line convenience. In well-structured scripts, variables are declared at the start of a script and are not unset. This prevents confusion because the programmer can be sure that the variables always exist while the script is running.

The results of a command can also be assigned to a variable. If a command is contained in backquotes (`), everything written to standard output is stored in the variable being assigned instead.

```
$ declare NUMBER_OF_FILES
$ NUMBER_OF_FILES='ls -1 | wc -l'
$ printf "%d" "$NUMBER_OF_FILES"
14
```

Predefined Variables

Bash has more than 50 predefined variables. These variables, created when Bash is first started, provide information about the Bash session and can be used to control some of the shell's features.

Some of these variables have special properties that might be lost if you unset the variable and then create a new one with the same name. For example, the variable RANDOM contains a random number. If you delete RANDOM with unset and declare a new variable called RANDOM, this new variable is a normal shell variable and does not contain random numbers. Therefore, it's best to avoid creating variables with the same name as the predefined variables.

The declare command, with no switches, lists all currently defined values.

- BASH—The full pathname of Bash.
- BASH_ENV—In a shell script, the name of the profile file executed before the script was started.
- BASH_VERSION—The version of Bash (for example, 2.04.0(1)-release).
- COLUMNS—The number of characters per line on your display (for example, 80).
- FUNCNAME—If inside a function, the name of the function.
- HOSTNAME—The name of the computer. Under some versions of Linux, this can be the machine name. On others, it can be a fully qualified domain name.
- HOSTTYPE—Type of computer.
- HOME—The name of your home directory.
- IFS—The *internal field separator*, a list of characters used to split a line into shell words.
- LINENO—The current line number in a script or function.
- LINES—The number of horizontal lines in your display (for example, 24).

- OSTYPE—The name of the operating system.
- PATH—Colon-separated list of search paths to find a command to execute.
- PPID—The process ID of the shell's parent process.
- PROMPT_COMMAND—Command to execute before the setting of the PS1 primary prompt string.
- PS1—The primary prompt string.
- PS2—The secondary prompt string.
- PS3—The select command prompt string.
- PS4—The trace command output prefix string.
- PWD—The current working directory (as set by the cd command).
- RANDOM—Returns a random number between 0 and 32767 each time it is referenced.
- SHELL—The preferred shell to use; for programs that start a shell for you.
- TERM—The terminal emulation type (for example, console).

Linux distributions define additional variables. The presence of these variables depends on your particular distribution. Many are declared for the use of applications.

- DISPLAY is the X Window display server.
- EDITOR is your default editor. Historically, this was used to indicate a line editor to use when a visual editor was not available (see VISUAL).
- ORGANIZATION is the name of your organization (usually the contents of /etc/organization).
- TERM is the terminal emulation (for example, xterm for an xterm session, or linux for the Linux console) .
- VISUAL is your default editor, usually the same as EDITOR.
- WINDOWMANAGER is the path to your current X Windows window manager.

A complete list appears in the reference section at the end of this chapter.

The Effect of Quotations

Those people familiar with other computer languages might be confused by the way Bash uses quotation marks. Single and double quotes are not used to delineate strings or characters, but to control how the shell groups characters and interprets special characters within a string. Bash calls this process *word splitting*.

```
$ COST=0
$ COST="0"
```

These two assignments produce the same result: COST is assigned a value of 0. The double quotes explicitly show that the value to assign to COST includes the character zero. Short alphanumeric values can be assigned to variables without quotations. However, when the string contains spaces, it's no longer apparent what value is to be assigned. Consider the following example.

```
$ DISTRIBUTION_CENTERS=London
$ printf "%s" $DISTRIBUTION_CENTERS
London
$ DISTRIBUTION_CENTERS=London ; Paris ; New York
bash: Paris: command not found
bash: New: command not found
$ printf "%s" $DISTRIBUTION_CENTERS
London
```

When Bash examines the second assignment statement, it sees a value of London terminated by a space. It assigns that value to the variable. It then sees the semicolon, the command separator, and expects a new statement to follow. It tries to execute the Paris command (there is none). It tries to do the same with the New command, giving it the York argument.

For this reason, it is a safe practice to enclose all assignment values in double quotation marks. Even if your company only has a distribution center in London, there's always the chance that a new distribution center will be added to the string, causing the shell script to crash. Always enclosing values in quotes ensures that Bash knows exactly what value is to be assigned.

```
$ DISTRIBUTION_CENTERS="London ; Paris ; New York"
$ printf "%s" $DISTRIBUTION_CENTERS
London;Paris;NewYork
```

The results are still not correct. Bash took the DISTRIBUTION_CENTERS value and removed the spaces so that printf doesn't interpret it as separate arguments of London, ;, Paris, ;, New, and York. The printf argument must also be enclosed in double quotes to keep the value of the variable as a single argument with the spacing intact.

```
$ printf "%s" "$DISTRIBUTION_CENTERS"
London ; Paris ; New York
```

Again, it is a safe practice to always enclose variable substitutions with quotes.

Because the quotation marks are not delimiters but hints on how to interpret special characters, they can be used back-to-back. This is a convenient way to separate variables from the surrounding text in a string.

```
$ TAX=7.25
$ TAX_MESSAGE="The tax is ""$TAX""%"
$ printf "%s" "$TAX_MESSAGE"
The tax is 7.25%
```

Separating each of the quoted pieces with a space would result in the same problem you saw previously: Bash would treat them as three individual values.

Alternatively, a variable substitution's variable name can be enclosed in curly braces to make it clear where the variable's name begins and ends.

```
$ TAX_MESSAGE="The tax is ${TAX}%"
```

Besides space interpretation, another effect of quotation marks is that no pattern matching is done. Normally, for example, the asterisk (*) represents all the files in the current directory. Quotation marks prevent the asterisk from being replaced with a list of files.

```
$ printf "%s\n" *
orders.txt
archive
calc.sh
$ printf "%s\n" "*"
*
```

To print strings without interpreting the special characters inside, use single quotes. Double quotes do not prevent Bash from interpreting the special characters $, `, and \, but single quotes leave all characters unchanged.

```
$ printf "%s" '$TAX_MESSAGE'
$TAX_MESSAGE
```

In this case, the single quotes prevent Bash from interpreting the value as a variable substitution because the dollar sign is not treated specially.

The backslash (\) acts like single quotes for one character, leaving the character unchanged. For example, to print a double quote mark, do this:

```
$ printf "%s" "\""
"
```

The backslash indicates that the second quote mark is to be treated as a character, not as the ending quote of a pair of quote marks.

The printf formatting code %q (*quoting*) prints backslashes before every character that has a special meaning to the shell. Use this to ensure that spacing is left intact.

```
$ printf "%q" "$TAX_MESSAGE"
The\ tax\ is\ 7.25%
```

For example, reading from files is affected by %q. If the printed variables contain spaces, read treats the spaces as separators unless they are protected with backslashes.

```
$ printf "%q %q\n" "Alpha Systems Inc" "Key West, Florida" > company.txt
$ read COMPANY LOCATION < company.txt
$ printf "%s\n" "$COMPANY"
Alpha Systems Inc
```

```
$ printf "%s %s\n" "Alpha Systems Inc" "Key West, Florida" > company.txt
$ read COMPANY LOCATION < company.txt
$ printf "%s\n" "$COMPANY"
Alpha
```

The read command has no knowledge of what text on the line belonged originally
to which variable. It assumes that the values are separated by spaces and assigns Alpha to
COMPANY. When %q is used, read knows that the backslash protected spaces belong with
the first value and it reads everything up to the first unprotected space, assigning Alpha
Systems Inc to COMPANY.

Word splitting is controlled by the value of the special variable IFS. Normally, IFS
treats spaces, tabs, and newline characters as *word delimiters*—that is, it uses whitespace
characters. If the content of IFS is changed, the new characters are used as word delimiters. However, this is an older feature for compatibility with the Bourne shell and the
IFS variable should not be altered by scripts because newer features such as %q formatting are available.

Whenever values are assigned or are substituted with a dollar sign, it is good practice
to always enclose the values in double quotes to prevent problems with values containing
spaces.

Variable Attributes

All Bash variables are stored as simple strings. Each variable has certain options called
attributes, which can be turned on or off by using the declare command in a similar
way to shell options and the shopt command.

If a variable is declared with the -i (integer) switch, Bash turns on the integer attribute for that variable. The shell will remember that the string should be treated as an integer value. If a non-numeric value is assigned to an integer variable, Bash does not report
an error but instead assigns a value of zero.

```
$ declare -i NUMBER_ACCOUNTS=15
$ printf "%d\n" "$NUMBER_ACCOUNTS"
15
$ NUMBER_ACCOUNTS="Smith" # mistake
$ printf "%d\n" "$NUMBER_ACCOUNTS"
0
$ NUMBER_ACCOUNTS=12
$ printf "%d\n" "$NUMBER_ACCOUNTS"
12
```

Sometimes an attempt to assign a string produces an error, but you can't rely on this
behavior.

```
$ NUMBER_ACCOUNTS="Smith Account" # mistake
bash: Smith Account: syntax error in expression (error token is "Account")
```

The attributes of a variable can be displayed with the -p (*print*) switch.

```
$ declare -p NUMBER_ACCOUNTS
declare -i NUMBER_ACCOUNTS="12"
```

The information is displayed in such a way that it can be saved for use in another script. This allows you to experiment with declarations at the command prompt and then write the declarations to a script file when you are satisfied with the results.

The integer attribute can be turned off with a plus sign.

```
$ declare +i NUMBER_ACCOUNTS # turn off integer attribute
$ printf "%d\n" "$NUMBER_ACCOUNTS"
bash: printf: Smith Account: invalid number
$ printf "%s\n" "$NUMBER_ACCOUNTS"
Smith Account
```

Although Bash does not consider the assignment of a non-numeric value an error, the printf command does report that the value can't be formatted as a number.

Like the printf command, integer variables can be assigned octal or hexadecimal numbers as well.

```
$ declare -i NUMBER_ACCOUNTS=0X0F
$ printf "%i\n" "$NUMBER_ACCOUNTS"
15
```

Constants are unchanging variables that are created with the -r (*read-only*) attribute. If you attempt to assign a value to a constant, Bash reports an error. Suppose the constant COMPANY has the name of a company.

```
$ declare -r COMPANY="Smith and Jones"
$ printf "%s\n" "$COMPANY"
Smith and Jones
$ COMPANY="Wilson Distribution"
bash: COMPANY: readonly variable
```

The readonly attribute can be turned off using a plus sign. However, this can make your scripts confusing to read because the reader will assume that a readonly variable is always read-only. Either remove the readonly attribute or change the structure of the script.

Arrays

Arrays are lists of values that are created with the -a (*array*) attribute. A number called an *index* refers to the position item in the array. Bash arrays differ from arrays in other computer languages because they are open-ended. Arrays can be any length and are initially filled with empty strings for items.

```
$ declare -a PRODUCTS
```

New items are assigned to the array using square brackets to indicate the position in the list. The first position is position zero (not one). If an initial value is specified, it is assigned to the first position. Assigning one value is not particularly useful but is included for compatibility with other shells. Alternatively, the initial values can be assigned to specific positions by including a position in square brackets.

```
$ declare -a DEPT[0]="accounting" DEPT [1]="shipping" \
DEPT [2]="customer service"
```

Because of the square brackets, use curly braces to delineate the variable name and supercede the shell's pathname matching process.

```
$ echo "${ DEPT [0]}"
accounting
$ echo "${ DEPT [2]}"
customer service
```

All unassigned positions in an array have no value. The position number 5 in the PRODUCTS array, for example, is initially an empty string. It can be assigned a value of hammers with an assignment statement.

```
$ printf "%s" "${PRODUCTS[5]}"

$ PRODUCTS[5]="hammers"
$ printf "%s" "${PRODUCTS[5]}"
hammers
```

If there is an item in position zero, it is also the value returned when no position is specified.

```
$ PRODUCTS[0]="screwdrivers"
$ printf "%s" "$PRODUCTS"
screwdrivers
$ printf "%s" "${PRODUCTS[0]}"
screwdrivers
```

The entire array can be accessed using an asterisk (*) or an at sign (@) for the array position. These two symbols differ only when double quotes are used: The asterisk returns one string, with each item separated with the first character of the IFS variable (usually space), and the at sign returns each item as a separate string with no separation character.

```
$ printf "%s" "${PRODUCTS[*]}"
screwdrivers hammers
/home/kburtch [bash]
$ printf "%s" "${PRODUCTS[@]}"
screwdrivershammers
```

In this example, the at sign version requires two separate %s formatting codes to display the array properly, one for each array item.

```
$ printf "%s %s\n" "${PRODUCTS[@]}"
screwdrivers hammers
```

Multiple values can be assigned with a list in parentheses.

```
$ DIVISIONS=("North America" "Europe" "Far East")
$ printf "%s\n" "${DIVISIONS[*]}"
North America Europe Far East
```

The list items can have an optional subscript.

```
$ DIVISIONS=([3]="North America" [2]="Europe" [1]="Far East")
$ printf "%s\n" "${DIVISIONS[*]}"
Far East Europe North America
```

Combining a list with a `declare` command, arrays can be assigned values at the time they are created.

The number of items in the array is returned when # is used in front of the variable name with a position of * or @. The items need not be assigned consecutively and the number doesn't reflect where the items are stored.

```
$ printf "%d" "${#PRODUCTS[*]}"
2
```

Individual array values can be removed with the `unset` command. Erasing a value by assigning the array position an empty string doesn't destroy it: The empty string is still treated as an array item whenever the items are counted.

The `read` command can read a list into an array using an -a (*array*) switch. When this switch is used, each item on the line of input is read into a separate array position.

The `array` attribute is the only variable attribute that cannot be turned off after it is turned on. If Bash allowed the attribute to be turned off, the data in the array would be lost when the array became a normal variable.

Exporting Variables and the Linux Environment

Shell variables exist in the script or interactive sessions only where they were declared. In order to make shell variables available outside of their place of origin, they have to be declared as exportable. Variables are marked as exportable with the export attribute using the `declare` -x (*export*) switch. The export attribute reminds the shell that you want to "export," or provide the variable, to all programs run by the script.

For example, the program CVS requires a variable called CVSROOT to exist for all its programs.

```
$ declare -x CVSROOT="/home/cvs/cvsroot"
```

In the same way, any variables declared in your profile scripts must be exported or they won't exist at the command prompt. They will disappear after the profile scripts are finished running.

When a variable is exported, any changes made by programs executed by the script are discarded when the program completes. If a second script were to change CVSROOT to the value /home/local/cvsroot, when the second script is finished, CVSROOT will once again be /home/cvs/cvsroot. The changes are "rolled back."

Create global constants by using both the export and read-only switches.

```
$ declare -rx COMPANY_BRANCH="West Coast Branch"
```

COMPANY_BRANCH is only a read-only variable in the current script. When it's exported to a second script, it's exported as a normal variable—the read-only effect is lost. The reason for this strange behavior is rooted in the way Linux shares environment variables between programs and has nothing to do with the Bash shell itself.

Environment variables are the variables Linux shares between a program and the program that executed it. Like layers of an onion, each program must explicitly export a variable into the environment for the next program to see it.

Although Linux has provisions for exporting environment variables, there is no way to assign any attributes to them. Linux has no notion of attributes. Bash attributes were thought up after environment variables were first invented. When Bash variables are given to Linux to share with a new program, the attributes are lost. When the second shell script starts, it has no way of knowing what the original attributes were.

The variables shared with a new program are copies of the original. If a script declares an exported variable and runs a second script, any changes made to the variable by the second script are invisible to the first. There is no way for a second script to assign a new value to a variable that the first script will see. Unlike other programming languages, exporting shell variables is a one-way street.

Suppose there are two scripts called outer.sh and inner.sh. outer.sh declares a variable and then runs the inner.sh script, as shown in Listings 5.1 and 5.2.

Listing 5.1   outer.sh

```
# outer.sh
#
# This script runs first.

declare -rx COMPANY_BRANCH="West Coast Branch"
bash inner.sh
printf "%s\n" "$COMPANY_BRANCH"

exit 0
```

Listing 5.2 `inner.sh`

```
# inner.sh
#
# This script is run by outer.sh.

printf "This is the inner script.\n"

declare -p COMPANY_BRANCH
COMPANY_BRANCH="East Coast Branch"
printf "%s\n" "$COMPANY_BRANCH"

printf "Inner script finished\n"

exit 0
```

When `outer.sh` is run, the `COMPANY_BRANCH` variable is read-only. However, inside `inner.sh`, the read-only attribute has been lost. `inner.sh` changes the variable to a new value, but when `inner.sh` is finished, `outer.sh` shows that the variable's value is unchanged.

```
$ bash outer.sh
This is the inner script.
declare -x COMPANY_BRANCH="West Coast Branch"
East Coast Branch
Inner script finished
West Coast Branch
```

The only way to return a value to the calling program is to write it to a file (or standard output) and have the calling program read (or assign) the value back into a variable.

The `eval` Command

Bash performs variable substitutions as variables are encountered in a command. Before a command is executed, Bash searches the command for all dollar signs and inserts the value of variables before the command is carried out. Bash performs this substitution once. If a variable contains a value with a dollar sign in it and the value is substituted into a command, the value with the dollar sign remains unchanged.

```
$ declare -rx COMPANY="Value Book Resellers"
$ declare -rx TITLE='$COMPANY'
$ printf "%s\n" "$TITLE"
$COMPANY
```

Before the `printf` is performed, Bash substitutes the value "`$COMPANY`" for `TITLE`. Bash does not repeat the substitution process to replace the `COMPANY` variable with "`Value Book Resellers`". Substitutions are performed only once.

Under rare cases, you might want to force Bash to perform an additional round of substitutions. The Bash eval command can do substitutions on demand and run the results. Take the following simple example, shown in Listing 5.3, whereby one of three variables is shown on the screen.

Listing 5.3 eval_example.sh

```
# eval_example.sh

shopt -s -o nounset

declare -r DISPLAY_VARIABLE='$SALES_EAST'

declare -i SALES_EAST=1000
declare -i SALES_WEST=2000
declare -i SALES_NORTH=3000


printf "DISPLAY_VARIABLE = %s\n" "$DISPLAY_VARIABLE"
printf "reprocessed with eval, DISPLAY_VARIABLE = %s\n" \
`eval printf "%s\n" "$DISPLAY_VARIABLE"`
```

This script can display the sales figures for one of three company branches. The constant DISPLAY_VARIABLE contains the variable to display, SALES_EAST, SALES_WEST, or SALES_NORTH. But if DISPLAY_VARIABLE is substituted, only the string "$SALES_EAST" is printed.

The backquotes run eval and perform a new set of substitutions. The results can be substituted into the original printf command. Now the results are as you expected.

```
$ bash eval_example.sh
DISPLAY_VARIABLE = $SALES_EAST
reprocessed with eval, DISPLAY_VARIABLE = 1000
```

In this example, Bash first processes the printf command as

```
printf "reprocessed with eval, DISPLAY_VARIABLE = %s\n" \
`eval printf "%s\n" $SALES_EAST`
```

This only prints $ SALES_EAST because Bash is finished substituting the values of variables. When Bash executes the eval command, there is a second examination of the echo command.

```
printf "reprocessed with eval, DISPLAY_VARIABLE = %s\n" ` printf "%s\n" 1000`
```

Because Bash also attempts to run the result, the echo command, a simpler version of printf, is required. eval tries to execute the re-evaluated $DISPLAY_VARIABLE as if it were a command. That is, with eval 1000, Bash would try to execute the number 1000, which is not what you want.

```
printf "reprocessed with eval, DISPLAY_VARIABLE = %s\n" 1000
```

Although not particularly realistic in this example, the eval command is useful when the user types commands to execute, or when reading commands to execute from a file. The commands can contain variables, dollar functions, and so forth, provided you use eval to process them.

A common pitfall is not following through the substitution process. Suppose, for example, that instead of assigning DISPLAY_VARIABLE the value $SALES_EAST, SALES_EAST was assigned and a second dollar sign was added to the printf statement.

```
printf "reprocessed with eval, DISPLAY_VARIABLE = %s\n" \
`eval printf "%s\n" "\$$DISPLAY_VARIABLE"
```

You would get a response similar to this:

```
reprocessed with eval, DISPLAY_VARIABLE = 14235SALES_EAST
```

In this case, the first substitution leaves the command:

```
 printf "reprocessed with eval, DISPLAY_VARIABLE = %s\n" \
`eval printf "%s\n" $$SALES_EAST'
```

But $$ is a built-in shell function. Bash doesn't understand that $SALES_EAST is supposed to be nested inside the first dollar sign: it simply reads from left to right, substituting as it does. The second substitution would execute the $$ function, not substitute the value of the SUM variable. To execute this properly, you have to escape the first dollar sign with a backslash to keep Bash from substituting it.

```
 printf "reprocessed with eval, DISPLAY_VARIABLE = %s\n" \
`eval printf "%s\n" "\\\$$DISPLAY_VARIABLE"'
```

After the first substitution, you get this:

```
 printf "reprocessed with eval, DISPLAY_VARIABLE = %s\n" \
`eval printf "%s\n" \$$SUM'
```

This prevents $$ from being treated as a built-in function: Bash substitutes for $SALES_EAST instead. You bypassed these issues in the first example when the dollar sign was inside DISPLAY_VARIABLE.

The same effect can be achieved by escaping some quotation marks in the right places.

Variables and constants form the building blocks of all scripts, but they only serve as storage containers without expressions. These are covered in the next chapter (Chapter 6, "Expressions").

story.bash: **A Story Generator**

Listing 5.4 is a complete example showing some of the concepts in this chapter. story.bash is a script that creates a story by substituting words chosen by the user.

Listing 5.4 `story.bash`

```bash
#!/bin/bash
#
# story.bash: a story generator
#
# Ken O. Burtch
# CVS: $Header$

shopt -s -o nounset

declare NAME          # a name
declare COLOR         # a color
declare DAY           # a day
declare RELATIONSHIP  # a person's relationship
declare OBJECT        # an everyday object
declare -a ACTIVITY   # a list of everyday activities

# Instructions

printf "%s\n" "This is a story generator.  I will ask you for some"
printf "%s\n" "common words.  Then I will compose a story."
printf "\n"

# Read the variables

read -p "Enter a man's name                       : " NAME
read -p "Enter a color (eg. red)                 : " COLOR
read -p "Enter a day (eg. Monday)                : " DAY
read -p "Enter a person's relationship (eg. uncle): " RELATIONSHIP
read -p "Enter an everyday object (eg. pencil)    : " OBJECT
read -p "Enter an everyday activity (eg. sleeping): " ACTIVITY[0]
read -p "Enter an everyday activity (eg. reading) : " ACTIVITY[1]
printf "\n"
read -p "Press return/enter to read your story"
printf "\n"

# Write the story

printf "%s\n" "$DAY at work, $NAME realized that he had forgotten to pack"
printf "%s\n" "a lunch.  Ignoring his $SHELL prompt, $NAME decided to head"
printf "%s\n" "out early and grab lunch from a street vendor."
printf "%s\n" "As he got outside of the front door of the office,"
printf "%s\n" "$NAME ran into his $RELATIONSHIP carrying a"
printf "%s\n" "$COLOR $OBJECT.  His $RELATIONSHIP remarked that it had"
printf "%s\n" "been $RANDOM days since $NAME had called.  $NAME"
```

Listing 5.4 **Continued**

```
printf "%s\n" "thought he would have been off surfing the net on his"
printf "%s\n" "$OSTYPE computer than running into his $RELATIONSHIP.  He"
printf "%s\n" "offered to take the $OBJECT to get polished." \
" He went ${ACTIVITY[0]}"
printf "%s\n" "down the street, wishing that his $RELATIONSHIP had stayed"
printf "%s\n" "home ${ACTIVITY[1]} instead."

exit 0
```

Reference Section

Declare Command Switches

- -a—Declares an array
- -f—Displays a function and its definition
- -F—Displays the function name
- -r—Declares a read-only variable
- -x—Declares an exported variable
- -I—Declares an integer variable

Bash Predefined Variables

- auto_resume—If set, allows command completion for the names of stopped jobs.
- BASH—The full pathname of the shell.
- BASH_ENV—In a shell script, displays the name of the profile file executed before the script was started.
- BASH_VERSION—The version of Bash (for example, 2.04.0(1)-release).
- BASH_VERSINFO—An array holding more detailed version information than BASH_VERSION.

BASH_VERSINFO[0]	The major version number (the release).
BASH_VERSINFO[1]	The minor version number (the version).
BASH_VERSINFO[2]	The patch level.
BASH_VERSINFO[3]	The build version.
BASH_VERSINFO[4]	The release status (for example, beta1).
BASH_VERSINFO[5]	The value of MACHTYPE.

- CDPATH—Colon-separated list of directories to search when using the cd command.
- COLUMNS—The number of characters per line on your display (for example, 80).
- COMP_WORDS—In a programmable completion function, an array of the individual words on the current command line.
- COMP_CWORD—In a programmable completion function, the current COMP_WORDS word.
- COMP_LINE—In a programmable completion function, the current command line.
- COMP_POINT—In a programmable completion function, the current command-line cursor position.
- COMPREPLY—In a programmable completion function, the list of completions returned.
- DIRSTACK—The list of directories used by dirs, popd, and pushd.
- EUID—The effective user ID of the current user.
- FCEDIT—The default text editor for the fc command.
- FIGNORE—Colon-separated list of prefixes or suffixes to ignore for filename completion.
- FUNCNAME—If inside a function, the name of the function.
- GLOBIGNORE—Colon-separated pattern list of filenames to be ignored by pathname expansion.
- GROUPS—The list of groups of which the user is a member (in numeric format).
- histchars—List of characters to be used for the history expansion in commands.
- HISTCMD—The position in the command history where the current command is placed.
- HISTCONTROL—Determines whether commands preceded by spaces, or repeated commands, are placed in the command history.
- HISTFILE—The file containing the command history.
- HISTFILESIZE—Maximum size of the HISTFILE command history file.
- HISTIGNORE—Colon-separated pattern list of commands to be kept in the command history.
- HISTSIZE—The number of commands kept in the command line history (for example, 1000).
- HOSTNAME—The name of the computer. Under some versions of Linux, this is the machine name. On others, it is a fully-qualified domain name.
- HOSTTYPE—Type of computer.
- HOME—The name of your home directory.

- IGNOREEOF—If this variable exists, it indicates the number of EOF characters that must be typed before Bash exits.
- IFS—The *internal field separator,* a list of characters used to split a line into sections by the read command.
- INPUTRC—The name of the Readline startup file.
- LANG—Used to determine the locale category for any category not specifically selected with a variable starting with LC_.
- LC_ALL—This variable overrides the value of LANG and any other LC_ variables specifying a locale category.
- LC_COLLATE—Controls the sorting order of pathname expansion and pattern matching.
- LC_CTYPE—Controls the character classes used by pathname expansion and pattern matching.
- LC_MESSAGES—Locale for translation of double-quoted string preceded by a dollar sign.
- LINENO—The current line number in a script or function.
- LINES—The number of horizontal lines in your display (for example, 24).
- MACHTYPE—A description of the computer; a combination of $HOSTTYPE and $OSTYPE.
- MAIL—The name of a file to check for incoming mail. It is superceded by MAILPATH.
- MAILCHECK—If this variable exists, the number of seconds to check MAILPATH for incoming mail. The default if no value is set is 60 seconds.
- MAILPATH—Colon-separated list of files to check for incoming mail.
- OSTYPE—The name of the operating system.
- OLDPWD—The previous working directory (as set by the cd command).
- OPTERR—If set, getopts shows error messages.
- PATH—Colon-separated list of search paths to find a command to execute.
- PIPESTATUS—An array with a list of exit status values for each command in the last pipe.
- PPID—The process ID of the shell's parent process.
- PROMPT_COMMAND—Command to execute before the setting of the PS1 primary prompt string.
- PS1—The primary prompt string.
- PS2—The secondary prompt string.
- PS3—The select command prompt string.

- PS4—The trace command output prefix string.
- PWD—The current working directory (as set by the cd command).
- RANDOM—Returns a random number between 0 and 32767 each time it is referenced.
- OPTARG—The last argument processed by the getopts command.
- OPTIND—The index of the next argument to be processed by the getopts command.
- SECONDS—The number of seconds since the Bash was started.
- SHELL—The preferred shell to use, for programs that start a shell for you.
- SHELLOPTS—Colon-separated list of currently enabled shell options.
- SHLVL—Each time a new Bash session is started inside Bash, this variable is incremented.
- TIMEFORMAT—The format for the time command.
- TMOUT—If greater than zero, indicates the timeout in seconds for an interactive session. Also, the default timeout for the read command.
- UID—The ID of the current user (the numeric equivalent of LOGNAME).

Linux distributions define additional variables. The presence of these variables depends on your particular distribution. Many are declared for the use of particular applications.

- _ETC_PROFILE—Displays 1 if /etc/profile was executed
- DISPLAY—The X Window display server
- CVSROOT—The location of the CVS repository
- EDITOR—Your default editor. Historically, this was used to indicate a line editor to use when a visual editor was not available (see VISUAL)
- KDEDIR—The parent directory for the KDE desktop
- HOST—The fully qualified hostname (for example, host.domain.com)
- INPUTRC—The location of the inputrc file (for example, /etc/inputrc)
- LESS—Contains the default switches for the less command
- LESSOPEN—The default command used by less to open a file (for example, |/usr/bin/lesspipe.sh %s)
- LESSCHARSET—The console character set to use for less (for example, latin1)
- LS_COLORS—The default colors for your ls output on the console, overriding /etc/DIR_COLORS
- LOGNAME—The name of the current login
- ORGANIZATION—The name of your organization (usually the contents of /etc/organization)

- PRINTER—The default printer
- QTDIR—The directory containing QT, the widget package for KDE desktop
- PAGER—The default paging program, usually less
- TEMPDIR—The path of the default temporary directory
- TERM—The terminal emulation (for example, xterm for an xterm session, or linux for the Linux console)
- USER—Your username for OpenLinux
- VISUAL—Your default editor, usually the same as EDITOR
- WINDOWMANAGER—The path to your current X Windows window manager

Expressions

AN EXPRESSION IS A FORMULA THAT CALCULATES a value. Bash has several built-in commands and functions to compute expressions, and not all have the same syntax or features. In some cases there is more than one way to calculate the same expression. There are also many specialized features for use in rare cases. As a result, few Bash programmers have all the nuances memorized.

During one of my many conversations with the late professor and author F. Ray Skilton, we were discussing the use of pull-down menus as a tool not for making selections but as a memory aid for commands. He turned away from his Atari computer and asked me, "Have you learned enough computer languages to start forgetting the syntax of commands you haven't used in while?" "Not really," I said. He chuckled. "Don't worry—you will."

Expansions

Expressions in Bash include more than arithmetic. Because variables are strings, many expressions involve replacing some kind of shorthand notation with the full value the string represents. This process of string substitution is called *expansion* because the string usually expands, becoming longer, after the substitution is performed.

Pathname pattern matching is an example of a string expansion. Asterisks, question marks, and other characters are replaced by the filenames they represent, creating a longer, complete string value.

Bash divides expansions into six separate categories. The shell always evaluates them in the following order:

- Filename brace expansion
- Pathname tilde expansion
- Dollar, variable, and arithmetic expressions
- Command substitution (performed left to right)

- Word splitting (that is, argument separation by whitespace or the contents of the IFS variable)
- Pathname expansion (that is, pathname pattern matching)

All these expansions are discussed in detail later in this section.

The order is important and can cause subtle problems in scripts. Suppose you assign a path with a tilde in it in a variable.

```
$ ls -d ~/tmp
/home/kburtch/tmp
$ TEMP="~/tmp"
$ ls $TEMP
~/tmp not found
```

The ls command cannot find the directory ~/tmp, despite the fact that it exists and ls can find it when typed directly into the command. This problem is caused by the order of expansion. Because variable expansion happens after tilde expansion, Bash first tries to replace any tildes. Finding only a variable, it substitutes the value of TEMP. Because tilde expansion has already finished, the tilde is left in the command and ls looks for a tmp directory inside another directory called ~. This wouldn't have happened if the order of expansion could be reversed.

As a result, tildes should never be used in paths assigned to variables. Use the HOME variable instead.

Other types of expansions not listed here are handled by commands. Because these are commands that must be executed, they only run after Bash completes its six expansions. There are two common built-in commands that interpret expressions.

The test command checks a wide variety of conditions and indicates whether the condition is true or not. Test can compare files, strings, or numbers. Don't confuse it with the Linux test command.

The let command computes an expression and assigns the results to a variable in a single command.

To test the results, you need a command that checks the result of a test and takes a course of action. The if command is a good choice.

The Basic if Command

The built-in if command runs a command and checks the results. If the command was successful, it executes another set of commands. The only command normally used with the if command is test. The other uses of if are described in more detail in Chapter 7, "Compound Commands."

The syntax for the basic if command is as follows

```
if test arguments ; then
    statements to run
fi
```

The keyword then is treated as a separate command, requiring a semicolon to separate it from the if command. The keyword fi appears after the final command to be executed inside the if.

For example, the test -f command checks for the existence of a file.

```
if test -f ./report.out ; then
  printf "The report file ./report.out exists!\n"
fi
```

The message "The report file ./report.out exists!" is printed only if the file exists. If the file does not exist, the printf command is skipped and execution proceeds after the fi.

File Expressions

The built-in test command contains a wide variety of tests for files. It can test the type of file, the accessibility of the file, compare the ages of files or other file attributes. The following is a complete list of Bash file tests:

- -b *file*—True if the file is a block device file
- -c *file*—True if the file is a character device file
- -d *file*—True if the file is a directory
- -e *file*—True if the file exists
- -f *file*—True if the file exists and is a regular file
- -g *file*—True if the file has the set-group-id permission set
- -h *file* (or -L *file*)—True if the file is a symbolic link
- -k *file*—True if the file has the sticky permission bit set
- -p *file*—True if the file is a pipe
- -r *file*—True if the file is readable (by your script)
- -s *file*—True if the file exists and is not empty
- -S *file*—True if the file is a socket
- -t fd—True if the file descriptor is opened on a terminal
- -u *file*—True if the file has the set-user-id permission set
- -w *file*—True if the file is writable (by your script)
- -x *file*—True if the file is executable (by your script)
- -O *file*—True if the file is (effectively) owned by you
- -G *file*—True if the file is (effectively) owned by your group
- -N *file*—True if the file has new content (since the last time it was read)
- *f1* -nt *f2*—(*newer than*) True if file *f1* is newer than *f2*

- *f1* -ot *f2*—(*older than*) True if file *f1* is older than *f2*
- *f1* -ef *f2*—(*equivalent file*) True if file *f1* is a hard link to *f2*

File testing is commonly used in the sanity checks at the beginning of a script. They can be used to check that all files are present and readable (and writable, if necessary). All commands must be executable (see Listing 6.1).

Listing 6.1 `archive.bash`

```
#!/bin/bash
#
# archive.bash - Archive old order files
#
# Ken O. Burtch
# CVS: $Header$
shopt -s -o nounset

# Global Declarations

declare -rx SCRIPT=${0##*/}          # SCRIPT is the name of this script
declare -rx who="/usr/bin/who"       # the who command - man 1 who
declare -rx TMP="/tmp/temp.$$"       # TMP is a temporary file

# Sanity Checks

if test ! -x "$who" ; then
   printf "$SCRIPT:$LINENO: the command $who is not available — aborting" >&2
   exit 192
fi
if test -f "$TMP" ; then
   if test ! -w "$TMP" ; then
      printf "$SCRIPT:$LINENO: the temp file $TMP exists and cannot "\
"be overwritten — aborting" >&2
      exit 192
   fi
fi
```

This script fragment ensures that the who command is executable and that the temp file named in TMP either doesn't exist or exists and can be overwritten.

Multiple Tests

Single tests can be combined together with -a (*and*) and -o (*or*) switches. The temp file test in the previous section can be rewritten as:

```
if test -f "$TMP" -a ! -w "$TMP" ; then
   printf "$SCRIPT:$LINENO: the temp file $TMP exists and cannot"\
 be overwritten — aborting" >&2
   exit 192
fi
```

This is not exactly the same as

```
if test -f "$TMP" && test ! -w "$TMP" ; then
   printf "$SCRIPT:$LINENO: the temp file $TMP exists and cannot"\
" be overwritten — aborting" >&2
   exit 192
fi
```

The version using && executes the test command twice and can run slower than the version using the -a switch, so the -a switch is preferred over using && in an if expression.

Parentheses can also be used as long as they are escaped with backslashes. Parentheses have special meaning to the shell. In certain cases, they are required.

One situation that tends to confuse shell programmers is when mixing the not operator with -a or -o switch. In most computer languages, not takes precedence as a unary operator and executes first. In Bash, -a and -o take precedence over the not operator, causing the following test to always be false:

```
if test ! -f "$TMP -o -f "$TMP" ; then
```

Bash interprets this command as "if the file neither exists nor exists." This odd behavior is in accordance with the POSIX standard. To get the expected result, you must use parentheses.

```
if test \( ! -f "$TMP" \) -o -f "$TMP" ; then
```

Square brackets are an alternative form of the test command. Using square brackets makes your if commands easier to read.

```
if [ -f "$TMP" -a ! -w "$TMP" ] ; then
   printf "$SCRIPT:$LINENO: the temp file $TMP exists and cannot"\
" be overwritten — aborting" >&2
   exit 192
fi
```

The square brackets version is in all ways identical to the normal test command.

The Korn shell introduced a variation of the test command that used double square brackets. This variation is supported by Bash for compatibility. The Korn shell test will not perform word splitting or pathname expansion between the brackets, making double quotes unnecessary around variable substitutions.

```
if [[ -f $FILE ]] ; then
   printf "%s\n" "The file exists"
fi
```

It also has enhanced pattern-matching features, but lacks many of the features of Bash's `test` command. Unless you are porting Korn shell scripts to Bash, you are well advised not to use the Korn shell `test` command.

Strings

The `test` command can compare a pair of strings.

- `-z` *s*—(*zero length*) True if the string is empty
- `-n` *s* (or just *s*)—(*not null*) True if the string is not empty
- *s1* `=` *s2*—True if string *s1* is equal to *s2*
- *s1* `!=` *s2*—True if string *s1* is not equal to *s2*
- *s1* `<` *s2*—True if string *s1* is less than *s2*
- *s1* `>` *s2*—True if string *s1* is greater than *s2*

```
DAY=`date '+%a'`
if [ "$DAY" = "Mon" ] ; then
    printf "The weekend is over...get to work!\n"
fi
```

The `-z` (*zero length*) and `-n` (*not zero length*) switches are short forms of `=` "" and `!=` "", respectively. Notice that there are no greater than or equal to, or less than or equal to, operators. You can simulate these operators by combining the two tests with the `-a` switch.

If you are used to other computer languages, remember that the quotation marks used in the `test` command are not being used for string delineation but for special character handling.

Because the less than and greater than operators are also used by the shell for redirection, the operator must be quoted to prevent Bash from interpreting them instead of passing them on to the `test` command.

```
COMPANY="Athabasca"
if [ "$COMPANY" \< "M" ] ; then
    printf "The company name begins with a letter less than M\n"
fi
```

A common use for string comparisons is the testing of shell flag variables. *Flags* are variables used to indicate whether a particular condition is true. They provide a way to remember previous tests.

Any pair of values can be used to represent the flag's condition, such as true and false or yes and no. However, this can lead to ambiguous conditions when the flag contains an unexpected string such as "NO". Traditionally, if the variable contains anything except a null string, the condition is considered true.

```
WEEKEND=
DAY=`date '+%a'`
if [ "$DAY" = "Sat" -o "$DAY" = "Sun" ] ; then
    WEEKEND=1
fi
```

To determine whether it is the weekend, use -n (*not null*) and -z (*null*).

```
if [ -n "$WEEKEND" ] ; then
    printf "%s" "The weekend is here"
else
    printf "%s" "It isn't the weekend"
fi
```

Arithmetic Expressions

The built-in let command performs math calculations. let expects a string containing a variable, an equals sign, and an expression to calculate. The result is assigned to the variable.

```
$ let "SUM=5+5"
$ printf "%d" "$SUM"
10
```

You don't need to use $ to expand a variable name in the string. let understands that any variable appearing on the right side of the equals sign needs to have its value substituted into the expression.

```
$ let "SUM=SUM+5"
$ printf "%d" "$SUM"
15
$ let "SUM=$SUM+5"
$ printf "%d" "$SUM"
20
```

The optional dollar sign is a special feature of the let command and does not apply to other commands.

If a variable is declared as an integer with the -i switch, the let command is optional.

```
$ SUM=SUM+5
$ printf "%d\n" $SUM
25
```

If SUM was a string variable, it would be assigned the string value "SUM+5":

```
$ unset SUM
$ declare SUM=0
$ SUM=SUM+5
$ printf "%s\n" "$SUM"
SUM+5
```

Any special characters appearing in the `let` expression have to be quoted to prevent Bash from expanding them.

The `let` command provides the four basic math operators, plus a remainder operator. Only integer expressions are allowed (no decimal points).

```
$ let "RESULT=5 + 2"
$ printf "5 plus 2 is %d\n" "$RESULT"
5 plus 2 is 7

$ let "RESULT=5 - 2"
$ printf "5 minus 2 is %d\n" "$RESULT"
5 minus 2 is 3

$ let "RESULT=5 * 2"
$ printf "5 times 2 is %d\n" "$RESULT"
5 times 2 is 10

$ let "RESULT=5 / 2"
$ printf "5 divided by 2 is %d\n" "$RESULT"
5 divided by 2 is 2

$ let "RESULT=5 % 2"
$ printf "remainder of 5 divided by 2 is %d\n" "$RESULT"
remainder of 5 divided by 2 is 1
```

Here are the arithmetic operators in order of precedence. Many of these operators will be familiar to C programmers:

- `-, +`—Unary minus and plus
- `!, ~`—Logical and bitwise negation (disable shell history to use `!`)
- `*, /, %`—Multiplication, division, and remainder
- `+, -`—Addition and subtraction
- `<<, >>`—Left and right bitwise shifts
- `<=, >=, <, >`—Comparison
- `==, !=`—Equality and inequality
- `&`—Bitwise AND
- `^`—Bitwise XOR
- `|`—Bitwise OR
- `&&`—Logical AND
- `||`—Logical OR
- `expr ? expr :`—Conditional expression
- `=, *=, /=, %=`—Assignment
- `+=, -=, <<=, >>=, &=, ^=, |=`—Self-referential operations

For example, to round to the nearest 10, do this:

```
$ declare -i COST=5234
$ COST=\(COST+5\)/10*10
$ printf "%d\n" $COST
5230
```

The parentheses must be escaped to prevent the shell from treating them as a reference to a subshell.

The `let` command will also handle octal and hexadecimal values.

```
$ declare -i OCTAL=0
$ let "OCTAL=0775"
$ printf "%i\n" "$OCTAL"
509
```

The operations are described in the next section.

Logical Expressions

In let, true is represented by the value of 1, and false by 0. Any value other than 1 or 0 is treated as true, but the logical operators themselves only return 1 or 0.

Remember that logical truth (a value greater than zero) is not the same as the success of a command (a status code of zero). In this respect, `test` and `let` are opposites of each other.

To use logical negation at the shell prompt, you must disable the shell history option or Bash will interpret the ! as a history look-up request.

```
$ let "RESULT=!0"
$ printf "logical negation of 0 is %d\n" "$RESULT"
logical negation of 0 is 1

$ let "RESULT=!1"
$ printf "logical negation of 1 is %d\n" "$RESULT"
logical negation of 1 is 0

$ let "RESULT=1 && 0"
$ printf "logical and of 1 with 0 is %d\n" "$RESULT"
logical and of 1 with 0 is 0

$ let "RESULT=1 || 0"
$ printf "logical or of 1 with 0 is %d\n" "$RESULT"
logical or of 1 with 0 is 1
```

There is no logical exclusive-or operator.

Relational Operations

Unlike string comparisons, `let` provides a full complement of numeric comparisons. These are of limited value because most of comparisons are tested with the `test` command in the `if` command, resulting in two sets of tests. In logical expressions, 0 is a failure.

```
$ let "RESULT=1 > 0"
$ printf "1 greater than 0 is %d\n" "$RESULT"
1 greater than 0 is 1

$ let "RESULT=1 >= 0"
$ printf "1 greater than or equal to 0 is %d\n" "$RESULT"
1 greater than or equal to 0 is 1

$ let "RESULT=1 < 0"
$ printf "1 less than 0 is %d\n" "$RESULT"
1 less than 0 is 0

$ let "RESULT=1 <= 0"
$ printf "1 less than or equal to 0 is %d\n" "$RESULT"
1 less than or equal to 0 is 0

$ let "RESULT=1 == 0"
$ printf "1 equal to 0 is %d\n" "$RESULT"
1 equal to 0 is 0

$ let "RESULT=1 != 0"
$ printf "1 equal to 0 is %d\n" "$RESULT"
1 equal to 0 is 1
```

Bitwise Operations

There is also a set of bitwise operators, as follows.

```
$ let "RESULT=~5"
$ printf "bitwise negation of 5 is %d\n" "$RESULT"
bitwise negation of 5 is -6

$ let "RESULT=5 >> 2"
$ printf "5 left-shifted by 2 is %d\n" "$RESULT"
5 left-shifted by 2 is 1

$ let "RESULT=5 << 2"
$ printf "5 right-shifted by 2 is %d\n" "$RESULT"
5 right-shifted by 2 is 20
```

```
$ let "RESULT=5 & 3"
$ printf "bitwise and of 5 with 3 is %d\n" "$RESULT"
bitwise and of 5 with 3 is 1

$ let "RESULT=5 | 3"
$ printf "bitwise or of 5 with 3 is %d\n" "$RESULT"
bitwise or of 5 with 3 is 7

$ let "RESULT=5 ^ 3"
$ printf "bitwise exclusive-or of 5 with 3 is %d\n" "$RESULT"
bitwise exclusive-or of 5 with 3 is 6
```

Self-Referential Operations

Self-referential operators are shorthand notations that combine assignment with one of the other basic operations. The operation is carried out using the assignment variable, and then the result is assigned to the assignment variable. For example, "RESULT+=5" is a short form of "RESULT=RESULT+5".

```
$ let "RESULT=5"
$ let "RESULT+=5"
$ printf "The result is %d" "$RESULT"
The result is 10
```

The other self-referential operators are multiplication (*=), division (/=), remainder (%=), subtraction (-=), right shift (<<=), left shift (>>=), bitwise AND (&=), bitwise exclusive OR (^=) , and bitwise OR (|=).

Notice that certain kinds of self-referential operations are impossible to express with the shorthand operators. RESULT=RESULT-10 can be written as RESULT-=10 but RESULT=10-RESULT must be written out in full.

The increment (++) operator adds one to a variable. The decrement operator (--) subtracts one from a variable.

```
$ let "CNT=0"
$ let "CNT++"
$ printf "%d\n" "$CNT"
1
```

When increment or decrement are used in another expression, the placement of the operator is important. If the operator is placed before a variable, it indicates that the variable should be updated prior to the rest of the expression. If the operator is placed after a variable, the update will occur after the expression is evaluated.

```
$ let "CNT=5"
$ let "PRODUCT=0"
$ let "PRODUCT=++CNT*5"
$ printf "%d\n" "$PRODUCT"
```

```
30
$ let "CNT=5"
$ let "PRODUCT=CNT++*5"
$ printf "%d\n" "$PRODUCT"
25
$ printf "%d\n" "$CNT"
6
```

In general, it's a good idea to avoid expressions with this kind of "side-effect," because it makes your script harder to maintain. Instead, perform increments and decrements on a separate line to make the results clear to read.

The self-referential operators cannot be used with integer variables without the `let` statement.

```
$ COST+=5
bash: COST+=5: command not found
```

Other `let` Features

Parentheses are allowed in the expressions.

```
$ let "RESULT=(5+3)*2"
$ printf "The expression is %d" "$RESULT"
The expression is 16
```

Assignment in the `let` command is an operator that returns the value being assigned. As a result, multiple variables can be assigned at once.

```
$ let "TEST=TEST2=5"
$ printf "The results are %d and %d\n" "$TEST" "$TEST2"
The results are 5 and 5
```

`let` can evaluate more than one expression at a time. Several, small assignments can be combined on one line.

```
$ let "SUM=5+5" "SUM2=10+5"
```

Excessive numbers of assignments in a single `let` command will lead to readability problems in a script. When each `let` is on a single line, it's easier to look through the script for a specific assignment.

The conditional expression operator (?) is shorthand for an `if` statement when one of two different expression are evaluated based on the left condition. Because this is a feature of the `let` command, it works only with numeric expressions, not strings. The following example constrains a truth value to a 1 or a 0.

```
$ VALUE=5
$ let "RESULT=VALUE > 1 ? 1 : 0"
$ printf "%d\n" "$VALUE"
1
```

More than one conditional expression operator can be chained together.

```
$ FILE_COUNT=`ls -1 | wc -1`
$ let "RESULT=FILE_COUNT==0 ? 0 : (FILE_COUNT%2 == 0 ? "\
"FILE_COUNT/2 : FILE_COUNT/2+1)"
$ printf "The files will fit in a report with 2 columns %d high\n" "$RESULT"
The files will fit in a report with 2 columns 11 high
$ printf "%d" "$FILE_COUNT"
22
```

Double parentheses are an alias for let. They are used to embed let expressions as parameters in another command. The shell replaces the double parentheses with the value of the expression.

```
declare -i X=5;
while (( X- > 0 )) ; do
  printf "%d\n" "$X"
done
```

This script fragment prints a list of numbers from four to zero. The embedded let reduces X by one each time through the loop and checks to see when the value of X reaches zero.

temperature.bash: Converting Fahrenheit to Celsius

To review let arithmetic, the script temperature.bash, shown in Listing 6.2, converts a temperature from Fahrenheit to Celsius.

Listing 6.2   temperature.bash

```
#!/bin/bash
#
# temperature.bash: Convert Fahrenheit to Celsius
#
# Ken O. Burtch
# CVS $Header$

shopt -s -o nounset

declare -i FTEMP  # Fahrenheit temperature
declare -i CTEMP  # Celsius temperature

# Title

printf "%s\n" "Fahrenheit-Celsius Conversion"
printf "\n"
```

Listing 6.2 **Continued**

```
# Get the value to convert

read -p "Enter a Fahrenheit temperature: " FTEMP

# Do the conversion

CTEMP="(5*(FTEMP-32) )/9"
printf "The Celsius temperature is %d\n" "$CTEMP"

exit 0
```

Arithmetic Tests

The test command can compare numeric values, but it uses different operators than the ones used to compare string values. Because all shell variables are stored as strings, variables can either be compared as numbers or strings depending on the choice of operator. Perl programmers will find this similar to Perl. Bash will not report an error if string operators are used with integer variables.

- $n1$ -eq $n2$—(*equal*) True if $n1$ is equal to $n2$
- $n1$ -ne $n2$—(*not equal*) True if $n1$ is not equal to $n2$
- $n1$ -lt $n2$—(*less than*) True if $n1$ is less than $n2$
- $n1$ -le $n2$—(*less than or equal*) True if $n1$ is less than or equal to $n2$
- $n1$ -gt $n2$—(*greater than*) True if $n1$ is greater than $n2$
- $n1$ -ge $n2$—(*greater than or equal*) True if $n1$ is greater than or equal to $n2$

For example, suppose RESULT contains the number of files in the current directory.

```
$ RESULT=`ls -1 | wc -l`
$ printf "%d" "$RESULT"
22
$ test "$RESULT" -gt 20 && printf "%s" "There are a lot of files."
There are a lot of files.
$ test "$RESULT" -le 20 && printf "There are few files"
$
```

These tests are not the same as the string comparison tests. Consider the following example.

```
$ test "$RESULT" \< 3 && printf "As a string, the result is less than 3"
As a string, the result is less than 3
```

In this case, the string 22 is compared with the string 3, and because the string 22 is alphabetically less than 3, the message is printed. Make sure you choose the correct operator to compare with.

Pattern Recognition

Bash pattern recognition is called *globbing*. Globbing is used to match filenames given to a command, and it is also used by the Korn shell test command to match strings.

```
$ ls *.txt
notes.txt  project_notes.txt
```

The pattern-recognition feature works by supplying wildcard symbols that Bash will attempt to match to a string or a filename.

The asterisk (*) character represents zero or more characters. The Korn shell test can be used to match the value of a variable to a string with an asterisk.

```
COMPANY="Athabasca"
if [[ $COMPANY = A* ]] ; then
    printf "The company name begins with a letter a A\n"
fi
if [[ $COMPANY = Z* ]] ; then
    printf "The company name begins with a letter a Z\n"
fi
```

This behavior doesn't work when quotation marks are used. Quotation marks tell the Korn shell test command not to interpret special characters. A test for "A*" would indicate a file named "A*".

```
COMPANY="Athabasca"
if [[ "$COMPANY" - "A*" ]] ; then
    printf "The company name is A*\n"
fi
```

The question mark (?) character is a wildcard representing any single character.

```
COMPANY="AIC"
if [[ $COMPANY = A?? ]] ; then
    printf "The company name is 3 characters beginning with A\n"
fi
```

You can specify a set of characters using square brackets. You can list individual characters or ranges.

```
if [[ $COMPANY = [ABC]* ]] ; then
    printf "The company name begins with a A, B or C\n"
fi
if [[ $COMPANY = [A-Z]* ]] ; then
    printf "The company name begins with a letter an uppercase letter\n"
```

```
fi
if [[ $COMPANY = [A-Z0-9]* ]] ; then
    printf "The company name begins with a letter an uppercase "\
"letter or number\n"
fi
```

Partial ranges are allowed. If the start of the range is omitted, the range is all ASCII values up to that character. Likewise, the end of the range can be omitted to specify any ASCII characters after the range start character.

If the first character in a square bracket set is a exclamation point (!) or caret (^), characters not in the set count as a match.

If the extending globbing option is on using `shopt -s extglob`, Bash supports several additional patterns:

- `?(pattern-list)`—Matches zero or one occurrence of the given patterns
- `*(pattern-list)`—Matches zero or more occurrences of the given patterns
- `+(pattern-list)`—Matches one or more occurrences of the given patterns
- `@(pattern-list)`—Matches exactly one of the given patterns
- `!(pattern-list)`—Matches anything except one of the given patterns

```
COMPANY="AAA Ballistics Ltd"
if [[ $COMPANY = +(A)*Ltd ]] ; then
  printf "The company name begins with one or more A's and finishes with Ltd\n"
fi
```

You can separate lists of patterns by using vertical bar characters (|).

```
COMPANY="Champion Ltd"
if [[ $COMPANY = Champion*@(Ltd|Corp|Inc) ]] ; then
    printf "The company name is Champion with a standard business ending\n"
fi
```

Bash defines short forms for common ranges called *character classes*:

- `[:alnum:]`—Alphanumeric
- `[:alpha:]`—Alphabetic
- `[:ascii:]`—ASCII characters
- `[:blank:]`—Space or tab
- `[:cntrl:]`—Control characters
- `[:digit:]`—Decimal digits
- `[:graph:]`—Non-blank characters
- `[:lower:]`—Lowercase characters
- `[:print:]`—Non-control characters
- `[:punct:]`—Punctuation characters

- `[:space:]`—Whitespace
- `[:upper:]`—Uppercase characters
- `[:xdigit:]`—Hexadecimal digits

For example, `[:lower:]` is equivalent to the range `[a-z]`.

```
COMPANY="2nd Rate Solutions"
if [[ $COMPANY = [[:digit:]]*]] ; then
   printf "Company name starts with a digit\n"
fi
```

For multilingual scripts, Bash will match a character based on "equivalence classes." If a range is a character surrounded by a pair of equal signs, the shell will match that letter or any similar letter from a related alphabet.

```
COMPANY="EZ Consulting Services"
if [[ $COMPANY = [=E=]* ]] ; then
   printf "Company name starts with an E (or a similar character)\n"
fi
```

This test will match strings with letters similar to E, such as the French É.

A particular collating symbol can be matched with `[.s.]` where *s* is the symbol to match.

Outside of the Korn shell `test` command, the behavior of the shell works in much the same way. Instead of matching characters in strings, pattern matching matches characters in files. All the features, including the extending globbing features, work the same.

```
$ ls *+(.c|.h)
actions.c coledit.c config.c   dump.c    form.c    form.h    main.c
```

The only difference is the use of the period (.). Because a leading period represents a Linux "hidden" file, these files normally remain invisible unless a leading period is specified in the pattern expression.

```
$ ls .*+(.c|.h)
.hidden.c
```

Because Bash does the expansion, all commands treat these patterns the same way.

```
$ wc -l *+(.c|.h)
96 actions.c
201 coledit.c
24 config.c
103 dump.c
88 form.c
12 form.h
305 main.c
829 total
```

If a pattern does not match any files, Bash assumes that the pattern is the filename you intended to give to the command.

```
$ ls X*
X* not found
```

In this case, there are no files that begin with the letter X. Bash, failing to find a match, gives the pattern X* as the filename to the ls command.

Globbing Options

There are a number of shell options that affect pattern matching. Filename pattern matching can be turned off completely by setting the noglob shell option (shopt -s -o noglob). If the nullglob option is set (with shopt -s nullglob), the pattern is discarded if not matched. In the previous example, ls would receive no argument and would list all the files in the current directory. You can disable case sensitivity by setting the nocaseglob option (shopt -s nocaseglob). Likewise, you can turn off the special treatment of leading periods in filenames by setting the dotglob option (shopt -s dotglob).

These shell options have a wide-ranging effect; use them with care. Change the setting for as few lines of a script as possible and clearly comment the effect of the change.

The GLOBIGNORE variable also affects how filenames are matched. This variable resembles the PATH variable; it's a colon-separated list of filenames that Bash will not attempt to match. If you are aware of files with pattern symbols in their names, adding them to the GLOBIGNORE list will ensure that Bash will treat them as files and not as globbing expressions.

If you need more sophisticated pattern recognition, or if you need to apply a pattern to an entire file, you can use the grep family of commands. These are described in Chapter 11, "Text File Basics" and Chapter 12, "Text File Processing."

Filename Brace Expansion ({ . . })

One filename can be expanded into multiple filenames using curly braces. Inside the curly braces, use commas to list each substring in order to build a new argument. Brace expansion is typically used to specify a root filename with different endings.

```
$ printf "%s %s %s\n" "Files should be named:" orders{.txt,.out}
Files should be named: orders.txt orders.out
```

Because Bash expands the first line to this:

```
$ printf "%s %s %s\n" "Files should be named:" orders.txt orders.out
```

three %s codes are necessary, one for each parameter to printf.

The braces can contain file-matching characters. The actual file matching occurs after the braces are processed by Bash.

Dollar Sign Substitutions

The dollar sign is used for more than variable substitution. There are a variety of dollar expansions, some substituting string values and others mimicking capabilities of Linux commands such as wc and sed. By using the dollar sign expressions, the shell doesn't have to start these programs and will run faster.

ANSI C Escape Expansion ($')

If a dollar sign is followed by a string in single quotes, the string is searched for ANSI C escape sequences and the sequences are replaced by the corresponding characters. The acceptable escape sequences are similar to the special format escape codes used by the printf command:

- \a—Alert (bell)
- \b—Backspace
- \cC—A control character C (for example, G for control-G)
- \e—Escape character
- \f—Form feed
- \n—New line
- \r—Carriage return
- \t—Horizontal tab
- \v—Vertical tab
- \\—A literal backslash
- \'—A single quote
- \nnn—The ASCII octal value for a character (up to three digits)
- \xnnn—The ASCII hexadecimal value for a character (up to three digits)

```
$ printf "%s\n" $'line 1\nline 2\nline 3'
line 1
line 2
line 3
```

Locale Translation ($")

If a dollar sign is followed by a string in double quotes, the string is translated into the character set of the current locale.

```
$ printf "%s\n" $"To a new locale"
To a new locale
```

Locales are discussed briefly in Chapter 18, "Final Topics."

Variable Name Matching (! *)

If the contents of curly braces start with an exclamation point (!) and end with an asterisk (*), a list of all variables starting with the specified letters is returned.

```
$ COMPANY="Nightlight Inc."
$ printf "%s\n" "${!COMP*}"
COMPANY
```

Variable Length (#)

A dollar sign with curly braces and a leading number sign (#) returns the length of the variable's contents.

```
$ printf "%s\n" "${#COMPANY}"
15
```

An asterisk or at sign returns the number of parameters to the shell script.

```
$ printf "%s\n" "${#*}"
0
```

This is similar to $*.

Default Values (: -)

If the content of the curly braces includes a trailing colon minus after the variable name, a default value can be specified which will be substituted if the variable is an empty string.

```
$ COMPANY=
$ printf "%s\n" "${COMPANY:-Unknown Company}"
Unknown Company
```

The actual value of the variable is left unchanged.
The colon can be removed to ignore the default:

```
$ COMPANY=
$ printf "%s\n" "${COMPANY-Nightlight Inc.}"
$
```

Assignment of Default Values (: =)

If, in curly braces, a trailing colon equals appears after the variable name, a default value is assigned to the variable if the variable is an empty string.

```
$ printf "%s\n" "${COMPANY:=Nightlight Inc.}"
Nightlight Inc.
$ printf "%s\n" "$COMPANY"
Nightlight Inc.
```

The actual value of the variable has changed.
By removing the colon, no assignment takes place.

Variable Existence Check (:?)

If a trailing colon question mark appears after the variable name, the message following the question mark is returned and the Bash script exits. This provides a crude form of a sanity check. The message is optional.

```
$ printf "Company is %s\n" \
"${COMPANY:?Error: Company has not been defined—aborting}"
```

By removing the colon, no check takes place.

Overriding a Default Value (:+)

If a trailing colon plus appears after the variable name, the message following the plus sign will replace the value of the string. Empty strings are not changed.

```
$ COMPANY="Nightlight Inc."
$ printf "%s\n" "${COMPANY:+Company has been overridden}"
Company has been overridden
```

By removing the colon, variables with empty strings are replaced as well.

Substrings (:n)

If a trailing colon followed by a number appears after the variable name, a substring is returned. The number indicates the first position of the substring, minus one. The first character in the string is character 0. Optionally, a colon and a second number can follow, which indicates the length of the substring.

```
$ printf "%s\n" "${COMPANY:5}"
light Inc.
$ printf "%s\n" "${COMPANY:5:5}"
light
```

Substring Removal by Pattern (%, #, %%, and ##)

If a trailing number sign appears after the variable name, the substring returned has the matching pattern removed. One number sign matches the smallest possible substring and two number signs matches the largest possible substring. The expression returns the characters to the right of the pattern.

```
$ printf "%s\n" "${COMPANY#Ni*}"
ghtlight Inc.
$ printf "%s\n" "${COMPANY##Ni*}"
$ printf "%s\n" "${COMPANY##*t}"
```

```
  Inc.
$ printf "%s\n" "${COMPANY#*t}"
light Inc.
```

Using percent signs (%), the expression returns the characters to the left of the pattern.

```
$ printf "%s\n" "${COMPANY%t*}"
Nightligh
$ printf "%s\n" "${COMPANY%%t*}"
Nigh
```

Substring Replacement by Pattern (/ /)

If the variable is followed by a slash (/), the first occurrence of the pattern following the slash is replaced. Following the pattern, there is a second slash and the replacement string. If the variable is followed by two slashes, all occurrences of the pattern are replaced.

```
$ printf "%s\n" "${COMPANY/Inc./Incorporated}"
Nightlight Incorporated
$ printf "You are the I in %s" "${COMPANY//i/I}"
You are the I in NIghtlIght Inc.
```

If the pattern begins with a number sign (#), the pattern matches at the beginning of the variable's value. If the pattern ends with a percent sign (%), the pattern matches at the end of the variable's value. Other occurrences are ignored.

```
$ COMPANY="NightLight Night Lighting Inc."
$ printf "%s\n" "$COMPANY"
NightLight Night Lighting Inc.
$ printf "%s" "${COMPANY//Night/NIGHT}"
NIGHTLight NIGHT Lighting Inc.
$ printf "%s" "${COMPANY//#Night/NIGHT}"
NIGHTLight Night Lighting Inc.
```

If no new value is indicated, the matching substring is deleted.

```
$ COMPANY="Nightlight Inc."
$ printf "%s\n" "${COMPANY/light}"
Night Inc.
```

Ranges can also be used. For example, to delete all the punctuation in a string, use the range [:punct:]:

```
$ printf "%s" "${COMPANY//[[:punct:]]}"
Nightlight Inc
```

Using an asterisk or at sign instead of a variable applies the substitutions to all the parameters to the shell script. Likewise, an array with an asterisk or at sign applies the substitutions to all elements in the array.

Command Result Substitution ((..))

When parentheses are used, the command inside them is executed. This has the same effect as enclosing the commands in backquotes.

```
$ printf "There are %d files in this directory\n" "$(ls -1 | wc -1)"
There are 28 files in this directory
$ printf "There are %d files in this directory\n" `ls -1 | wc -1`
There are 28 files in this directory
```

Arithmetic Expression Substitution (((..)))

When two pairs of parentheses are used, the arithmetic expression inside them is evaluated and the result is returned. The format is identical to the ((..)) short form of the let command except that the result of the expression is substituted into the command.

```
$ ORDERS=50
$ COST=25
$ printf "There are $%d worth of orders in this directory\n" "$((ORDERS*COST))"
There are $1250 worth of orders in this directory
```

Other Test Expressions

The -o (*option*) switch of the test command determines whether a particular shell option is set.

```
if [ -o noglob ] ; then
    printf "Globbing is off\n"
fi
```

There are many types of expressions in Bash, and each has its own syntax and order of operation. To paraphrase Professor Skilton, "Have you learned so many that you've started forgetting the syntax of the ones you don't use very often?" The next chapter is far more straightforward.

mixer.bash: HTML Color Mixer

mixer.bash, shown in Listing 6.3, is a script that calculates HTML hexadecimal color codes of the kind used in Web pages. It uses many of the concepts discussed in this chapter, including the test command, dollar substitutions, and the let command.

Listing 6.3 mixer.bash

```
#!/bin/bash
#
# mixer.bash: HTML color mixer
#
```

Listing 6.3 **Continued**

```
# Ken O. Burtch
# CVS: $Header$

shopt -s -o nounset

declare -rx SCRIPT=${0##*/}
declare -i RED    # amount of red in color
declare -i GREEN  # amount of green in color
declare -i BLUE   # amount of blue in color

# Title

printf "%s\n" "This program mixes color values for Web pages"
printf "\n"

# Choose percent or absolute
# If none is given, default to 'p'

printf "%s\n" "Mix the color by (p)ercent or (a)bsolute amount?"
printf "%s\n" "The default is percentage."
read -p "Select p or a: " REPLY
REPLY="${REPLY:=p}"
printf "\n"

# Read absolute values

if [ "$REPLY" = "a" ] ; then
   read -p "How much red (0..255)?" RED
   if [ $RED -gt 255 ] ; then
      printf "$SCRIPT: too much red\n" >&2
      exit 192
   fi
   if [ $RED -lt 0 ] ; then
      printf "$SCRIPT: too little red\n" >&2
      exit 192
   fi
   read -p "How much green (0..255)?" GREEN
   if [ $GREEN -gt 255 ] ; then
      printf "$SCRIPT: too much green\n" >&2
      exit 192
   fi
   if [ $GREEN -lt 0 ] ; then
      printf "$SCRIPT: too little green\n" >&2
      exit 192
   fi
```

```
      read -p "How much blue (0..255)?" BLUE
      if [ $BLUE -gt 255 ] ; then
         printf "$SCRIPT: too much blue\n" >&2
         exit 192
      fi
      if [ $BLUE -lt 0 ] ; then
         printf "$SCRIPT: too little blue\n" >&2
         exit 192
      fi
   fi
fi

# Read percentage values and convert to absolute

if [ "$REPLY" = "p" ] ; then
   read -p "How much red (0..100)?" RED
   if [ $RED -gt 100 ] ; then
      printf "$SCRIPT: too much red\n" >&2
      exit 192
   fi
   if [ $RED -lt 0 ] ; then
      printf "$SCRIPT: too little red\n" >&2
      exit 192
   fi
   read -p "How much green (0..100)?" GREEN
   if [ $GREEN -gt 100 ] ; then
      printf "$SCRIPT: too much green\n" >&2
      exit 192
   fi
   if [ $GREEN -lt 0 ] ; then
      printf "$SCRIPT: too little green\n" >&2
      exit 192
   fi
   read -p "How much blue (0..100)?" BLUE
   if [ $BLUE -gt 100 ] ; then
      printf "$SCRIPT: too much blue\n" >&2
      exit 192
   fi
   if [ $BLUE -lt 0 ] ; then
      printf "$SCRIPT: too little blue\n" >&2
      exit 192
   fi
   RED="255*RED/100"
   GREEN="255*GREEN/100"
   BLUE="255*BLUE/100"
fi
```

Listing 6.3 **Continued**

```
# Show the result

printf "HTML color code is #%x%x%x\n" "$RED" "$GREEN" "$BLUE"

exit 0
```

Reference Section

Test Command Switches

- -b *file*—True if the file is a block device file
- -c file—True if the file is a character device file
- -d *file*—True if the file is a directory
- -e *file*—True if the file exists
- *f1* -ef *f2*—(equivalent file) True if file *f1* is a hard link to *f2*
- *n1* -eq *n2*—(equal) True if *n1* is equal to *n2*
- -f *file*—True if the file exists and is a regular file
- *n1* -ge *n2*—(greater than or equal) True if *n1* is greater than or equal to *n2*
- *n1* -gt *n2*—(greater than) True if *n1* is greater than *n2*
- -g *file*—True if the file has the set-group-id permission set
- -G *file*—True if the file is (effectively) owned by your group
- -h *file* (or -L *file*)—True if the file is a symbolic link
- -k *file*—True if the file has the sticky permission bit set
- *n1* -le *n2*—(*less than or equal*) True if *n1* is less than or equal to *n2*
- *n1* -lt *n2*—(*less than*) True if *n1* is less than *n2*
- -n *s* (or just *s*)—(*not null*) True if the string is not empty
- -N *file*—True if the file has new content (since the last time it was read)
- *n1* -ne *n2*—(*not equal*) True if *n1* is not equal to *n2*
- *f1* -nt *f2*—(newer than) True if file *f1* is newer than *f2*
- -O *file*—True if the file is (effectively) owned by you
- *f1* -ot *f2*—(*older than*) True if file *f1* is older than *f2*
- -p *file*—True if the file is a pipe
- -r *file*—True if the file is readable (by your script)
- -s *file*—True if the file exists and is not empty

- -s *file*—True if the file is a socket
- -t fd—True if the file descriptor is opened on a terminal
- -u *file*—True if the file has the set-user-id permission set
- -w *file*—True if the file is writable (by your script)
- -x *file*—True if the file is executable (by your script)
- -z *s*—(*zero length*) True if the string is empty

Test Command String Tests

- *s1* = *s2*—True if string *s1* is equal to *s2*
- *s1* != *s2*—True if string *s1* is not equal to *s2*
- *s1* < *s2*—True if string *s1* is less than *s2*
- *s1* > *s2*—True if string *s1* is greater than *s2*

Character Classes

- [:alnum:]—Alphanumeric
- [:alpha:]—Alphabetic
- [:ascii:]—ASCII characters
- [:blank:]—Space or tab
- [:cntrl:]—Control characters
- [:digit:]—Decimal digits
- [:qraph:]—Non-blank characters
- [:lower:]—Lowercase characters
- [:print:]—Non-control characters
- [:punct:]—Punctuation characters
- [:space:]—Whitespace
- [:upper:]—Uppercase characters
- [:xdigit:]—Hexadecimal digits

ASCII C Escape Expansion

- \a—Alert (bell)
- \b—Backspace
- \e—Escape character

- \f—Form feed
- \n—New line
- \r—Carriage return
- \t—Horizontal tab
- \v—Vertical tab
- \\—A literal backslash
- \'—A single quote
- \nnn—The ASCII octal value for a character (up to three digits)
- \xnnn—The ASCII hexadecimal value for a character (up to three digits)

7

Compound Commands

Except for the simplest scripts, you seldom want to execute every command. It's helpful to execute one set of commands instead of another, or repeat a set of commands several times. *Compound commands* are commands that enclose a group of other commands.

For readability, the enclosed commands are indented to make it clear that their execution depends on the compound command. I once had a supervisor complain that I occasionally indented my lines one space less than the standard he insisted on. (I had to put a ruler up to the screen to see whether it was true.) I figured this was a minor problem because he went to another programmer and pointed out that his program crashed when a zero was typed.

Compound commands always consist of two commands that bracket the commands inside. The ending command is usually the name of the first command spelled backwards. The mysterious sounding `esac` command is actually the ending command for the compound command `case`.

Command Status Codes

Every Linux command returns a *status code* (or exit status), which is a number between 0 and 255 that indicates what problems the command experienced. A status code of zero indicates that the last command ran successfully. Any other status code indicates some kind of error.

The status code is contained in the variable `$?`.

```
$ unzip no_file.zip
unzip:  cannot find no_file.zip, no_file.zip.zip or no_file.zip.ZIP.
$ printf "%d\n" "$?"
9
```

When `unzip` command doesn't find a file to decompress, the status code returned is 9 (an error).

The unofficial Linux convention uses codes 127 and below for Linux standard error codes. In this case, `ls` returned a status code of 9, which is the Linux error code for "bad file number". The complete set of Linux error codes is listed in Appendix D, "Error Codes."

If a command is interrupted by a signal, Bash returns a status code of 128, plus the signal number. As a result, user-defined error codes should be above 191, and the code returned by Bash for the final Linux signal, number 63. The list of signal codes is in Appendix E, "Signals."

```
if test ! -x "$who" ; then
    printf "$SCRIPT:$LINENO: the command $who is not available - "\
"aborting\n " >&2
    exit 192
fi
```

Unfortunately, most Linux commands simply return a one or zero to indicate failure or success. This is often all the information needed by a script if it stops immediately when an error occurs. The particular error message is still displayed on standard output.

```
$ ls po_1473.txt
po_1473.txt
$ printf "%d\n" $?
0
$ ls no_file
no_file not found
$ printf "%d\n" $?
1
```

The status code is different from the truth values returned by the `let` command as discussed in Chapter 6, in the section called "Logical Expressions." In `let`, `false` (a failed comparison) has the value of 0. This follows the conventions of computer languages such as C. However, a status code of 0 is success, not a failure.

```
$ let "RESULT=1>0"
$ printf "%d %d\n" "$RESULT" $?
1 0
$ test 1 -gt 0
$ printf "%d\n" $?
0
```

`let` assigns 1 to RESULT, indicating that 1 is greater than 0. The `test` command returns a status code of 0 to indicate that 1 is greater than 0. What's more, the `let` command has a status code of 0, indicating the `let` command successfully performed the comparison.

These opposite codes and conventions can lead to mistakes that are hard to debug. Bash has two built-in commands called `true` and `false`. These return status codes, not `let` truth values.

```
$ true
$ printf "%d\n" "$?"
0
$ false
$ printf "%d\n" "$?"
1
```

true assigns a successful status code (0). false assigns an error status code (1).

Confused yet?

If you need to save the success of a logical comparison, it's best to use the test command for consistency. Most shell commands expect status codes, not truth values.
In a pipeline, several commands run at once. The status code returned from a pipe is the status code of the final command. In the following example, the status code is for the wc command, not ls.

```
$ ls badfile.txt | wc -l
ls: badfile.txt: No such file or directory
       0
$ printf "%d\n" "$?"
0
```

Although ls reported an error, the result of the pipeline is zero because wc was successful at counting no lines.

Bash also defines an array called PIPESTATUS that contains the individual status codes for each command in the last pipeline.

```
$ ls badfile.txt | wc -l
ls: badfile.txt: No such file or directory
       0
$ printf "%d %d\n" "${PIPESTATUS[0]}" "${PIPESTATUS[1]}"
1 0
```

$? is essentially another name for the final PIPESTATUS Value.

A command or pipeline can be preceded by a ! to negate the status code. If the status is 0, it becomes 1. If the status is greater than 0, it becomes 0.

if **Command**

The if command executes one of two or more alternative series of commands based on a status code returned by other commands.

Normally, the if statement is used in conjunction with the test command.

```
NUM_ORDERS=`ls -1 | wc -l`
if [ "$NUM_ORDERS" -lt "$CUTOFF" ] ; then
    printf "%s\n" "Too few orders...try running again later"
    exit 192
fi
```

This example counts customer orders stored as files in a directory. If there are not enough order files in the current directory, the script will run the statements between the then and fi keywords, printing a message and stopping the script.

The semicolon before the then is required. then is technically a separate command, although it works in conjunction with if. Because they are on one line, the semicolon is needed to separate the commands.

if commands can have an else part that is only executed when the condition fails.

```
NUM_ORDERS=`ls -1 | wc -l`
if [ "$NUM_ORDERS" -lt "$CUTOFF" ] ; then
    printf "%s\n" "Too few orders...but will process them anyway"
else
    printf "%s\n" "Starting to process the orders"
fi
```

if commands can be nested inside other if commands.

```
NUM_ORDERS=`ls -1 | wc -l`
if [[ $NUM_ORDERS -lt $TOOFEW ]] ; then
    printf "%s\n" "Too few orders...but will process them anyway"
else
    if [[ $NUM_ORDERS -gt $TOOMANY ]] ; then
        printf "%s\n" "There are many orders.  Processing may take a long time"
    else
        printf "%s\n" "Starting to process the orders"
    fi
fi
```

The commands cannot be cross-nested; the inner if must always be completed before the outer if.

To choose between a series of alternatives, if commands can have an elif part. elif is a shortcut for else if and reduces unnecessary if nesting. The elif part can be followed by a final else part that, if it is present, is executed only when there are no alternatives. Combining these ideas, you can rewrite the previous example as follows.

```
NUM_ORDERS=`ls -1 | wc -l`
if [ "$NUM_ORDERS" -lt "$TOOFEW" ] ; then
    printf "%s\n" "Too few orders...but will process them anyway"
elif [ "$NUM_ORDERS" -gt "$TOOMANY" ] ; then
    printf "%s\n" "There are many orders.  Processing may take a long time"
else
    printf "%s\n" "Starting to process the orders"
fi
```

The if command doesn't have to be used with the test command. It can run and test the status code of any command.

```
if rm "$TEMPFILE" ; then
    printf "%s\n" "$SCRIPT:temp file deleted"
else
    printf "%s - status code %d\n" \
"$SCRIPT:$LINENO: unable to delete temp file" $? 2>&
fi
```

Embedding complex commands into an `if` command can make a script difficult to read and debug; you should avoid doing this. In this case, the `rm` command is not as prominent as it would be if it appeared on a line of its own. Likewise, it is possible to declare variables inside of an `if` command, but it makes it very difficult to determine which variables exist and which do not.

case **Command**

The `case` command compares a variable against a series of values or patterns. If the value or pattern matches, the corresponding statements are executed. The name comes from the fact that the variable is tested on a case-by-case basis.

Unlike `elif` commands that test the status code for individual commands, `case` tests the value of a variable. The `case` command is preferable to a long set of `elif`s when testing string values.

Each individual `case` must end with a pair of semicolons. Without the semicolons, Bash will attempt to execute the next `case` designation and report an error.

```
printf "%s -> " "1 = delete, 2 = archive.  Please choose one"
read REPLY
case "$REPLY" in
1) rm "$TEMPFILE" ;;
2) mv "$TEMPFILE" "$TEMPFILE.old" ;;
*) printf "%s\n" "$REPLY was not one of the choices" ;;
esac
```

The pattern asterisk (*) is the catch-all case; it matches all values that were not handled by a previous case. Although this case is optional, it's good design to always include a catch-all case, even if it only contains a null statement (:).

The pattern-matching rules follow the file globbing rules, as discussed in the previous chapter. For example, vertical bars can separate multiple patterns.

The cases don't "fall through" as some computer languages do, notably C. When one case is selected, only those commands are executed. The commands in the following cases are not executed.

while **Loop**

There are several commands for repeating a set of commands.

The `while` command repeats the enclosed commands while the command being tested succeeds. If the command fails on the first try, the enclosed commands are never executed.

```
printf "%s\n" "Enter the names of companies or type control-d"
while read -p "Company ?" COMPANY; do
  if test -f "orders_$COMPANY.txt" ; then
     printf "%s\n" "There is an order file from this company"
  else
     printf "%s\n" "There are no order files from this company"
  fi
done
```

A while loop is completed with the done command, not elihw as you might expect.

An *infinite loop* can be created using the true command. Because true always succeeds, the loop will continue indefinitely.

```
printf "%s\n" "Enter the names of companies or type quit"
while true ; do
  read -p "Company ?" COMPANY
  if [ "$COMPANY" = "quit" ] ; then
     break
  elif test -f "orders_$COMPANY.txt" ; then
     printf "%s\n" "There is an order file from this company"
  else
     printf "%s\n" "There are no order files from this company"
  fi
done
```

A while loop can be stopped prematurely with the break command. On reaching a break, Bash stop executing commands and "breaks out" of the loop and begins executing the first command after the loop.

break can be followed by a number indicating how many enclosing loops to break out of. For example

```
break 2
```

breaks out of the current loop as well as the loop enclosing the current loop.

The counterpart to break is continue, which causes the remainder of the enclosed statements to be ignored; the loop is resumed at the top. continue can be followed by a number indicating how many enclosing statements to break out of before continuing.

until **Loop**

The counterpart of the while loop is the until loop. The until command is identical to the while command except that it repeats the enclosed statements until the condition is successful, essentially the same as while !.

```
until test -f "$INVOICE_FILE" ; do
  printf "%s\n" "Waiting for the invoice file to arrive..."
  sleep 30
done
```

Using until with the false command creates an infinite loop.

The break and continue commands can be used with an until loop.

for **Loops**

The standard Bourne *for in loop* is a variation on the here file. The for command reads a sequence of values into a variable and repeats the enclosed commands once for each value.

```
for FILE_PREFIX in order invoice purchase_order; do
  if test -f "$FILE_PREFIX""_vendor1.txt" ; then
    printf "%s\n" "There is a $FILE_PREFIX file from vendor 1..."
  fi
done
```

If the *in* part is missing, the for command will execute the enclosed statements for each argument to the shell script.

The break and continue commands can be used with a for loop.

Because of the other shell features, this kind of for loop isn't commonly used.

Embedded let (((..)))

The let command returns a status code of 1 if an expression is zero, or 0 if the expression is a value other than zero. In the same way that the test command can be expressed with a pair of square brackets for easier reading in compound statements, the let command also has a form for easier reading: double parentheses.

The for loop, as found in other programming languages, is created using an embedded let, as shown in Listing 7.1.

Listing 7.1   forloop.sh

```
#!/bin/bash
# forloop.sh: Count from 1 to 9
for (( COUNTER=1; COUNTER<10; COUNTER++ )) ; do
    printf "The counter is now %d\n" "$COUNTER"
done
exit 0
```

The first expression in the double parentheses is executed when the loop is started. Each time the loop is restarted, the third expression is executed and the second expression is checked. When the second expression returns false, the loop ends.

```
$ bash forloop.sh
The counter is now 1
The counter is now 2
The counter is now 3
```

```
The counter is now 4
The counter is now 5
The counter is now 6
The counter is now 7
The counter is now 8
The counter is now 9
```

Grouping Commands ({ . . })

Commands can be grouped together using curly braces ({ . . . }).

```
ls -1 | {
  while read FILE ; do
    echo "$FILE"
  done
}
```

In this example, the results of the `ls` command become the input for all the statements in the group.

```
$ test -f orders.txt && { ls -l orders.txt ; rm orders.txt; } \
|| printf "no such file"
```

If the file `orders.txt` exists, the file will be listed and deleted; otherwise, "no such file" is printed. The semicolon after the last braced command is required only when the braces are on a single line.

Commands can also be grouped using subshells. Subshells are described in Chapter 9, "Parameters and Subshells."

`report.bash`: Report Formatter

`report.bash` is a script that reads a list of sales figures and creates a simple report. The sales figure file consists of product names, local country sales, and foreign country sales. For example, `report.bash` turns this

```
binders 1024 576
pencils 472  235
rules 311   797
stencils 846 621
```

into the following report:

```
Report created on Thu Aug 22 18:27:07 EDT 2002 by kburtch

Sales Report
```

Product	Country	Foreign	Total	Average
—	—	—	—	—
binders	1024	576	1600	800
pencils	472	235	707	353
rules	311	797	1108	554
stencils	846	621	1467	733
—	—	—	—	—

Total number of products: 4

End of report

Listing 7.2   report.bash

```bash
#!/bin/bash
#
# report.bash: simple report formatter
#
# Ken O. Burtch
# CVS: $Header$

# The report is read from DATA_FILE.  It should contain
# the following columns:
#
#   Column 1: PRODUCT = Product name
#   Column 2: CSALES  = Country Sales
#   Column 3: FSALES  = Foreign Sales
#
# The script will format the data into columns, adding total and
# average sales per item as well as a item count at the end of the
# report.

# Some Linux systems use USER instead of LOGNAME

if [ -z "$LOGNAME" ] ; then          # No login name?
   declare -rx LOGNAME="$USER"       # probably in USER
fi

shopt -s -o nounset

# Global Declarations

declare -rx SCRIPT=${0##*/}          # SCRIPT is the name of this script
declare -rx DATA_FILE="report.txt"   # this is raw data for the report
declare -i  ITEMS=0                   # number of report items
declare -i  LINE_TOTAL=0              # line totals
declare -i  LINE_AVG=0                # line average
```

Listing 7.2 **Continued**

```
declare    PRODUCT                   # product name from data file
declare -i CSALES                   # country sales from data file
declare -i FSALES                   # foreign sales from data file
declare -rx REPORT_NAME="Sales Report" # report title
# Sanity Checks

if test ! -r "$DATA_FILE" ; then
   printf "$SCRIPT: the report file is missing—aborting\n" >&2
   exit 192
fi

# Generate the report

printf "Report created on %s by %s\n" "`date`" "$LOGNAME"
printf "\n"
printf "%s\n" "$REPORT_NAME"
printf "\n"
printf "%-12s%12s%12s%12s%12s\n" "Product" "Country" "Foreign" "Total" "Average"
printf "%-12s%12s%12s%12s%12s\n" "—" "—" "—" "—" "—"

{ while read PRODUCT CSALES FSALES ; do
   let "ITEMS+=1"
   LINE_TOTAL="CSALES+FSALES"
   LINE_AVG="(CSALES+FSALES)/2"
   printf "%-12s%12d%12d%12d%12d\n" "$PRODUCT" "$CSALES" "$FSALES" \
"$LINE_TOTAL" "$LINE_AVG"
done } < $DATA_FILE

# Print report trailer

printf "%-12s%12s%12s%12s%12s\n" "—" "—" "—" "—" "—"
printf "Total number of products: %d\n" "$ITEMS"
printf "\n"
printf "End of report\n"

exit 0
```

8

Debugging and Version Control

W̲HEN I WAS IN BROCK UNIVERSITY, the Macquarium lab was filled with used Macintosh Plus computers passed down from professors who had outgrown them. One day I was working on a program for my third-year operating system course. The short C program I was working on was reported to be error free. When I ran it, vertical bars appeared in the monochrome desktop, my floppy disk ejected, and the computer rebooted. Upon closer inspection, I noticed that I used an = instead of a == in an if statement. That small mistake created unforeseen results. Ever since then, I treat the C language as a psychotic roommate; we might live and work together, but I never take my eye off it for a minute in case it tries to stab me in the back.

Unfortunately, shell scripts are almost as difficult to debug as C programs. Like C, shell commands usually assume you know what you are doing and issue an error only when the offending line actually runs. Unless shell scripts are thoroughly tested, bugs can linger for months or years until the faulty command is finally executed. A solid knowledge of shell debugging tools is essential for professional script development.

Shell Debugging Features

There are several Bash switches and options useful in tracking down problems in scripts.

The -n (*no execution*) switch checks a script for syntax errors without running it. Use this switch to check a script during development.

```
$ bash -n bad.sh
bad.sh: line 3: syntax error near unexpected token 'fi'
bad.sh: line 3: 'fi'
```

In this example, there is an error on or before line 3 of the script. The term *token* refers to a keyword or another piece of text near the source of the error.

The -o errexit option terminates the shell script if a command returns an error code. The exceptions are loops, so the if command cannot work properly if commands can't return a non-zero status. Use this option only on the simplest scripts without any other error handling; for example, it does not terminate the script if an error occurs in a subshell.

The -o nounset option terminates with an error if unset (or nonexistent) variables are referenced. This option reports misspelled variable names. nounset does not guarantee that all spelling mistakes will be identified (see Listing 8.1).

Listing 8.1 nounset.bash

```
#!/bin/bash
#
# A simple script to list files

shopt -o -s nounset

declare -i TOTAL=0

let "TOTAL=TTOAL+1"         # not caught
printf "%s\n" "$TOTAL"

if [ $TTOAL -eq 0 ] ; then  # caught
    printf "TOTAL is %s\n" "$TOTAL"
fi
```

The -o xtrace option displays each command before it's executed. The command has all substitutions and expansions performed.

```
declare -i TOTAL=0
if [ $TOTAL -eq 0 ] ; then
    printf "%s\n" "$TOTAL is zero"
fi
```

If this script fragment runs with the xtrace option, you should see something similar to the following results:

```
+ alias 'rm=rm -i'
+ alias 'cp=cp -i'
+ alias 'mv=mv -i'
+ '[' -f /etc/bashrc ']'
+ . /etc/bashrc
+++ id -gn
+++ id -un
+++ id -u
++ '[' root = root -a 0 -gt 99 ']'
++ umask 022
++ '[' '' ']'
+ declare -i TOTAL=0
+ '[' 0 -eq 0 ']'
+ printf '%s\n' '0 is zero'
0 is zero
```

The first 11 lines are the commands executed in the profile scripts on the Linux distributions. The number of plus signs indicate how the scripts are nested. The last four lines are the script fragment after Bash has performed all substations and expansions. Notice the compound commands (like the `if` command) are left out (see Listing 8.2).

Listing 8.2 `bad.bash`

```
#!/bin/bash
#
# bad.bash: A simple script to list files

shopt -o -s nounset
shopt -o -s xtrace

declare -i RESULT
declare -i TOTAL=3

while [ $TOTAL -ge 0 ] ; do
  let "TOTAL—"
  let "RESULT=10/TOTAL"
  printf "%d\n" "$RESULT"
done
```

`xtrace` shows the line-by-line progress of the script. In this case, the script contains a mistake resulting in an extra cycle through the `while` loop. Using `xtrace`, you can examine the variables and see that `-ge` should be replaced by `-gt` to prevent a cycle when `TOTAL` is zero.

```
$ bash bad.bash
+ declare -i RESULT
+ declare -i TOTAL=3
+ '[' 3 -ge 0 ']'
+ let TOTAL—
+ let RESULT=10/TOTAL
+ printf '%d\n' 5
5
+ '[' 2 -ge 0 ']'
+ let TOTAL—
+ let RESULT=10/TOTAL
+ printf '%d\n' 10
10
+ '[' 1 -ge 0 ']'
+ let TOTAL—
+ let RESULT=10/TOTAL
bad.sh: let: RESULT=10/TOTAL: division by 0 (error token is "L")
+ printf '%d\n' 10
```

```
10
+ '[' 0 -ge 0 ']'
+ let TOTAL—
+ let RESULT=10/TOTAL
+ printf '%d\n' -10
-10
+ '[' -1 -ge 0 ']'
```

You can change the trace plus sign prompt by assigning a new prompt to the PS4 variable. Setting the prompt to include the variable LINENO will display the current line in the script or shell function. In a script, LINENO displays the current line number of the script, starting with 1 for the first line. When used with shell functions at the shell prompt, LINENO counts from the first line of the function.

Debug Traps

The built-in trap command (discussed in more detail in Chapter 10, "Job Control and Signals") can be used to execute debugging commands after each line has been processed by Bash. Usually debug traps are combined with a trace to provide additional information not listed in the trace.

When debug trapping is combined with a trace, the debug trap itself is listed by the trace when it executes. This makes a printf rather redundant because the command is displayed with all variable substitutions completed prior to executing the printf. Instead, using the null command (:) displays variables without having to execute a shell command at all (see Listing 8.3).

Listing 8.3 debug_demo.sh

```
#!/bin/bash
#
# debug_demo.sh : an example of a debug trap

trap ': CNT is now $CNT' DEBUG

declare -i CNT=0

while [ $CNT -lt 3 ] ; do
    CNT=CNT+1
done
```

When it runs with tracing, the value of CNT is displayed after every line.

```
$ bash -x debug_demo.sh
+ trap ': CNT is now $CNT' DEBUG
+ declare -i CNT=0
++ : CNT is now 0
```

```
+ '[' 0 -lt 3 ']'
++ : CNT is now 0
+ CNT=CNT+1
++ : CNT is now 1
+ '[' 1 -lt 3 ']'
++ : CNT is now 1
+ CNT=CNT+1
++ : CNT is now 2
+ '[' 2 -lt 3 ']'
++ : CNT is now 2
+ CNT=CNT+1
++ : CNT is now 3
+ '[' 3 -lt 3 ']'
++ : CNT is now 3
```

Version Control (CVS)

In a business environment, where money and careers are at stake, it's not enough to create a flawless program. There's always a chance some last-minute change will cause a program to produce the wrong result or even to crash. When that happens, the changes need to be undone or corrected as quickly as possible with no data loss.

A *version control system* is a program that maintains a master copy of the data files, scripts, and source programs. This master copy is kept in a directory called a *repository*. Every time a program is added or changed, it's resubmitted to the repository with a record of which changes were made, who made them, and when.

CVS (Concurrent Versions System) is the version control software supplied with most Linux distributions. Based on an older program called RCS (Revision Control System), CVS can share a script among multiple programmers and log any changes. It can work with individual files, whole directories, or large projects. They can be organized into groups of files called *modules*. CVS timestamps files, maintains version numbers, and identifies possible problems when two programmers update the same section of a program simultaneously.

CVS is also very popular for open source development. It can be configured to enable programmers all over the world to work on a project.

To use CVS, the project or team leader must create a directory to act as the version control repository as well as a subdirectory called CVSROOT. Then you define an environment variable called CVSROOT so CVS knows where to find the repository directory. For example, to make /home/repository the repository for your team, you set up the CVS-ROOT under Bash as follows

```
$ declare -rx CVSROOT=/home/repository
```

The repository holds copies of all the files, change logs, and other shared resources related to your project.

There are no special requirements for the software being added to the repository. However, when a program is added or updated, CVS reads through the file looking for special strings. If they are present, CVS replaces these strings with the latest information about this copy of the program. CVS documentation refers to these strings as *keywords*, although they are not keywords in the Bash sense.

- $Author$—The login name of the user who checked in the revision.
- $Date$—The date and time (UTC) the revision was checked in.
- $Header$—A standard header containing the full pathname of the RCS file, the revision number, the date (UTC), the author, and so forth.
- Id—Same as $Header$, except that the RCS filename is without a path.
- $Name$—If tags are being used, this is the tag name used to check out this file.
- $Locker$—The login name of the user who locked the revision (empty if not locked, which is the normal case unless cvs admin -l is in use).
- Log—The log message supplied during the commit, preceded by a header containing the RCS filename, the revision number, the author, and the date (UTC). Existing log messages are not replaced. Instead, the new log message is inserted after Log.
- $RCSfile$—The name of the CVS file without a path.
- $Revision$—The revision number assigned to the revision.
- $Source$—The full pathname of the CVS file.
- $State$—The state assigned to the revision.

The CVS keywords can be added anywhere in a script, but they should appear in a comment or in a quoted string if not in a comment. This prevents the keyword from being treated as an executable shell command.

```
# CVS: $Header$
```

When the script is added to the repository, CVS will fill in the header information.

```
# CVS: $Header: /home/repository/scripts/ftp.sh,v 1.1 2001/03/26
20:35:27 kburtch Exp $
```

The CVS keyword header should be placed in the header of a script.

```
#!/bin/bash
#
# flush.sh: Flush disks if nobody is on the computer
#
# Ken O. Burtch
# CVS: $Header$
```

CVS is controlled using the Linux cvs command. cvs is always followed by a CVS command word and any parameters for that command.

To add a new project directory to the CVS repository, use the import command. Import places the current directory's files in the repository under the specified name. Import also requires a short string to identify who is adding the project and a string to describe the state of the project. These strings are essentially comments and can be anything: Your login name and init-rel for initial release are good choices.

```
$ cvs import scripts kburtch init-rel
```

CVS starts your default text editor as indicated by the environment variables EDITOR or CVSEDITOR. CVS doesn't recognize the VISUAL variable. The file to be edited contains comment lines marked by a leading CVS:.

```
CVS: ─────────────────────────────
CVS: Enter Log. Lines beginning with 'CVS: ' are removed automatically
CVS:
CVS: ─────────────────────────────
```

When you are finished editing, CVS adds your program to the repository, recording your comments in the change log. The results are written to screen.

```
N scripts/ftp.sh
No conflicts created by this import
```

The N scripts/ftp.sh line indicates that CVS created a new project called scripts and added the Bash script ftp.sh to it. ftp.sh is now stored in the CVS repository, ready to be shared among the development team members. It is now safe to delete the project directory from your directory. In fact, it must be deleted before work can continue on the project.

Use the CVS command checkout (or co) to work on a project. This CVS command saves a copy of the project in the current directory. It also creates a CVS directory to save private data files used by CVS.

To use checkout, move to your home directory and type:

```
$ cvs checkout scripts
cvs checkout: Updating .
U scripts/ftp.sh
```

The subdirectory called scripts contains personal copies of project files from the repository. CVS maintains the original copy of ftp.sh. Another programmer can also checkout ftp.sh while you are working on your personal copy.

To add new files or directories to the project directory, use the add command. To add a file called process_orders.sh, use this:

```
$ cvs add process_orders.sh
```

As you work on your scripts, periodically check your work against the repository using the update command. If another programmer makes changes to the scripts, CVS will update your project directory to reflect the changes to the scripts. Any changes you have made, however, will not yet be added to the repository copies.

```
$ cvs update
cvs update: Updating .
```

Sometimes the changes involve the same part of the script and CVS can't combine the changes automatically. CVS calls this a conflict and notes this with a c during an update. CVS marks the place where the conflict occurred; you have to edit the script yourself to resolve the conflict.

If there are no other problems after an update, you can continue working on your source code.

To delete a script that is already in the repository, remove it using the rm command and perform a CVS update. CVS will delete the file.

While working on your source code, changes are not distributed to the rest of your team until you are ready. When the script is tested and you're ready to make it available, use commit (or ci, which stands for *check in*). Before committing changes, delete non-essential files (such as temporary files) to save space in the repository.

```
$ cvs commit
```

Like import, CVS commit commandstarts your editor and prompts you for a description of the changes you've made.

CVS commit also increments the version number of your changed scripts automatically. By convention, CVS begins numbering your project with 1.1. To start a new version 2.1, edit the version number in the $Header$ line (or any other CVS keywords in your script) and change the number to 2.0. CVS saves the script as version 2.1.

At any time, you can retrieve the log for a script or an entire project. The CVS log command displays all the related log entries, scripts, and version numbers:

```
$ cvs log project
cvs log: Logging project
RCS file: /home/repository/scripts/ftp.sh,v
Working file: scripts/ftp.sh
head: 1.1
branch: 1.1.1
locks: strict
access list:
symbolic names:
p1: 1.1.1.1
keyword substitution: kv
total revisions: 2; selected revisions: 2
description:
----------------
revision 1.1
date: 1999/01/13 17:27:33; author: kburtch; state: Exp;
branches: 1.1.1;
Initial revision
----------------
revision 1.1.1.1
```

```
date: 1999/01/13 17:27:33; author: kburtch; state: Exp; lines: +0 -0
Project started
=============================================================================
```

The `status` command gives you an overview of a project directory and a list of the scripts that have not been committed to the repository.

```
$ cvs status scripts
cvs status: Examining scripts
===================================================================
File: ftp.sh Status: Up-to-date
Working revision: 1.1.1.1 Wed Jan 13 17:27:33 1999
Repository revision: 1.1.1.1 /home/repository/scripts/ftp.sh,v
Sticky Tag: (none)
Sticky Date: (none)
Sticky Options: (none)
```

CVS has many other specialized capabilities not discussed here. Consult the CVS man page for further information.

Creating Transcripts

The output of a command can be saved to a file with the `tee` command. The name symbolizes a pipe that splits into two at a *T* connection: A copy of the output is stored in a file without redirecting the original standard output. To capture both standard output and standard error, redirect standard error to standard output before piping the results to `tee`.

```
$ bash buggy_script.sh >& | tee results.txt
```

The `tee` —append (`-a`) switch adds the output to the end of an existing file. The —ignore-interrupts (`-i`) switch keeps `tee` running even if it's interrupted by a Linux signal.

This technique doesn't copy what is typed on standard input. To get a complete recording of a script's run, Linux has a `script` command. When a shell script is running under script, a file named `typescript` is created in the current directory. The typescript file is a text file that records a list of everything that appears in the shell session.

You can stop the recording process with the `exit` command.

```
$ script
Script started, file is typescript
$ bash buggy_script.sh
...
$ exit
exit
Script done, file is typescript
```

Watching Running Scripts

To test cron scripts without installing them under cron, use the `watch` command. `watch` periodically re-runs a command and displays the results on the screen. `watch` runs the command every two seconds, but you can specify a different number of seconds with the —interval= (or -n) switch. You can filter the results so that only differences are shown (—differences or -d) or so that all the differences so far are shown (—differences= cumulative).

Timing Execution with Time

There are two commands available for timing a program or script.

The Bash built-in command `time` tells you how long a program took to run. You can also use `time` to time a series of piped commands. Except for the real time used, the statistics returned by time refer to the system resources used by the script and not any of the commands run by the script.

The results are formatted according to the value of the `TIMEFORMAT` variable. The layout of `TIMEFORMAT` is similar to the `date` command formatting string in that it uses a set of % format codes.

- `%%`—A literal `%`.
- `%[precision][l]R`—The real time; the elapsed time in seconds.
- `%[precision][l]U`—The number of CPU seconds spent in user mode.
- `%[precision][l]S`—The number of CPU seconds spent in system mode.
- `%P`—The CPU percentage, computed as (`%U` + `%S`) / `%R`.

The precision indicates the number decimal positions to show, with a default of 3. The character l (`long`) prints the value divided into minutes and seconds. If there is no `TIMEFORMAT` variable, Bash uses `\nreal\t%3lR\nuser\t%3lU\nsys%3lS`.

```
$ unset TIMEFORMAT
$ time ls > /dev/null

real    0m0.018s
user    0m0.010s
sys     0m0.010s
$ declare -x TIMEFORMAT="%P"
$ time ls > /dev/null
75.34
$ declare -x TIMEFORMAT="The real time is %1R"
$ time ls > /dev/null
The real time is 0m0.023s
```

Notice the times can vary slightly between the runs because other programs running on the computer affect them. To get the most accurate time, test a script several times and take the lowest value.

Linux also has a `time` command. This variation cannot time a pipeline, but it displays additional statistics. To use it, use the `command` command to override the Bash time.

```
$ command time myprog
3.09user 0.95system 0:05.84elapsed 69%CPU(0avgtext+0avgdata 0maxresident)k
0inputs+0outputs(4786major+4235minor)pagefaults 0swaps
```

Like Bash time, Linux time can format the results. The format can be stored in a variable called TIME (not TIMEFORMAT) or it can be explicitly indicated with the —format (-f) switch.

- %%—A literal %.
- %E—The real time; the elapsed time in the hours:minutes:seconds format.
- %e—The real time; the elapsed time in seconds.
- %S—The system time in CPU seconds.
- %U—The user time in CPU seconds.
- %P—The percentage of the CPU used by the program.
- %M—The maximum size in memory of the program in kilobytes.
- %t—The average resident set size of the program in kilobytes.
- %D —The average size of the unshared data area.
- %p—The average size of the unshared stack in kilobytes.
- %X—The average size of the shared text area.
- %Z—The size of system pages, in bytes.
- %F—The number of major page faults.
- %R—The number of minor page faults (where a page was previously loaded and is still cached by Linux).
- %W—The number of times the process was swapped.
- %c—The number of time-slice context switches.
- %w—The number of voluntary context switches.
- %I—The number of file system inputs.
- %O—The number of file system outputs.
- %r—The number of socket messages received.
- %s—The number of socket messages sent.
- %k—The number of signals received.
- %C—The command line.
- %x—The exit status.

Statistics not relevant to your hardware are shown as zero.

```
$ command time grep ken /etc/aliases
Command exited with non-zero status 1
0.00user 0.00system 0:00.02elapsed 0%CPU (0avgtext+0avgdata 0maxresident)k
0inputs+0outputs (142major+19minor)pagefaults 0swaps
$ command time —format "%P" grep ken /etc/aliases
Command exited with non-zero status 1
0%
$ command time —format "Major faults = %F" grep ken /etc/aliases
Command exited with non-zero status 1
Major faults = 141
```

The —portability (-p) switch forces time to adhere to the POSIX standard, the same as Bash time -p, turning off many of the extended features.

```
$ command time —portability grep ken /etc/aliases
Command exited with non-zero status 1
real 0.00
user 0.00
sys 0.00
```

The results can be redirected to a file with —output (-o), or appended to a file with —append (-a). The —verbose (-v) option gives a detailed explanation of each statistic.

Creating Man Pages

Linux man pages are special text files formatted for the *groff* program (*GNU run off*). groff is based on the older Unix programs troff (*for printers*) and nroff (*for terminals*). Troff was originally created in 1973 by Joseph F. Ossanna. By creating short man pages for important scripts, a single access point can be created for online information about your projects.

Place man pages for your own projects in section 9 of the manual. Originally, section 9 was used to document the Linux kernel, but it now follows the traditional Unix interpretation as being free for your personal use. Manual pages for section 9 are usually stored in /usr/share/man/man9. If you don't have access to this directory, make a man9 directory your home directory and store your personal manual pages there. By adding $HOME to the MANPATH environment variable in your Bash profile file, man will search the pages stored in your man9 directory.

```
$ mkdir ~/man9
$ declare -x MANPATH="$HOME:/usr/share/man "
```

man pages are text files containing groff markup codes (or macros) embedded in the text. These codes, much like HTML tags in a Web page, control the spacing, layout, and graphics used in the pages. You can also define your own groff codes. These codes always appear at the start of a line and begin with a period.

Here's an example of some groff markup codes:

```
.\"$Id$
.TH MAN 9 "25 July 1993" "Linux" "Nightlight Corporation Manual"
.SH NAME
ftp.sh \- script to FTP orders to suppliers
.SH SYNOPSIS
.B ftp.sh
.I file
```

The groff codes begin on lines by themselves with a period (.), followed by a one- or two-letter code. For example, the .B code indicates that the text that follows is bold (similar to the HTML <b> tag).

The groff predefined macros pertaining to manual pages are documented in the section 7 manual page on man (man 7 man). Some of the more commonly used groff codes are as follows:

- .B—Bold
- .I—Italics
- .PP—Begin new paragraph
- .RS *i*—Indent by *i* characters
- .RE—End last RS indentation
- .UR *u*—Begin text linked by a URL
- .UE—End linked test started by .UR
- .\"—Indicate a comment
- .TH—Heading of the page
- .SH—A subheading

Although there are no firm requirements for a manual page, most man pages include one or more of the following sections: SYNOPSIS, DESCRIPTION, RETURN VALUES, EXIT STATUS, OPTIONS, USAGE, FILES, ENVIRONMENT, DIAGNOSTICS, SECURITY, CONFORMING TO, NOTES, BUGS, AUTHOR, and SEE ALSO. If you are using CVS, you can include a CVS keyword such as Id in a VERSION section.

The easiest way to create a simple man page for your program is to find a similar man page and make a modified copy.

Listing 8.4 shows an example of a short, complete man page.

Listing 8.4 **Sample Man Page**

```
.\"man page supply_ftp.sh.9
.TH "SUPPLY_FTP.SH" 9 "25 May 2001" "Nightlight" "Nightlight Corporation Manual"
.SH NAME
supply_ftp.sh \- Bash script to FTP orders to suppliers
.SH SYNOPSIS
```

Listing 8.4 **Continued**

```
.B supply_ftp.sh
.I file
.I supplier
.SH DESCRIPTION
.B supply_ftp.sh
sends orders via FTP to suppliers.
.I file
is the name of the file to send.
.I supplier
is the name of the supplier.  The suppliers and their FTP account information
are stored in the text file
.I supplier.txt
.SH RETURN VALUES
The script returns 0 on a successful FTP and 1 if the FTP failed.
.SH AUTHOR
Created by Ken O. Burtch.
.SH FILES
/home/data/supplier.txt
.SH VERSION
$Id$
```

This page is displayed as

```
SUPPLY_FTP.SH(9)  Nightlight Corporation Manual  SUPPLY_FTP.SH(9)


NAME
       supply_ftp.sh - Bash script to FTP orders to suppliers


SYNOPSIS
       supply_ftp.sh file supplier


DESCRIPTION

       supply_ftp.sh sends orders via FTP to suppliers. file is the
       name of the file to send. supplier is the name of the supplier.
       The suppliers and their FTP account information are stored in
       the text file supplier.txt


RETURN VALUES
       The script returns 0 on a successful FTP and 1 if the FTP failed.


AUTHOR
       Created by Ken O. Burtch.


FILES
```

```
        /home/data/supplier.txt

VERSION
        $Id$

Nightlight              25 May 2001                    1
```

Id is updated when the page is committed using CVS.

The less command knows how to display a man page. Use this command to test a man page before installing it.

Some Linux distributions include a command called man2html that can convert a man page to a Web page. To convert a simple man page called my_man_page.9, type this

```
$ man2html < my_man_page.9 > my_man_page.html
```

Post the resulting page to your Web server.

Source Code Patches

The Linux diff command lists the changes between two or more files.

When used with the proper switches, diff creates a *patch file* containing a list of changes necessary to upgrade one set of files to another.

```
$ diff -u —recursive —new-file older_directory newer_directory > update.diff
```

For example, suppose you have a script to count the files in the current directory, as shown in Listing 8.5.

Listing 8.5   file_count.bash

```
#!/bin/bash
#
# file_count: count the number of files in the current directory.
# There are no parameters for this script.

shopt -s -o nounset

declare -rx SCRIPT=${0##*/}          # SCRIPT is the name of this script
declare -rx ls="/bin/ls"             # ls command
declare -rx wc="/usr/bin/wc"         # wc command

# Sanity checks

if test -z "$BASH" ; then
  printf "Please run this script with the BASH shell\n" >&2
  exit 192
fi
```

Listing 8.5 **Continued**

```
if test ! -x "$ls" ; then
  printf "$SCRIPT:$LINENO: the command $ls is not available — aborting\n " >&2
  exit 192
fi
if test ! -x "$wc" ; then
  printf "$SCRIPT: $LINENO: the command $wc is not available — aborting\n " >&2
exit 192
fi


ls -l | wc -l


exit 0
```

You decide that the script is better with exit $? instead of exit 0. This code

```
$ diff -u —recursive —new-file older.sh newer.sh > file_count.diff
```

creates the patch file containing

```
@@ -26,5 +26,5 @@

 ls -l | wc -l

-exit 0
+exit $?
```

The - indicates the exit 0 line will be removed. The + indicates that exit $? will be inserted. Then the old script will be upgraded to the new script.

The Linux patch command applies a patch file created by diff. Use the -p1 and -s switches.

```
$ cd older_directory
$ patch -p1 -s < update.diff
```

In the file_count script example, because the patch was created for one file and not for a directory, patch asks for the name of the older file to patch.

```
$ patch -p1 -s < file_count.diff
The text leading up to this was:
--------------
|—- older.sh   Tue Feb 26 10:52:55 2002
|+++ newer.sh   Tue Feb 26 10:53:56 2002
--------------
File to patch: older.sh
```

The file older.sh is now identical to newer.sh.

Shell Archives

A *shell archive* (or a *shar* file) is a collection of text files or scripts encoded as a single shell script. The data in the scripts is represented here as files. Binary files are converted to text with the Linux uuencode command. Shell archives are self-extracting archives; when the shell script executes, the files in the archive are unpacked.

The Linux shar (*shell archive*) command is a utility to create new shell archives.

To save a file called orders.txt as a shell archive, use this

```
$ shar orders.txt > orders.shar
shar: Saving orders.txt (text)
```

To extract the file, run the shell archive with Bash.

```
$ bash orders.shar
x - creating lock directory
x - extracting orders.txt (text)
```

To create a shell archive of the files in the current directory, use this

```
$ shar * > myproject.shar
```

The shar command recursively archives any subdirectories when a directory is being archived.

There are a large number of switches for shar. These are primarily for handling special cases. A complete list appears in the reference section of this chapter.

There is also an unshar command. Not exactly the opposite of shar, this command extracts shar archives from a saved email message and then uses Bash to unpack the files.

Shell archives were a popular method of sharing files over newsgroups during the early days of the Internet. Shell archives are not particularly efficient, but they provide an example of an unusual use for shell scripts and support for them is available on all Linux distributions.

Although shell scripts might not run vertical bars down your screen and eject your disks as my C program did in my third-year O/S course, they can be equally as difficult to debug. Knowing that there are debugging features in Bash makes it much easier to find and repair scripts. With version control, patches, and transcripts, your work can be shared with other programmers and problems caused by updates to scripts can be quickly isolated. These tools come in handy in the next chapter on subshells.

Reference Section

tee Command Switches

- —append (or -a)—Adds the output to the end of an existing file.
- —ignore-interrupts (or -i)—Keeps tee running even if it's interrupted by a Linux signal.

Linux Time Command Switches

- —portability (or -p)—Adheres to the POSIX standard.
- —output (or -o)—Directs output to a file.
- —append (or -a)—Appends results to a file.
- —verbose (or -v)—Gives a detailed explanation of each statistic.

Bash Time Command Format Codes

- %%—A literal %.
- %[precision][l]R—The real time; the elapsed time in seconds.
- %[precision][l]U—The number of CPU seconds spent in user mode.
- %[precision][l]S—The number of CPU seconds spent in system mode.
- %P—The CPU percentage, computed as (%U + %S) / %R.

Linux Time Command Format Codes

- %%—A literal %.
- %E—The real time; the elapsed time in the hours:minutes:seconds format.
- %e—The real time; the elapsed time in seconds.
- %S—The system time in CPU seconds.
- %U—The user time in CPU seconds.
- %P—The percentage of the CPU used by the program.
- %M—The maximum resident set size of the program in kilobytes.
- %t—The average resident set size of the program in kilobytes.
- %D—The average size of the unshared data area.
- %p—The average size of the unshared stack in kilobytes.
- %X—The average size of the shared text area.
- %Z—The size of system pages, in bytes.
- %F—The number of major page faults.
- %R—The number of minor page faults (where a page was previously loaded and is still cached by Linux).
- %W—The number of times the process was swapped.
- %c—The number of time-slice context switches.
- %w—The number of voluntary context switches.
- %I—The number of file system inputs.

- %O—The number of file system outputs.
- %r—The number of socket messages received.
- %s—The number of socket messages sent.
- %k—The number of signals received.
- %C—The command line.
- %x—The exit status.

Shell Debugging Options

- -o errexit—Terminates the shell script if a command returns an error code.
- -o nounset—Terminates with an error if unset (or non-existent) variables are referenced.
- -o xtrace—Displays each command before it's executed.

shar **Command Switches**

- —quiet (–silent or -q)—Hides status message while creating archives.
- —intermix-type (-p)—Allows packing options to be applied individually on the command line as opposed to being applied to all files.
- —stdin-file-list (or -S)—Reads a list of files to pack from standard input.
- —output-prefix=s (or -o s)—Names of the resulting *shar* files (when used with -whole-size-limit).
- —whole-size-limit=k (or -l *k*)—Limits the size of the resulting shar files to the specified number of kilobytes, but doesn't split individual files.
- —split-size-limits=k (or -L *k*)—Limits the size of the resulting shar files to the specified number of kilobytes, and splits individual files.
- —archive-name=*name* (or -n *name*)—Adds an archive name line to the header.
- —submitter=*email* (or -n *email*)—Adds a submitted by line to the header.
- —net-headers—Adds submitted by and archive name headers.
- —cut-mark (or -c)—Adds a CUT HERE line for marking the beginning of an archive embedded in the body of an email message.
- —mixed-uuencode (or -M)—(default) Allows text and uuencoded binary files.
- —text-files (or -T)—Forces all files to be treated as text.
- —uuencode (or -B)—Treats all files as binary data to be uuencoded.
- —gzip (or -z)—Compresses all data with gzip and uuencodes it.
- —level-for-gzip=L (or -G *L*)—Sets the compression level (1–9).

- —compress (or -z)—Compresses all data with the Linux compress command and uuencodes it.
- —bits-per-code=B (or -b B)—Sets the compress compression word size (default 12 bits).
- —no-character-count (or -w)—Suppresses the character count check.
- —no-md5-digest (or -D)—Suppresses the MD5 checksum.
- —force-prefix (or -F)—Prefixes lines with the prefix character.
- —here-delimiter=d (or -d d)—Changes the here file delimiter to d.
- —vanilla-operation (or -V)—Creates an archive that can be decompressed using a minimum number of Linux commands.
- —no-piping (or -P)—Doesn't use pipelines in the shar file.
- —no-check-existing (or -x)—Overwrites existing shar files.
- —query-user (or -X)—When extracting, prompts before overwriting.
- —no-timestamp (or -m)—Doesn't fix the modified timestamps when unpacking.
- —quiet-unshar (or -Q)—Discards extract comments.
- —basename (or -f)—Discards pathnames when extracting, storing all files in current directory.
- —no-i18n—No internationalization in shell archives.
- —print-text-domain-dir—Displays the directory shar uses for messages in different languages.

9

Parameters and Subshells

To serve as a flexible tool, a script has to be qualified when it is called, given additional information about how and where to perform its task. Like commands, a script is qualified using parameters. Switches and arguments make a script reusable, which in turn reduces costs and time.

Positional Parameters

There are three methods available to extend Linux scripts using parameters. The first method uses *positional parameters*. A script can refer to the parameters on the command line by the position (or order) in which they appear. Because the other two methods rely on positional parameters, they are discussed first.

The Bash variable $0 is the pathname of the script. It is not necessarily the full pathname, but rather the path used to specify the script when it was executed.

```
$ printf "%s\n" "$0"
/bin/bash
```

In this case, the Bash session was started with the command /bin/bash.

When combined with the basename command, the name of the script is removed from the rest of the pathname.

```
$ declare -rx SCRIPT='basename $0'
$ printf "%s\n" "$SCRIPT"
bash
```

A slightly faster version uses Bash's substring features and avoids running an outside program.

```
$ declare -rx SCRIPT=${0##*/}
$ printf "%s\n" "$SCRIPT"
bash
```

By finding the name of the script from $0, there is no danger that the wrong name will be printed after the script has been copied or renamed. SCRIPT is always the correct name of the script.

The variable $# contains the number of parameters to a script or a shell session. If there are no parameters, $# is zero. The number doesn't include the script name in $0.

```
$ printf "%d\n" $#
0
```

The first nine parameters are placed in the variables $1 through $9. (Parameters beyond nine can be accessed if curly braces surround the number.) When the nounset shell option is used, accessing an undefined parameter results in an error, just as if it were an undeclared variable name.

```
$ printf "%s\n" $9
bash: $9: unbound variable
```

The variable ?* (or $@) returns a complete list of all the parameters as a single string.

When using positional parameters, Bash doesn't differentiate between switches and arguments. Each item on the command line is a separate parameter to the script. Consider the following script, shown in Listing 9.1.

Listing 9.1 `params.sh`

```
#!/bin/bash
#
# params.sh: a positional parameter demonstration

printf "There are %d parameter(s)\n" "$#"
printf "The complete list is %s\n" "$@"
printf "The first parameter is %s\n" "$1"
printf "The second parameter is %s\n" "$2"
```

When the script runs using the parameters -c and t2341, $1 refers to -c and $2 refers to t2341.

```
$ bash parms.sh -c t2341
There are 2 parameter(s)
The complete list is -c t2341
The first parameter is -c
The second parameter is t2341
```

Although both $@ and $* refer to all the parameters, they differ when they are enclosed in double quotes. $* parameters are separated by the first character of the IFS variable, or by spaces if IFS is empty, or without anything when IFS is unset. $* treats the set of parameters as a single group.

$@, on the other hand, always separates the parameters by spaces and treats the parameters as individual items, even when they are enclosed in double quotes. $@ is often used to transfer the entire set of switches to another command (for example, ls $@).

Although positional parameters are a straightforward way to view switches and arguments, they do not "walk through" the list. There is a built-in `shift` command that discards the parameter in `$1` and moves the remaining parameters down one number to take its place. Using `shift`, you can check each parameter in turn as if it were the first parameter.

Listing 9.2 shows a complete example, using `shift`.

Listing 9.2 `param2.sh`

```
#!/bin/bash
#
# param2.sh
#
# This script expects the switch -c and a company name.  --help (-h)
# is also allowed.

shopt -s -o nounset

declare -rx SCRIPT=${0##*/}

# Make sure there is at least one parameter or accessing $1
# later will be an error.

if [ $# -eq 0 ] ; then
    printf "%s\n" "Type --help for help."
    exit 192
fi

# Process the parameters

while [ $# -gt 0 ] ; do
  case "$1" in
  -h | --help) # Show help
      printf "%s\n" "usage: $SCRIPT [-h] [--help] -c companyid"
      exit 0
      ;;
  -c ) shift
      if [ $# -eq 0 ] ; then
          printf "$SCRIPT:$LINENO: %s\n" "company for -c is missing" >&2
          exit 192
      fi
      COMPANY="$1"
      ;;
  -* ) printf "$SCRIPT:$LINENO: %s\n" "switch $1 not supported" >&2
      exit 192
```

Listing 9.2   Continued

```
      ;;
  * ) printf "$SCRIPT:$LINENO: %s\n" "extra argument or missing switch" >&2
      exit 192
      ;;
  esac
  shift
done
if [ -z "$COMPANY" ] ; then
   printf "%s\n" "company name missing" >&2
   exit 192
fi


# <-- begin work here


exit 0
```

A final parameter-related switch is $_ (dollar underscore). This switch has two purposes. First, it represents the pathname to the shell or shell script when the shell (or shell script) is first started. Second, after each command is executed, the command is placed in the environment as a variable containing the pathname of the command.

```
$ /bin/date
Fri Jun 29 14:39:58 EDT 2001
$ printf "%s\n" "$_"
/bin/date
$ date
Fri Jun 29 14:40:04 EDT 2001
$ printf "%s\n" "$_"
date
```

You can use $_ to repeat the last argument.

The getopts Command

There are two limitations to the positional parameter approach. First, it requires the script writer to test for errors and create the corresponding messages. Second, the shift command destroys all the parameters. If you want to access them later, you can't.

To deal with these issues, Bash includes a built-in getopts (*get options*) command that extracts and checks switches without disturbing the positional parameter variables. Unexpected switches, or switches that are missing arguments, are recognized and reported as errors.

Using getopts requires some preparation by the script writer. First, you must define a string containing a list of expected switch letters. By convention, this variable is called OPTSTRING. If any switch requires an argument, add a colon after the switch character.

For example, if the param2.sh script expects -h (*help*) and -c (*company ID*) with a company ID argument, the OPTSTRING would be hc:.

There is a second required parameter after the list of options: The name of a shell variable into which to record each option encountered.

Each time the getopts command runs, the next switch on the command line is examined and the name of the switch is saved in the variable SWITCH. The position of the next parameter to be examined is in a variable called OPTIND. If it doesn't exist, OPTIND automatically set to 1 before the first script parameter is checked. If there is any argument to the script, it is saved in a variable called OPTARG. Listing 9.3 shows a short script that tests the first parameter of the script.

Listing 9.3   getopts.sh

```
#!/bin/bash
#
# getopts.sh

declare SWITCH
getopts "hc:" SWITCH
printf "The first switch is SWITCH=%s OPTARG=%s OPTIND=%s\n" \
  "$SWITCH" "$OPTARG" "$OPTIND"
```

In this short script, unknown switches assign a question mark (?) to the SWITCH variable; an error message is displayed.

```
$ bash getopts.sh -h
The first switch is SWITCH=h OPTARG= OPTIND=2
$ bash getopts.sh -c a4327
The first switch is SWITCH=c OPTARG=a4327 OPTIND=3
$ bash gettopts.sh -a
t.sh: illegal option -- a
The first switch is SWITCH=? OPTARG= OPTIND=1
```

The error message can be hidden using a colon as the first character in the switch list. By using :hc:, the error on the bad switch -a disappears, but the bad option is saved in OPTARG to be used in a custom error message.

```
$ bash getopts.sh -a
The first switch is SWITCH=? OPTARG=a OPTIND=1
```

You can also hide errors by creating an OPTERR variable with the value of 0. This overrides the contents of the legal switches string.

Switches are usually checked with a while and case statement. See Listing 9.4.

Listing 9.4   getopts_demo.sh

```
# getopts_demo.sh
#
```

Listing 9.4   Continued

```
# This script expects the switch -c and a company name.  --help (-h)
# is also allowed.

shopt -s -o nounset

declare -rx SCRIPT=${0##*/}
declare -r OPTSTRING="hc:"
declare SWITCH
declare COMPANY
# Make sure there is at least one parameter

if [ $# -eq 0 ] ; then
   printf "%s\n" "Type --help for help."
   exit 192
fi

# Examine individual options

while getopts "$OPTSTRING" SWITCH ; do
  case $SWITCH in
  h) printf "%s\n" "usage: $SCRIPT [-h] -c companyid"
     exit 0
     ;;
  c) COMPANY="$OPTARG"
     ;;
  \?) exit 192
     ;;
  *) printf "$SCRIPT:$LINENO: %s\n" "script error: unhandled argument"
     exit 192
     ;;
  esac
done

printf "$SCRIPT: %s\n" "Processing files for $COMPANY..."
```

This script is shorter than the positional parameter version. The only error the script must look for is a legitimate switch listed in OPTSTRING that isn't handled by the switch statement.

As a special case, getopts can process variables instead of script parameters if they are supplied with the getopts command as extra arguments. This can be used to test a switch using specific parameters.

The getopt **Command**

Although the getopts command makes programming scripts somewhat easier, it doesn't adhere to the Linux switch standards. In particular, getopts doesn't allow double minus long switches.

To get around this limitation, Linux includes its own getopt (singular, *not* getopts) command. Similar to getopts, getopt allows long switches and has other features that getopts does not, and it is used in scripts in an entirely different way.

Because getopt is an external command, it can't save switches into variables the way getopts does. It has no way to export environment variables back to the script. Likewise, getopt doesn't know what switches the shell has unless they are copied to the getopt command using $@. As a result, instead of being run in a loop, getopt runs once to process all the parameters as a single group.

Like getopts, getopt uses a OPTSTRING list of options. The list can be proceeded by --options (or -o) to make it clear that these are the list of switches. The items can be listed as in getopts or as a comma-separated list.

The list of options given to the script must be appended to the getopt command using a double minus and $@. The double minus indicates where the getopt switches end and where the script switches begin.

Listing 9.5 contains a script that duplicates the getopts.sh using getopt. Notice that the --name (or -n) switch is used to give getopt the name of the script to be used in any error messages.

Listing 9.5   getopt.sh

```
#!/bin/bash
#
#getopt.sh - a demonstration of getopt
declare -rx SCRIPT-${0##*/}
declare RESULT
RESULT='getopt --name "$SCRIPT" --options "-h, -c:" -- "$@"'
printf "status code=$? result=\"$RESULT\"\n"
```

Here are the results:

```
$ bash getopt.sh -h
status code=0 result=" -h --"
$ bash getopt.sh -c
getopt.sh: option requires an argument -- c
status code=1 result=" --"
$ bash getopt.sh -x
getopt.sh: invalid option -- x
status code=1 result=" --"
```

The status code indicates whether getopt was successful. Status code 1 indicates getopt printed error messages. Status code 2 indicates a problem with options given to the getopt command itself.

Long switches are supported using the `--longoptions` (or -l) switch. Include a comma-separated list of expected long options. For example, to allow a `--help` switch, do this

```
RESULT='getopt --name "$SCRIPT" --options "-h, -c:" \

  --longoptions "help" -- "$@"'
```

getopt has other enhancements. To specify an optional argument for a long option, add an equals sign and the name of the argument.

If a double colon follows a switch name, it indicates an optional argument to the switch instead of a required one. If the POSIXLY_CORRECT variable exists and the option list begins with a +, arguments are not allowed for switches and the first argument is treated as the end of the switches.

If the GETOPT_COMPATIBLE shell variable exists, getopt behaves more like the C language getopt standard library function. Some older versions of getopt have this behavior by default. If you need to check for this behavior, use the `--test` (or -T) switch to test for C compatibility mode: If it is not running in compatibility mode, the status code is 4.

What do you do with the switches after getopt examines them? They can replace the original parameters using the set command

```
eval set - "$RESULT"
```

Now the parameters can be examined using positional parameters or using the built-in getopts, as shown in Listing 9.6.

Listing 9.6 getopt_demo.sh

```
#!/bin/bash
#
# getopt_demo.sh
#
# This script expects the switch -c and a company name.  --help (-h)
# is also allowed.

shopt -s -o nounset

declare -rx SCRIPT=${0##*/}
declare -r OPTSTRING="-h,-c:"
declare COMPANY
declare RESULT

# Check getopt mode

getopt -T
if [ $? -ne 4 ] ; then
    printf "$SCRIPT: %s\n" "getopt is in compatibility mode" >&2
```

Listing 9.6   Continued

```
    exit 192
fi

# Test parameters

RESULT='getopt --name "$SCRIPT" --options "$OPTSTRING" \
  --longoptions "help" \  -- "$@"'
if [ $? -gt 0 ] ; then
    exit 192
fi

# Replace the parameters with the results of getopt

eval set -- "$RESULT"

# Process the parameters

while [ $# -gt 0 ] ; do
  case "$1" in
  -h | --help) # Show help
      printf "%s\n" "usage: $SCRIPT [-h] [--help] -c companyid"
      exit 0
      ;;
  -c ) shift
      if [ $# -eq 0 ] ; then
          printf "$SCRIPT:$LINENO: %s\n" "company for -c is missing" >&2
          exit 192
      fi
      COMPANY="$1"
      ;;
  esac
  shift
done
if [ -z "$COMPANY" ] ; then
    printf "%s\n" "company name missing" >&2
    exit 192
fi

printf "$SCRIPT: %s\n" "Processing files for $COMPANY..."

# <-- begin work here

exit 0
```

This might seem like a lot of work, but for scripts with many complex switches, getopt makes the job of handling them much easier.

There are also a number of special switches. The `--alternative` (or -a) switch allows long options with only a single leading minus sign. Using this switch violates Linux convention. `--quiet-output` (or -Q) can be used to check the switches without returning the processed list to standard output. `--quiet` (or -q) indicates any errors by the status code but hides the error messages so that you can create your own custom messages. The `--shell` (or -u) switch uses quotation marks to protect special characters like spaces that might be treated in a special way by a shell. (This is necessary only in C compatibility mode.)

Subshells

Chapter 7, "Compound Commands," mentioned that a set of commands can be grouped together using curly braces. These commands act as a group and return a single status code.

```
$ { sleep 5 ; printf "%s\n" "Slept for 5 seconds" ; }
Slept for 5 seconds
```

A subshell is a set of commands grouped using round parentheses instead of curly braces. Unlike a command group, if a subshell appears on a single line, a semicolon is not required after the last command.

```
$ ( sleep 5 ; printf "%s\n" "Slept for 5 seconds" )
Slept for 5 seconds
```

Subshells act like a hybrid of a curly braces command set and a separate script. Like a statement group, a subshell is a set of statements that returns a single status code. Like a separate shell script, a subshell has its own environment variables.

```
$ declare -ix COUNT=15
$ { COUNT=10 ; printf "%d\n" "$COUNT" ; }
10
$ printf "%d\n" "$COUNT"
10
$ ( COUNT=20 ; printf "%d\n" "$COUNT" )
20

$ printf "%d\n" "$COUNT"
10
```

In this example, a command group can change the value of the variable COUNT in the shell session because the group runs as part of the session. The subshell cannot change the value of COUNT in the main program because it runs as if it were a separate shell script. COUNT is a copy of the variable from the session and the subshell can only change its private copy of COUNT.

Subshells are often used in conjunction with pipes. Using a pipe (or file redirection), the results of a command can be redirected to the subshell for processing. The data appears on the standard input of the subshell, as shown in Listing 9.7.

Listing 9.7 `subshell.sh`

```
#!/bin/bash
#
# subshell.sh
#
# Perform some operation to all the files in a directory

shopt -s -o nounset

declare -rx SCRIPT=${0##*/}
declare -rx INCOMING_DIRECTORY="incoming"

ls -1 "$INCOMING_DIRECTORY" |
  (
    while read FILE ; do
       printf "$SCRIPT: Processing %s...\n" "$FILE"
       # <-- do something here
    done
  )
printf "Done\n"
exit 0
```

The `read` command in the subshell reads one line at a time from standard input. In this case, it is reading the list of files created by the `ls` command.

```
$ bash subshell.sh
subshell.sh: Processing alabama_orders.txt...
subshell.sh: Processing new_york_orders.txt...
subshell.sh: Processing ohio_orders.txt...
Done
```

Subshells inherit more than just environment variables. This topic is discussed in detail in Chapter 14, "Functions and Script Execution."

Argument handling greatly increases the flexibility of scripts, and subshells are an indispensable tool. But there is still more fundamental material to master before a script can be truly called professional. A script without job control and signal handling is still incomplete.

Reference Section

getopt Command Switches

- --longoptions (or -l)—A comma-separated list of expected long options.
- --alternative (or -a)—Allows long options with only a single leading minus sign.
- --quiet-output (or -Q)—Checks the switches without returning the processed list to standard output.
- --quiet (or -q)—Indicates any errors by the status code but hides the error messages.
- --shell (or -u)—Uses quotation marks to protect special characters.
- --test (or -T)—Tests for C compatibility mode.

10

Job Control and Signals

ALTHOUGH I GREW UP ON A GRAPE FARM, I didn't spend a lot of time out in the fields. I suppose that was my father's way of not biasing me towards a life of sweat and sunburns. Somehow one farming skill that I never mastered was the use of hand signals. It seemed like those who had spent years outdoors were used to gesticulating over distances and noise, able to understand the most incomprehensible motioning. Not so for me.

One summer my father was trying to place a heavy piece of equipment into the back of a pickup truck using his tractor. He had me stationed at the base of the truck to line up the equipment and tell him when to start lowering. When everything looked in position, I gave him the signal. Unfortunately, my glasses are thick enough that they cause spherical aberration—that is, things sometimes appear crooked because the light passing through the lenses is bent. Almost at once I saw that the equipment wasn't centered and I started hopping up and down, gesturing wildly. But my father didn't notice anything was wrong until the equipment caved in the side of the truck with a sickening crunch.

Whether it was my bad signaling or his failure to pay attention is beside the point. An important condition had risen that was unable to be communicated. Similarly, scripts need to be able to delegate responsibilities to other scripts and to interrupt each other when pressing matters arise. This cooperation is achieved through job control and Linux signal handling.

Job Control

You can start background tasks by typing an ampersand (&) at the end of a command. Bash refers to background tasks as *jobs*. Any command or script running in the background is a job. During an interactive session, the shell keeps a list of all outstanding jobs. Managing background tasks using Bash commands is called *job control*.

Job control is available by default at the command prompt but must be enabled in scripts with the `-o monitor` shell option. Without job control, background tasks can still be started from a script, but Bash's job-management commands are unavailable.

The built–in `jobs` command lists active jobs. When a background task completes, the job is removed from the list.

```
$ sleep 60 &
[1] 28875
$ jobs
[1]+  Running                 sleep 60 &
```

In interactive sessions, Bash automatically checks and reports any changes to the background jobs before showing the command prompt. The job status is shown in the same format as the `jobs` command. The `set -b` command causes changes in job status to be displayed immediately when they occur, even if it means interrupting the user while he or she types. In scripts running with job control, the status of background tasks is also checked and printed.

The plus sign indicates the current running job, the one that moves into the foreground when the `fg` command is used. A minus sign indicates the last job started.

Linux assigns all jobs a unique *process identification number* (or *PID*). You can view it by using the `-l` (*long*) switch.

```
$ jobs -l
[1]+ 28875 Running                 sleep 60 &
```

The number in square brackets is the position of the job in the shell's job list. The PID number for the job can be expanded into a command using a percent sign (`%`). The `kill` command can stop a job. To kill the first background task, use a `%1`. The following example produces the same results as typing `kill 28875`.

```
$ kill %1
[1]+  Terminated              sleep 60
```

Other job list percent codes include `%%` and `%+` for the current background task, `%-` for the last background task started, and `%name` for a job with the name *name*. You can search the job names by using `%?`, which matches a job containing a particular substring.

```
$ sleep 10 &
[1] 13692
$ kill %?sle
$
[1]+  Terminated              sleep 10
```

The job number substitution is not the same as variable substitution, although the jobs command `-x` (*execute*) switch makes it behave that way.

```
$ printf "%d\n" %1
bash: printf: %1: invalid number
$ jobs -x printf "%d\n" %1
6259
```

In this case, the `printf` command (unlike `kill`) is not a job control command and has no knowledge of job numbers. The `jobs -x` command substitutes PID numbers for job numbers and then runs the `printf` command.

The `-p` (*PID*) switch lists only the process identification number. The jobs displayed can be narrowed to three types: Jobs with status changes `-n` (*new status*) , running jobs `-r` (*running*) , and stopped jobs `-s` (*stopped*) .

You can remove background tasks from Bash's job list using the built-in `disown` command.

```
$ sleep 10 &
[1] 14611
$ sleep 10 &
[2] 14623
$ sleep 10 &
[3] 14628
$ disown %2
$ jobs
[1]   Running                 sleep 10 &
[3]+  Running                 sleep 10 &
```

A disowned task continues to run even though it is no longer appears in the shell's job list, but job control commands will not accept the task. In this case, the second job continues to run, but %2 is no longer defined. When the second job is complete, Bash cannot notify the user because it is no longer monitoring the task. The `disown` command is useful when removing background commands you are not interested in tracking, such as MP3 players, Web browsers, or other background applications on the X Window desktop.

The `-a` (*all*) switch disowns all jobs just as if the background tasks were started in a script without job control. The `-r` (*running*) switch disowns all running jobs.

You can force a script to wait for one or more background tasks to complete by using the built-in `wait` command. If no jobs are specified, `wait` suspends the script until all the background tasks are finished.

```
$ sleep 5 &
[1] 7338
$ wait
[1]+  Done                    sleep 5
```

Signals

A *signal* is sometimes referred to as a *software interrupt*; it's a request to break away from a program and perform an urgent task. When a Bash receives the signal, it finishes the current command, identifies which signal was received, and takes the appropriate action. If it is able to continue executing the script afterwards, it does so, advancing to the next command.

Signals are sent to scripts with the built-in `kill` command. Despite what its name implies, `kill` can do more than just terminate programs with its default SIGTERM signal.

Suppose a slow command is running in the background.

```
$ { sleep 60; echo "DONE"; } &
[1] 7613
```

The `kill` command can suspend the command using the SIGSTOP signal.

```
$ kill -SIGSTOP 7613
[1]+  Stopped                 { sleep 60; echo "DONE"; }
```

After the command is stopped, it remains inactive until it receives another signal, such as SIGCONT.

```
$ kill -SIGCONT 7613
$ DONE

[1]+  Done                    { sleep 60; echo "DONE"; }
```

The SIGCONT signal continues execution at the point of interruption.

Linux defines 63 different signals. The signals most commonly sent to scripts are SIGTERM (immediately exit the script), SIGSTOP (stop the script, putting it to sleep temporarily), SIGHUP (hang up a connection), and SIGCONT (continue a stopped script). A complete list appears in Appendix E, "Signals."

The built-in `disown` command affects how signals are shared with background tasks. If the -h (SIGHUP) switch is used, Bash does not share SIGHUP with the background jobs of a particular task when a SIGHUP is received (such as when a user logs out).

The `suspend` Command

The built-in `suspend` command stops a script until a signal is received, just as if the script received a SIGSTOP signal. It is equivalent to using the command `kill -SIGSTOP $$` to force the script to stop itself. When used in a script, `suspend` requires job control to be enabled. See Listing 10.1.

Listing 10.1 `suspend_demo.sh`

```
#!/bin/bash
#
# suspend_demo.sh
#
# Wait for a SIGCONT signal and then print a message

shopt -s -o nounset
shopt -s -o monitor # enable job control

# wait for SIGCONT
```

Listing 10.1   Continued

```
suspend
printf "%s\n" "Who woke me up?"
exit 0
```

When this script runs, it is stopped until a SIGCONT is received.

```
$ bash suspend_demo.sh &
[1] 9185
$
[1]+  Stopped                 bash suspend_demo.sh
$ kill -SIGCONT 9185
$ Who woke me up?

[1]+  Done                    bash suspend_demo.sh

$
```

Traps

While Bash is running interactively, it handles most signals on behalf of the user. When a script is running and special actions need to be taken, it is the responsibility of the script to handle the appropriate signals. The action taken by Bash depends on which signal was received.

- SIGQUIT is always ignored
- SIGTTIN is ignored if job control is enabled; otherwise, it suspends the script
- SIGTTOU is ignored if job control is enabled; otherwise, it suspends the script
- SIGTSTP is ignored if job control is enabled; otherwise, it suspends the script
- SIGHUP is sent to all background tasks started by the script, waking up stopped tasks if necessary

For example, Bash normally handles the SIGHUP signal by passing the signal to all sub-scripts (unless disown -h is used). You can activate the same behavior in an interactive session by setting the huponexit shell option: When a session is terminated, SIGHUP is sent to all running jobs.

Other signals terminate a script unless a signal handler (or *trap*) is created. A trap is a set of commands that executes when a signal is received. The built-in trap command manages the signal handlers for a script.

The -l (*list*) switch lists all signals and their corresponding numbers.

Not all signals can be caught with traps. Some signals, such as SIGKILL, always terminate a script even if a signal handler is installed.

Signal handlers are created by supplying a command and a list of handlers to the trap command. Either the signal name or number can be used. SIGWINCH, for example, is the signal generated when a window changes its size. By installing a trap, a message can be displayed each time the window is resized.

```
$ trap `printf "There are %s lines\n" "$LINES"' SIGWINCH
```

Altering the window size results in:

```
$ There are 32 lines
$ There are 43 lines
$ There are 37 lines
```

You can view the current trap with the -p (*print*) switch.

```
$ trap -p SIGWINCH
trap -- `printf "There are %s lines\n" "$LINES"' SIGWINCH
```

To restore the default handler, don't supply a trap.

```
$ trap SIGWINCH
$ trap -p SIGWINCH
$
```

SIGUSR1 and SIGUSR2 are user-defined signals that have no pre-defined meaning. They can be freely used in scripts. When the following script receives a SIGUSR1 signal, it waits for the current command to complete, prints the message SIGUSR1, and resumes the script, as shown in Listing 10.2.

Listing 10.2 trap_demo.sh

```
#!/bin/bash
#
# trap_demo.sh
#
# Wait indefinitely for SIGUSR1, print a message when one arrives.

shopt -s -o nounset
trap `printf "SIGUSR1\n"' SIGUSR1

# Infinite loop!

while true ; do
  sleep 1
done

printf "%s\n" "Should never get here!" >&2
exit 192
```

The script continues until killed.

```
$ bash trap_demo.sh &
[1] 544
```

```
$ kill -SIGUSR1 544
SIGUSR1
$ kill 544
[1]+  Terminated              bash trap_demo.sh
```

The two most common uses for signal handlers are to awaken suspended scripts and to temporarily block signals for some critical commands that must not be interrupted. To temporarily ignore a signal, use empty quote marks or the `null` command as a signal handler and restore the original signal handler after the uninterruptable commands are finished.

```
trap : SIGINT SIGQUIT SIGTERM
# some command that must not be interrupted
trap SIGINT SIGQUIT SIGTERM
```

Exit Handlers

An exit handler is a set of commands executed whenever a script is finished. Exit handlers use the non-existent signal EXIT (signal number 0), as shown in Listing 10.3.

Listing 10.3 `exittrap_demo.sh`

```
#!/bin/bash
#
# exittrap_demo.sh
#
# Display "Goodbye" when this script exits.

shopt -s -o nounset
trap 'printf "Goodbye\n"' EXIT

sleep 5

exit 0
```

When the shell is exited, the message `Goodbye` is printed.

```
$ bash exittrap_demo.sh
Goodbye
```

When there is a lot of cleaning up to do, exit handlers usually invoke a shell function to perform the work. Shell functions are described Chapter 14, "Functions and Script Execution."

The `killall` Command

The Linux `killall` command kills by a program name instead of by a process ID number. As the name suggests, all matching jobs are killed. If an absolute path is specified, only processes running a particular file are killed.

```
$ sleep 15 &
[1] 1225
$ killall sleep
[1]+ Terminated          sleep
```

There are a number of switches for `killall`. The `-e` switch doesn't kill swapped out processes with long filenames. The `-g` switch kills the process group. The `-i` switch prompts before killing. The `-q` switch suppresses the warning when no processes are killed. The `-w` switch forces `killall` to wait until all processes have finished running.

Being Nice

All Linux programs run with a priority number between –20 and 19. The priority indicates the importance of the program, with lower numbers getting more time running than higher numbers.

The Linux `nice` command changes the priority of a command. `nice` should always be used when a script consumes a lot of resources in order to prevent more important jobs, such as handling user sessions, from being slowed or interrupted. Background tasks are automatically *niced* by Bash when they are started.

By default, `nice` reduces the priority (that is, it increases the priority number) by 10. Any number can be used, but the priority can only be reduced and it can never be less than 19. (The superuser, however, can reduce or increase the priority of any program.) The adjustment can be specified as a number after a minus sign, or by using the more readable `--adjustment=VALUE` (or `-n VALUE`) switch.

```
$ nice --adjustment=20 big_script.sh &
```

A corresponding `renice` command changes the priority of a running background task. As with `nice`, the priority can only be reduced. Unlike `nice`, the priority is a specific priority, not an offset.

The priority is a number immediately after the command (with no -). The optional -p (*PID*) switch indicates the parameters are process identification numbers. The `-g` switch indicates a list of process groups. The `-u` switch indicates usernames to change. Obviously, you can only `renice` programs that you own.

```
$ bash big_script.sh &
[1] 22516
$ renice 10 22516
22516: old priority 0, new priority 10
```

Process Status

The `jobs` command shows basic information about a background task. For more detailed information, Linux has a `ps` (*process status*) command. This command has many switches, some with leading minus signs and some without. Some of these switches are for compatibility with other operating systems. A complete list is given in the chapter's reference section.

For purposes of shell scripting, the most useful switches are -lu, which lists all the processes running for a particular user in long format.

```
$ ps -lu ken
  F S   UID   PID  PPID  C PRI  NI ADDR SZ WCHAN  TTY            TIME CMD
100 S   500  1838  1837  0  62   0 -    547 wait4  pts/1      00:00:01 bash
000 R   500  2274  1838  0  72   0 -    611 -      pts/1      00:00:00 ps
```

The important columns in the long format are as follows:

- s—Process state
- UID—User ID of the session running the program
- PID—The process identification number
- PPID—The process identification number of the program that ran the program listed
- PRI—The Linux priority value
- NI—The nice value
- TTY—The tty device used by the program, as returned by the tty command
- TIME—CPU time used by the process
- CMD—The name of the command

The state of the process is a general indication as to whether it is running and, if not, why not:

- D—Uninterruptible sleep usually caused by waiting on input or output
- R—Running or waiting to run
- S—Sleeping
- T—Traced or stopped
- Z—A defunct ("zombie") process waiting to be deleted

Be aware that ps has been known to change significantly between different versions of Linux. For best portability, ps should be used only for debugging unless the more advanced switches are avoided.

Using signals and traps allows scripts to work in tandem and alert each other to important events. Exit handlers guarantee that whenever a script exits, all necessary cleanup commands are executed. The nice command ensures that priority scripts get the most attention by Linux. The next couple of chapters examine the tools provided by Linux for scripts to work with data.

Reference Section

jobs Command Switches

- -l—Lists process IDs in addition to the normal information
- -p—Lists process IDs only
- -n—Prints only the processes that have changed status since the last notification
- -r—Shows running jobs
- -s—Shows stopped jobs
- -x c args—Runs command c after all job specifications that appear in the optional args have been replaced with the process ID of that job's process group leader

kill Command Switches

- -l n—Lists signal names; n is an optional list of signal numbers
- -s—Specifies a signal name to send
- -n—Specifies a signal number to send

renice Command Switches

- -p pids—renice by a list of process identification numbers
- -g gids—renice by a list of process groups
- -u users—renice by a list of users

ps Command Switches

- -A—Selects all processes
- -a—Selects all processes with a tty except any session leaders
- a—Selects all processes on a terminal, including those of other users
- -C—Selects processes by command name
- -c—Different scheduler info for -l option
- c—Uses raw CPU time for %CPU instead of decaying average
- c—Uses the true command name
- --columns (or -cols or --width)—Sets the screen width
- --cumulative (or S)—Includes some dead child process data (as a sum with the parent)

- -d—Selects all processes, but omits session leaders
- --deselect—Negates the selection
- -e—Selects all processes
- e—Shows the environment after the command
- -f—Displays a full listing
- --forest (or -H or f)—Shows process hierarchy (the forest)
- --format (or u)—Displays user-oriented format
- --Group (or -G)—Selects by real group name or ID
- --group (or -g)—Selects by effective group name or ID
- --no-headers (or h)—Does not print header lines
- --html—Shows HTML-escaped output
- --headers—Repeats header lines
- -j (or j)—Uses jobs format
- -l (or l)—Uses long format
- L—Lists all format specifiers
- --lines (or --rows)—Sets screen height
- -m—Shows threads
- m—Shows all threads
- -N—Same as --deselect
- -n (or N)—Sets namelist file
- n—Numeric output for WCHAN and USER
- --no-headers—Prints no header line
- --nul (or -null or -zero)—Shows unjustified output with NULLs
- -o (or O)—Is preloaded -o
- -o (or o)—User-defined format
- --pid (or -p)—Selects by process ID
- p—Selects by process ID
- r—Restricts output to running processes
- --sid (or -s or -n or n)—Selects processes belonging to the sessions given, where n is the SID
- s—Displays signal format
- --sort—Specifies sorting order
- T—Selects all processes on this terminal
- --tty (or -t)—Selects by terminal
- --User (or -U)—Selects by real username or ID

- `--user` (or `-u`)—Selects by effective username or ID
- `U`—Selects processes for specified users
- `--version` (or `-V` or `V`)—Prints version
- `-w` (or `w`)—Shows wide output
- `x`—Selects processes without controlling ttys
- `X`—Old Linux i386 register format
- `-y`—Does not show flags; shows `rss` in place of `addr`

`ps` **Command Sort Codes**

- `c` (or `cmd`)—Simple name of executable
- `C` (or `cmdline`)—Full command line
- `f` (or `flags`)—Flags as in long format `F` field
- `g` (or `pgrp`)—Process group ID
- `G` (or `pgid`)—Controlling tty process group ID
- `j` (or `cutime`)—Cumulative user time
- `J` (or `cstime`)—Cumulative system time
- `k` (or `utime`)—User time
- `K` (or `stime`)—System time
- `m` (or `min_flt`)—Number of minor page faults
- `M` (or `maj_flt`)—Number of major page faults
- `n` (or `cmin_flt`)—Cumulative minor page faults
- `N` (or `cmaj_flt`)—Cumulative major page faults
- `o` (or `session`)—Session ID
- `p` (or `pid`)—Process ID
- `P` (or `ppid`)—Parent process ID
- `r` (or `rss`)—Resident set size
- `R` (or `resident`)—Resident pages
- `s` (or `size`)—Memory size in kilobytes
- `S` (or `share`)—Amount of shared pages
- `t` (or `tty`)—The minor device number of tty
- `T` (or `start_time`)—Time process was started
- `U` (or `uid`)—User ID number
- `u` (or `user`)—Username
- `v` (or `vsize`)—Total `virtual memory usage` in bytes
- `y` (or `priority`)—Kernel scheduling priority

11

Text File Basics

A TEXT FILE IS A FILE CONTAINING human-readable text. Each line ends with a line feed character, a carriage return, or both, depending on the operating system. By Linux convention, each line ends with a line feed, the \n (newline) character in printf.

The examples in this chapter use a text file that lists several pieces of furniture by name, price, quantity, and supplier number, as shown in Listing 11.1.

Listing 11.1 orders.txt

```
Birchwood China Hutch,475.99,1,756
Bookcase Oak Veneer,205.99,1,756
Small Bookcase Oak Veneer,205.99,1,756
Reclining Chair,1599.99,1,757
Bunk Bed,705.99,1,757
Queen Bed,925.99,1,757
Two-drawer Nightstand,125.99,1,756
Cedar Toy Chest,65.99,1,757
Six-drawer Dresser,525.99,1,757
Pine Round Table,375.99,1,757
Bar Tool,45.99,1,756
Lawn Chair,55.99,1,756
Rocking Chair,287.99,1,757
Cedar Armoire,825.99,1,757
Mahogany Writing Desk,463.99,1,756
Garden Bench,149.99,1,757
Walnut TV Stand,388.99,1,756
Victorian-style Sofa,1225.99,1,757
Chair - Rocking,287.99,1,75
Grandfather Clock,2045.99,1,756
```

Linux contains many utilities for working with text files. Some can act as filters, processing the text so that it can be passed on to yet another command using a pipeline. When a text file is passed through a pipeline, it is called a *text stream,* that is, a stream of text characters.

Working with Pathnames

Linux has three commands for pathnames.

The `basename` command examines a path and displays the filename. It doesn't check to see whether the file exists.

```
$ basename /home/kburtch/test/orders.txt
orders.txt
```

If a suffix is included as a second parameter, `basename` deletes the suffix if it matches the file's suffix.

```
$ basename /home/kburtch/test/orders.txt .txt
orders
```

The corresponding program for extracting the path to the file is `dirname`.

```
$ dirname /home/kburtch/test/orders.txt
/home/kburtch/test
```

There is no trailing slash after the final directory in the path.

To verify that a pathname is a correct Linux pathname, use the `pathchk` command. This command verifies that the directories in the path (if they already exist) are accessible and that the names of the directories and file are not too long. If there is a problem with the path, `pathchk` reports the problem and returns an error code of 1.

```
$ pathchk "~/x" && echo "Acceptable path"
Acceptable path
$ mkdir a
$ chmod 400 a
$ pathchk "a/test.txt"
pathchk: directory 'a' is not searchable
$ pathchk "~/xxxxxxxxxxxxxxxxxxxxxxxxxxxxxxxxxxxxxxxxxxxxxxxxxxxxxxxx\
xxxxxxxxxxxxxxxxxxxxxxxxxxxxxxxxxxxxxxxxxxxxxxxxxxxxxxxxxxxxxxxxxxxxxxx\
xxxxxxxxxxxxxxxxxxxxxxxxxxxxxxxxxxxxxxxxxxxxxxxxxxxxxxxxxxxxxxxxxxxxxxx\
xxxxxxxxxxxxxxxxxxxxxxxxxxxxxxxxxxxxxxxxxxxxxxxxxxxxxxxxxxxxxxxxxxxxxxx\
xxxxxxxxxxxxxxxxxxxxxxxxxxxxxxxxxxxxxxxxxxxxxxxxxxxxxxxxxxxxxxxxxxxxxxx\
xxxxxxxxxxxxxxxxxxxxxxxxxxxxxxxxxxxxxxxx" && echo "Acceptable path"
pathchk: name
'xxxxxxxxxxxxxxxxxxxxxxxxxxxxxxxxxxxxxxxxxxxxxxxxxxxxxxxxxxxxxxxxxxxxxxx
xxxxxxxxxxxxxxxxxxxxxxxxxxxxxxxxxxxxxxxxxxxxxxxxxxxxxxxxxxxxxxxxxxxxxxx
xxxxxxxxxxxxxxxxxxxxxxxxxxxxxxxxxxxxxxxxxxxxxxxxxxxxxxxxxxxxxxxxxxxxxxx
xxxxxxxxxxxxxxxxxxxxxxxxxxxxxxxxxxxxxxxxxxxxxxxxxxxxxxxxxxxxxxxxxxxxxxx
xxxxxxxxxxxxxxxxxxxxxxxxxxxxxxxxxxxxxxxxxxxxxxxxxxxxxxxxxxxxxxxxxxxxxxx
xxxxxxxxxxxxxxxxxxxxxxxxxxxxxxxxx' has length 388; exceeds limit of 255
```

With the –portability (-p) switch, pathchk enforces stricter portability checks for all POSIX-compliant Unix systems. This identifies characters not allowed in a pathname, such as spaces.

```
$ pathchk "new file.txt"
$ pathchk -p "new file.txt"
pathchk: path 'new file.txt' contains nonportable character ' '
```

pathchk is useful for checking pathnames supplied from an outside source, such as pathnames from another script or those typed in by a user.

File Truncation

A particular feature of Unix-based operating systems, including the Linux ext3 file system, is the way space on a disk is reserved for a file. Under Linux, space is never released for a file. For example, if you overwrite a 1MB file with a single byte, Linux still reserves one megabyte of disk space for the file.

If you are working with files that vary greatly in size, you should remove the file and re-create it in order to free up the disk space rather than simply overwriting it.

This behavior affects all files, including directories. If a program removes all 5,000 files from a large directory, and puts a single file in that directory, the directory will still have space reserved for 5,000 file entries. The only way to release this space is to remove and re-create the directory.

Identifying Files

The built-in type command, as discussed in Chapter 3, "Files, Users, and Shell Customization," identifies whether a command is built-in or not, and where the command is located if it is a Linux command.

To test files other than commands, the Linux file command performs a series of tests to determine the type of a file. First, file determines whether the file is a regular file or is empty. If the file is regular, file consults the /usr/share/magic file, checking the first few bytes of the file in an attempt to determine what the file contains. If the file is an ASCII text file, it performs a check of common words to try to determine the language of the text.

```
$ file empty_file.txt
empty_file.txt: empty
$ file orders.txt
orders.txt: ASCII text
```

file also works with programs. If check-orders.sh is a Bash script, file identifies it as a shell script.

```
$ file check-orders.sh
check-orders.sh: Bourne-Again shell script text
$ file /usr/bin/test
```

```
/usr/bin/test: ELF 32-bit LSB executable, Intel 80386, version 1,
dynamically linked (uses shared libs), stripped
```

For script programming, file's -b (*brief*) switch hides the name of the file and returns only the assessment of the file.

```
$ file -b orders.txt
ASCII text
```

Other useful switches include -f (*file*) to read filenames from a specific file. The -i switch returns the description as MIME type suitable for Web programming. With the -z (*compressed*) switch, file attempts to determine the type of files stored inside a compressed file. The -L switch follows symbolic links.

```
$ file -b -i orders.txt
text/plain, ASCII
```

Creating and Deleting Files

As discussed in Chapter 3, "Files, Users, and Shell Customization," files are deleted with the rm (*remove*) command. The -f (*force*) command removes a file even when the file permissions indicate the script cannot write to the file, but rm never removes a file from a directory that the script does not own. (The sticky bit is an exception and is discussed in Chapter 15, "Shell Security.")

As whenever you deal with files, always check that the file exists before you attempt to remove it. See Listing 11.2.

Listing 11.2   rm_demo.sh

```
#!/bin/bash
#
# rm_demo.sh: deleting a file with rm
shopt -s -o nounset

declare -rx SCRIPT=${0##*/}
declare -rx FILE2REMOVE="orders.bak"
declare -x  STATUS

if [ ! -f "$FILE2REMOVE" ] ; then
    printf "%s\n" "$SCRIPT: $FILE2REMOVE does not exist" >&2
    exit 192
else
    rm "$FILE2REMOVE" >&2
    STATUS=$?
```

```
   if [ $STATUS -ne 0 ] ; then
      printf "%s\n" "$SCRIPT: Failed to remove file $FILE2REMOVE" >&2
      exit $STATUS
   fi
fi

exit 0
```

When removing multiple files, avoid using the -r (*recursive*) switch or filename glob-bing. Instead, get a list of the files to delete (using a command such as find, discussed next) and test each individual file before attempting to remove any of them. This is slow-er than the alternatives but if a problem occurs no files are removed and you can safely check for the cause of the problem.

New, empty files are created with the touch command. The command is called touch because, when it's used on an existing file, it changes the modification time even though it makes no changes to the file.

touch is often combined with rm to create new, empty files for a script. Appending output with >> does not result in an error if the file exists, eliminating the need to remember whether a file exists.

For example, if a script is to produce a summary file called run_results.txt, a fresh file can be created with Listing 11.3.

Listing 11.3   touch_demo.sh

```
#!/bin/bash
#
# touch_demo.sh: using touch to create a new, empty file

shopt -s -o nounset

declare -rx RUN_RESULTS="./run_results.txt"

if [ -f "$RUN_RESULTS" ] ; then
   rm -f "$RUN_RESULTS"
   if [ $? -ne 0 ] ; then
      printf "%s\n" "Error: unable to replace $RUN_RESULTS" >&2
   fi
   touch "$RUN_RESULTS"
fi

printf "Run stated %s\n" "'date'" >> "$RUN_RESULTS"
```

The -f switch forces the creation of a new file every time.

Moving and Copying Files

Files are renamed or moved to new directories using the mv (*move*) command. If -f (*force*) is used, move overwrites an existing file instead of reporting an error. Use -f only when it is safe to overwrite the file.

You can combine touch with mv to back up an old file under a different name before starting a new file. The Linux convention for backup files is to rename them with a trailing tilde (~). See Listing 11.4.

Listing 11.4   backup_demo.sh

```
#!/bin/bash
#
# backup_demo.sh

shopt -s -o nounset

declare -rx RUN_RESULTS="./run_results.txt"

if [ -f "$RUN_RESULTS" ] ; then
    mv -f "$RUN_RESULTS" "$RUN_RESULTS""~"
    if [ $? -ne 0 ] ; then
        printf "%s\n" "Error: unable to backup $RUN_RESULTS" >&2
    fi
    touch "$RUN_RESULTS"
fi

printf "Run stated %s\n" "'date'" >> "$RUN_RESULTS"
```

Because it is always safe to overwrite the backup, the move is forced with the -f switch. Archiving files is usually better than outright deleting because there is no way to "undelete" a file in Linux.

Similar to mv is the cp (*copy*) command. cp makes copies of a file and does not delete the original file. cp can also be used to make links instead of copies using the —link switch.

More Information About Files

There are two Linux commands that display information about a file that cannot be easily discovered with the test command.

The Linux stat command shows general information about the file, including the owner, the size, and the time of the last access.

```
$ stat ken.txt
  File: "ken.txt"
  Size: 84        Blocks: 8        Regular File
```

```
Access: (0664/-rw-rw-r—)      Uid: (  503/ kburtch)  Gid: (  503/ kburtch)
Device: 303      Inode: 131093    Links: 1
Access: Tue Feb 20 16:34:11 2001
Modify: Tue Feb 20 16:34:08 2001
Change: Tue Feb 20 16:34:08 2001
```

To make the information more readable from a script, use the -t (*terse*) switch. Each stat item is separated by a space.

```
$ stat -t orders.txt
orders.txt 21704 48 81fd 503 503 303 114674 1 6f 89 989439402
981490652 989436657
```

The Linux `statftime` command has similar capabilities to `stat`, but has a wider range of formatting options. `statftime` is similar to the `date` command: It has a string argument describing how the status information should be displayed. The argument is specified with the -f (*format*) switch.

The most common `statftime` format codes are as follows:

- %c—Standard format
- %d—Day (zero filled)
- %D—mm/dd/yy
- %H—Hour (24-hr clock)
- %I—Hour (12-hr clock)
- %j—Day (1..366)
- %m—Month
- %M—Minute
- %S—Second
- %U—Week number (Sunday)
- %w—Weekday (Sunday)
- %Y—Year
- %%—Percent character
- %_A—Uses file last access time
- %_a—Filename (no suffix)
- %_C—Uses file inode change time
- %_d—Device ID
- %_e—Seconds elapsed since epoch
- %_f—File system type
- %_i—Inode number
- %_L—Uses current (local) time

- `%_l`—Number of hard links
- `%_M`—Uses file last modified time
- `%_m`—Type/attribute/access bits
- `%_n`—Filename
- `%_r`—Rdev ID (char/block devices)
- `%_s`—File size (bytes)
- `%_U`—Uses current (UTC) time
- `%_u`—User ID (uid)
- `%_z`—Sequence number (1,2,...)

A complete list appears in the reference section at the end of this chapter.

By default, any of formatting codes referring to time will be based on the file's modified time.

```
$ statftime -f "%c" orders.txt
Tue Feb  6 15:17:32 2001
```

Other types of time can be selected by using a time code. The format argument is read left to right, which means different time codes can be combined in one format string. Using `%_C`, for example, changes the format codes to the inode change time (usually the time the file was created). Using `%_L` (*local time*) or `%_U` (*UTC time*) makes statftime behave like the date command.

```
$ statftime -f "modified time = %c current time = %_L%c" orders.txt
modified time = Tue Feb  6 15:17:32 2001 current time = Wed May
  9 15:49:01 2001
$ date
Wed May  9 15:49:01 2001
```

statftime can create meaningful archive filenames. Often files are sent with a name such as orders.txt and the script wants to save the orders with the date as part of the name.

```
$ statftime -f "%_a_%_L%m%d.txt" orders.txt
orders_0509.txt
```

Besides generating new filenames, statftime can be used to save information about a file to a variable.

```
$ BYTES='statftime -f "%_s" orders.txt'
$ printf "The file size is %d bytes\n" "$BYTES"
The file size is 21704 bytes
```

When a list of files is supplied on standard input, the command processes each file in turn. The `%_z` code provides the position of the filename in the list, starting at 1.

Transferring Files Between Accounts (wget)

Linux has a convenient tool for downloading files from other logins on the current computer or across a network. wget (*web get*) retrieves files using FTP or HTTP. wget is designed specifically to retrieve files, making it easy to use in shell scripts. If a connection is broken, wget tries to reconnect and continue to download the file.

The wget program uses the same form of address as a Web browser, supporting ftp:// and http:// URLs. Login information is added to a URL by placing user: and password@ prior to the hostname. FTP URLs can end with an optional ;type=a or ;type=i for ASCII or IMAGE FTP downloads. For example, to download the info.txt file from the kburtch login with the password jabber12 on the current computer, you use:

```
$ wget ftp://kburtch:jabber12@localhost/info.txt;type=i
```

By default, wget uses –verbose message reporting. To report only errors, use the –quiet switch. To log what happened, append the results to a log file using –append-output and a log name and log the server responses with the –server-response switch.

```
$ wget –server-response –append-output wget.log \ ftp://kburtch:\
jabber12@localhost/info.txt;type=i
```

Whole accounts can be copied using the –mirror switch.

```
$ wget –mirror ftp://kburtch:jabber12@localhost;type=i
```

To make it easier to copy a set of files, the –glob switch can enable file pattern matching. –glob=on causes wget to pattern match any special characters in the filename. For example, to retrieve all text files:

```
$ wget –glob=on 'ftp://kburtch:jabber12@localhost/*.txt'
```

There are many special-purpose switches not covered here. A complete list of switches is in the reference section. Documentation is available on the wget home page at http://www.gnu.org/software/wget/wget.html.

Transferring Files with FTP

Besides wget, the most common way of transferring files between accounts is using the ftp command. FTP is a client/server system: An FTP server must be set up on your computer if there isn't one already. Most Linux distributions install an FTP server by default.

With an FTP client, you'll have to redirect the necessary download commands using standard input, but this is not necessary with wget.

To use ftp from a script, you use three switches. The -i (*not interactive*) switch disables the normal FTP prompts to the user. -n (*no auto-login*) suppresses the login prompt, requiring you to explicitly log in with the open and user commands. -v (*verbose*) displays more details about the transfer. The ftp commands can be embedded in a script using a here file.

```
ftp -i -n -v <<!
open ftp.nightlight.com
user incoming_orders password
cd linux_lightbulbs
binary
put $1
!
if [ $? -ne 0 ] ; then
    printf "%s\n" "$SCRIPT: FTP transfer failed" >&2
    exit 192
fi
```

This script fragment opens an FTP connection to a computer called `ftp.`
`nightlight.com`. It deposits a file in `linux_lightbulbs` directory in the
`incoming_orders` account. If an error occurs, an error message is printed and the
script stops.

Processing files sent by FTP is difficult because there is no way of knowing whether
the files are still being transferred. Instead of saving a file to a temp file and then moving
it to its final location, an FTP server will create a blank file and will slowly save the data
to the file. The mere presence of the file is not enough to signify the transfer is complete. The usual method of handling this situation is to wait until the file has been
modified within a reasonable amount of time (perhaps an hour). If the file hasn't been
modified recently, the transfer is probably complete and the file can be safely renamed
and moved to a permanent directory.

Some distributions have an `ftpcopy` (or a `ftpcp`) command, which will copy whole
directories at one time. Care must be taken with `ftpcopy` because it is primarily intended as a mirroring tool and it will delete any local files not located at the remote account.

Transferring Files with Secure FTP (`sftp`)

Part of the OpenSSH (Open Source Secure Shell) project, Secure FTP (`sftp`) is another
file-transfer program that works in a similar way to FTP but encrypts the transfer so that
it cannot be intercepted or read by intermediary computers. The encryption process
increases the amount of data and slows the transfer but provides protection for confiden-
tial information.

You must specify the computer and user account on the `sftp` command line. SFTP
prompts you for the password.

```
$ sftp root@our_web_site.com:/etc/httpd/httpd.conf
Connecting to our_web_site.com...
root@our_web_site.coms password:
Fetching /etc/httpd/httpd.conf to httpd.conf
```

For security purposes, SFTP normally asks the user for the Linux login password. It
doesn't request the password from standard input but from the controlling terminal. This

means you can't include the password in the batch file. The solution to this problem is to use SSH's public key authentication using the `ssh-keygen` command. If you have not already done so, generate a new key pair as follows.

```
$ ssh-keygen -t rsa
```

A pair of authentication keys are stored under `.ssh` in your home directory. You must copy the public key (a file ending in `.pub`) to the remote machine and add it to a text file called `~/.sshd/authorized_keys`. Each local login accessing the remote login needs a public key in `authorized_keys`. If a key pair exists, SFTP automatically uses the keys instead of the Linux login password.

Like FTP, SFTP needs a list of commands to carry out. SFTP includes a `-b` (*batch*) switch to specify a separate batch file containing the commands to execute. To use a convenient here file in your script, use a batch file called `/dev/stdin`.

The commands that SFTP understands are similar to FTP. For purposes of shell scripting, the basic transfer commands are the same. Transfers are always "binary." There is a `-v` (*verbose*) switch, but it produces a lot of information. When the `-b` switch is used, SFTP shows the commands that are executed so the `-v` switch is not necessary for logging what happened during the transfer.

```
sftp -C -b /dev/stdin root@our_web_site.com <<!
cd /etc/httpd
get httpd.conf
!
STATUS=$?
if [ $STATUS -ne 0 ] ; then
    printf "%s\n" "Error: SFTP transfer failed" >&2
    exit $STATUS
fi
```

The `-C` (*compress*) option attempts to compress the data for faster transfers.

For more information about `ssh`, `sftp`, and related programs, visit http://www.openssh.org/.

Verifying Files

Files sent by FTP or wget can be further checked by computing a checksum. The Linux `cksum` command counts the number of bytes in a file and prints a cyclic redundancy check (CRC) checksum, which can be used to verify that the file arrived complete and intact. The command uses a POSIX-compliant algorithm.

```
$ cksum orders.txt
491404265 21799 orders.txt
```

There is also a Linux `sum` command that provides compatibility with older Unix systems, but be aware that `cksum` is incompatible with `sum`.

For greater checksum security, some distributions include a md5sum command to compute an MD5 checksum. The –status switch quietly tests the file. The –binary (or -b) switch treats the file as binary data as opposed to text. The –warn switch prints warnings about bad MD5 formatting. –check (or -c) checks the sum on a file.

```
$ md5sum orders.txt
945eecc13707d4a23e27730a44774004  orders.txt
$ md5sum orders.txt > orderssum.txt
$ md5sum –check orderssum.txt
file1.txt: OK
```

Differences between two files can be pinpointed with the Linux cmp command.

```
$ cmp orders.txt orders2.txt
orders.txt orders2.txt differ: char 179, line 6
```

If two files don't differ, cmp prints nothing.

Splitting Large Files

Extremely large files can be split into smaller files using the Linux split command. Files can be split by bytes or by lines. The –bytes=*s* (or -b *s*) switch creates files of no more than *s* bytes. The –lines=*s* (or -l *s*) switch creates files of no more than *s* lines. The –line-bytes=*s* (or -C *s*) switch constraints each line to no more than *s* bytes. The size is a number with an optional b (512 byte blocks), k (kilobytes), or m (megabytes). The final parameter is the prefix to use for the new filenames.

```
$ split –bytes=10k huge_file.txt small_file
$ ls -l small_file*
-rw-rw-r—   1 kburtch  kburtch     10240 Aug 28 16:19 small_fileaa
-rw-rw-r—   1 kburtch  kburtch     10240 Aug 28 16:19 small_fileab
-rw-rw-r—   1 kburtch  kburtch      1319 Aug 28 16:19 small_fileac
```

You reassemble a split file with the Linux cat command. This command combines files and writes them to standard output. Be careful to combine the split files in the correct order.

```
$ cksum huge_file.txt
491404265 21799 huge_file.txt
$ cat small_fileaa small_fileab small_fileac > new_file
$ cksum new_file
491404265 21799 new_file
```

If the locale where the split occurred is the same as the locale where the file is being reassembled, it is safe to use wildcard globbing for the cat filenames.

The Linux csplit (*context split*) command splits a file at the points where a specific pattern appears.

The basic `csplit` pattern is a regular expression in slashes followed by an optional offset. The regular expression represents lines that will become the first line in the next new file. The offset is the number of lines to move forward or back from the matching line, which is by default zero. The pattern `"/dogs/+1"` will separate a file into two smaller files, the first ending with the first occurrence of the pattern `dogs`.

Quoting the pattern prevents it from being interpreted by Bash instead of the `csplit` command.

The –prefix=*P* (or -f *P*) switch sets the prefix for the new filenames. The –suffix=*S* (or -b *S*) writes the file numbers using the specified C `printf` function codes. The –digits=*D* (or -n *D*) switch specifies the maximum number of digits for file numbering. The default is two digits.

```
$ csplit –prefix "chairs" orders.txt "/Chair/"
107
485
$ ls -l chairs*
-rw-rw-r—    1 kburtch  kburtch        107 Oct  1 15:33 chairs00
-rw-rw-r—    1 kburtch  kburtch        485 Oct  1 15:33 chairs01
$ head -1 chairs01
Reclining Chair,1599.99,1,757
```

The first occurrence of the pattern `Chair` was in the line `Reclining Chair`.

Multiple patterns can be listed. A pattern delineated with percent signs (%) instead of with slashes indicates a portion of the file that should be ignored up to the indicated pattern. It can also have an offset. A number by itself indicates that particular line is to start the next new file. A number in curly braces repeats the last pattern a specific number of times, or an asterisk to match all occurrences of a pattern.

To split the `orders.txt` file into separate files, each beginning with the word `Chair`, use the all occurrences pattern.

```
$ csplit –prefix "chairs" orders.txt "/Chair/" "{*}"
107
222
23
179
61
$ ls -l chairs*
-rw-rw-r—    1 kburtch  kburtch        107 Oct  1 15:37 chairs00
-rw-rw-r—    1 kburtch  kburtch        222 Oct  1 15:37 chairs01
-rw-rw-r—    1 kburtch  kburtch         23 Oct  1 15:37 chairs02
-rw-rw-r—    1 kburtch  kburtch        179 Oct  1 15:37 chairs03
-rw-rw-r—    1 kburtch  kburtch         61 Oct  1 15:37 chairs04
```

The –elide-empty-files (or -z) switch doesn't save files that contain nothing. –keep-files (or -k) doesn't delete the generated files when an error occurs. The –quiet (or –silent or -q or -s) switch hides progress information.

`csplit` is useful in splitting large files containing repeated information, such as extracting individual orders sent from a customer as a single text file.

Tabs and Spaces

The Linux `expand` command converts Tab characters into spaces. The default is eight spaces, although you can change this with –tabs=n (or -t n) to n spaces. The –tabs switch can also use a comma-separated list of Tab stops.

```
$ printf "\tA\tTEST\n" > test.txt
$ wc test.txt
      1       2       8 test.txt
$ expand test.txt | wc
      1       2      21
```

The –initial (or -i) switch converts only leading Tabs on a line.

```
$ expand –initial test.txt | wc
      1       2      15
```

The corresponding `unexpand` command converts multiple spaces back into Tab characters. The default is eight spaces to a Tab, but you can use the –tabs=n switch to change this. By default, only initial tabs are converted. Use the –all (or -a) switch to consider all spaces on a line.

Use `expand` to remove tabs from a file before processing it.

Temporary Files

Temporary files, files that exist only for the duration of a script's execution, are traditionally named using the $$ function. This function returns the process ID number of the current script. By including this number in the name of the temporary files, it makes the name of the file unique for each run of the script.

```
$ TMP="/tmp/reports.$$"
$ printf "%s\n" "$TMP"
/tmp/reports.20629
$ touch "$TMP"
```

The drawback to this traditional approach lies in the fact that the name of a temporary file is predictable. A hostile program can see the process ID of your scripts when it runs and use that information to identify which temporary files your scripts are using. The temporary file could be deleted or the data replaced in order to alter the behavior of your script.

For better security, or to create multiple files with unique names, Linux has the `mktemp` command. This command creates a temporary file and prints the name to standard output so it can be stored in a variable. Each time `mktemp` creates a new file, the file is given a unique name. The name is created from a filename template the program supplies, which ends in the letter X six times. `mktemp` replaces the six letters with a unique, random code to create a new filename.

```
$ TMP='mktemp /tmp/reports.XXXXXX'
$ printf "%s\n" "$TMP"
/tmp/reports.3LnWVw
$ ls -l "$TMP"
-rw------    1 kburtch  kburtch         0 Aug  1 14:34 reports.3LnWVw
```

In this case, the letters XXXXXX are replaced with the code 3LnWvw.

mktemp creates temporary directories with the -d (*directories*) switch. You can suppress error messages with the -q (*quiet*) switch.

Lock Files

When many scripts share the same files, there needs to be a way for one script to indicate to another that it has finished its work. This typically happens when scripts overseen by two different development teams need to share files, or when a shared file can be used by only one script at a time.

A simple method for synchronizing scripts is the use of lock files. A *lock file* is like a flag variable: The existence of the file indicates a certain condition, in this case, that the file is being used by another program and should not be altered.

Most Linux distributions include a directory called /var/lock, a standard location to place lock files.

Suppose the invoicing files can be accessed by only one script at a time. A lock file called invoices_lock can be created to ensure only one script has access.

```
declare -r INVOICES_LOCKFILE="/var/lock/invoices_lock"
while test ! -f "$INVOICES_LOCKFILE" ; do
  printf "Waiting for invoices to be printed...\n"
  sleep 10
done
touch "$INVOICES_LOCKFILE"
```

This script fragment checks every 10 seconds for the presence of invoices_lock. When the file disappears, the loop completes and the script creates a new lock file and proceeds to do its work. When the work is complete, the script should remove the lock file to allow other scripts to proceed.

If a lock file is not removed when one script is finished, it causes the next script to loop indefinitely. The while loop can be modified to use a timeout so that the script stops with an error if the invoice files are not accessible after a certain period of time.

```
declare -r INVOICES_LOCKFILE="/var/lock/invoices_lock"
declare -ir INVOICES_TIMEOUT=1800    # 30 minutes
declare -i TIME=0
TIME_STARTED='date +%s'
while test ! -f "$INVOICES_LOCKFILE" ; do
  printf "Waiting for the invoices to be printed...\n"
```

```
   sleep 10
   TIME='date +%s'
   TIME=TIME-TIME_STARTED
   if [ $TIME -gt $INVOICES_TIMEOUT ] ; then
      printf "Timed out waiting for the invoices to print\n"
      exit 1
   fi
done
```

The date command's %s code returns the current clock time in seconds. When two executions of date are subtracted from each other, the result is the number of seconds since the first date command was executed. In this case, the timeout period is 1800 seconds, or 30 minutes.

Named Pipes

Lock files are convenient when a small number of scripts share the same file. When too many scripts are waiting on a lock file, a *race condition* occurs: the computer spends a lot of time simply checking for the presence of the lock file instead of doing useful work. Fortunately, there are other ways to share information.

Two scripts can share data using a special kind of file called a *named pipe*. These pipes (also called FIFOs or queues) are files that can be read by one script while being written to by another. The effect is similar to the pipe operator (|), which forwards the results of one command as the input to another. Unlike a shell pipeline, the scripts using a named pipe run independently of one another, sharing only the pipe file between them. No lock files are required.

The mkfifo command creates a new named pipe.

```
$ mkfifo website_orders.fifo
$ ls -l website_orders.fifo
prw-rw-r—   1 kburtch kburtch        0 May 22 14:14 orders.fifo
```

The file type p to the left of the ls output indicates this is a named pipe. If the ls filename typing option (-F) is used, the filename is followed by a vertical bar (|) to indicate a pipe.

The named pipe can be read like a regular file. Suppose, for example, you want to create a script to log incoming orders from the company Web site, as shown in Listing 11.5.

Listing 11.5 do_web_orders.sh

```
#!/bin/bash
#
# do_web_orders.sh: read a list of orders and show date read

shopt -s -o nounset
```

```
declare -rx SCRIPT=${0##*/}
declare -rx QUEUE="website_orders.fifo"
declare DATE
declare ORDER

if test ! -r "$QUEUE" ; then
   printf "%s\n" "$SCRIPT:$LINENO: the named pipe is missing or \
not readable" >&2
   exit 192
fi

{
  while read ORDER; do
    DATE='date'
    printf "%s: %s\n" "$DATE" "$ORDER"
  done
} < $QUEUE

printf "Program complete"
exit 0
```

In this example, the contents of the pipe are read one line at a time just as if it was a regular file.

When a script reads from a pipe and there's no data, it sleeps (or blocks) until more data becomes available. If the program writing to the pipe completes, the script reading the pipe sees this as the end of the file. The while loop will complete and the script will continue after the loop.

To send orders through the pipe, they must be printed or otherwise redirected to the pipe. To simulate a series of orders, write the orders file to the named pipe using the cat command. Even though the cat command is running in the background, it continues writing orders to the named pipe until all the lines have been read by the script.

```
$ cat orders.txt > website_orders.fifo &
$ sh do_web_orders.sh
Tue May 22 14:23:00 EDT 2001: Birchwood China Hutch,475.99,1,756
Tue May 22 14:23:00 EDT 2001: Bookcase Oak Veneer,205.99,1,756
Tue May 22 14:23:00 EDT 2001: Small Bookcase Oak Veneer,205.99,1,756
Tue May 22 14:23:00 EDT 2001: Reclining Chair,1599.99,1,757
Tue May 22 14:23:00 EDT 2001: Bunk Bed,705.99,1,757
Tue May 22 14:23:00 EDT 2001: Queen Bed,925.99,1,757
Tue May 22 14:23:00 EDT 2001: Two-drawer Nightstand,125.99,1,756
Tue May 22 14:23:00 EDT 2001: Cedar Toy Chest,65.99,1,757
Tue May 22 14:23:00 EDT 2001: Six-drawer Dresser,525.99,1,757
Tue May 22 14:23:00 EDT 2001: Pine Round Table,375.99,1,757
Tue May 22 14:23:00 EDT 2001: Bar Stool,45.99,1,756
Tue May 22 14:23:00 EDT 2001: Lawn Chair,55.99,1,756
```

```
Tue May 22 14:23:00 EDT 2001: Rocking Chair,287.99,1,757
Tue May 22 14:23:00 EDT 2001: Cedar Armoire,825.99,1,757
Tue May 22 14:23:00 EDT 2001: Mahogany Writing Desk,463.99,1,756
Tue May 22 14:23:00 EDT 2001: Garden Bench,149.99,1,757
Tue May 22 14:23:00 EDT 2001: Walnut TV Stand,388.99,1,756
Tue May 22 14:23:00 EDT 2001: Victorian-style Sofa,1225.99,1,757
Tue May 22 14:23:00 EDT 2001: Chair - Rocking,287.99,1,757
Tue May 22 14:23:00 EDT 2001: Grandfather Clock,2045.99,1,756
```

Using `tee`, a program can write to two or more named pipes simultaneously.

Because a named pipe is not a regular file, commands such as `grep`, `head`, or `tail` can behave unexpectedly or block indefinitely waiting for information on the pipe to appear or complete. If in doubt, verify that the file is not a pipe before using these commands.

Process Substitution

Sometimes the vertical bar pipe operators cannot be used to link a series of commands together. When a command in the pipeline does not use standard input, or when it uses two sources of input, a pipeline cannot be formed. To create pipes when normal pipelines do not work, Bash uses a special feature called *process substitution*.

When a command is enclosed in `<(...)`, Bash runs the command separately in a subshell, redirecting the results to a temporary named pipe instead of standard input. In place of the command, Bash substitutes the name of a named pipe file containing the results of the command.

Process substitution can be used anywhere a filename is normally used. For example, the Linux `grep` command, a file-searching command, can search a file for a list of strings. A temporary file can be used to search a log file for references to the files in the current directory.

```
$ ls -1 > temp.txt
$ grep -f temp.txt /var/log/nightrun_log.txt
Wed Aug 29 14:18:38 EDT 2001 invoice_error.txt deleted
$ rm temp.txt
```

A pipeline cannot be used to combine these commands because the list of files is being read from `temp.txt`, not standard input. However, these two commands can be rewritten as a single command using process substitution in place of the temporary file-name.

```
$ grep -f <(ls -1) /var/log/nightrun_log.txt
Wed Aug 29 14:18:38 EDT 2001 invoice_error.txt deleted
```

In this case, the results of `ls -1` are written to a temporary pipe. `grep` reads the list of files from the pipe and matches them against the contents of the `nightrun_log.txt` file. The fact that Bash replaces the `ls` command with the name of a temporary pipe can be checked with a `printf` statement.

```
$ printf "%s\n" <(ls -1)
/dev/fd/63
```

Bash replaces -f <(ls -1) with -f /dev/fd/63. In this case, the pipe is opened as file descriptor 63. The left angle bracket (<) indicates that the temporary file is read by the command using it. Likewise, a right angle bracket (>) indicates that the temporary pipe is written to instead of read.

Opening Files

Files can be read by piping their contents to a command, or by redirecting the file as standard input to a command or group of commands. This is the easiest way to see what a text file contains, but it has two drawbacks. First, only one file can be examined at a time. Second, it prevents the script from interacting with the user because the read command reads from the redirected file instead of the keyboard.

Instead of piping or redirection, files can be opened for reading by redirecting the file to a descriptor number with the exec command, as shown in Listing 11.6.

Listing 11.6   open_file.sh

```
#!/bin/bash
#
# open_file.sh: print the contents of orders.txt

shopt -s -o nounset

declare LINE

exec 3< orders.txt
while read LINE <&3 ; do
   printf "%s\n" "$LINE"
done
exit 0
```

In this case, the file orders.txt is redirected to file descriptor 3. Descriptor 3 is the lowest number that programs can normally use. File descriptor 0 is standard input, file descriptor 1 is standard output, and file descriptor 2 is standard error.

The read command receives its input from descriptor 3 (orders.txt), which is being redirected by <. read can also read from a particular file descriptor using the Korn shell -u switch.

If the file opened with exec does not exist, Bash reports a "bad file number" error. The file descriptor must also be a literal number, not a variable.

If exec is not used, the file descriptor can still be opened but it cannot be reassigned.

```
3< orders.txt
3< orders2.txt
```

In this example, file descriptor 3 is `orders.txt`. The second line has no effect because descriptor 3 is already opened. If `exec` is used, the second line re-opens descriptor 3 as `orders2.txt`.

To save file descriptors, `exec` can copy a descriptor to a second descriptor. To make input file descriptor 4 the same file as file descriptor 3, do this

```
exec 4<&3
```

Now descriptor 3 and 4 refer to the same file and can be used interchangeably. Descriptor 3 can be used to open another file and can be restored to its original value by copying it back from descriptor 4. If descriptor 4 is omitted, Bash assumes that you want to change standard input (descriptor 0).

You can move a file descriptor by appending a minus sign to it. This closes the original file after the descriptor was copied.

```
exec 4<&3-
```

You can likewise duplicate output file descriptors with `>&` and move them by appending a minus sign. The default output is standard output (descriptor 1).

To open a file for writing, use the output redirection symbol (`>`).

```
exec 3<orders.txt
exec 4>log.out
while read LINE <&3 ; do
  printf "%s\n" "$LINE" >&4
done
```

The `<>` symbol opens a file for both input and output.

```
exec 3<>orders.txt
```

The reading or writing proceeds sequentially from the beginning of the file. Writing to the file overwrites its contents: As long as the characters being overwritten are the same length as the original characters, the new characters replace the old. If the next line in a file is `dog`, for example, writing the line `cat` over `dog` replaces the word `dog`. However, if the next line in the file is `horse`, writing `cat` creates two lines—the line `cat` and the line `se`. The linefeed character following `cat` overwrites the letter `r`. The script will now read the line `se`.

`<>` has limited usefulness with regular files because there is no way to "back up" and rewrite something that was just read. You can only overwrite something that you are about to read next.

The script in Listing 11.7 reads through a file and appends a "`Processed on`" message to the end of the file.

Listing 11.7   open_files2.sh

```bash
#!/bin/bash
#
# open_files2.sh

shopt -o -s nounset

declare LINE

exec 3<>orders.txt
while read LINE <&3 ; do
  printf "%s\n" "$LINE"
done
printf "%s\n" "Processed on "'date' >&3
exit 0
```

<> is especially useful for socket programming, which is discussed in Chapter 16, "Network Programming."

As files can be opened, so they can also be closed. An input file descriptor can be closed with <&-. Be careful to include a file descriptor because, without one, this closes standard input. An output file descriptor can be closed with >&-. Without a descriptor, this closes standard output.

As a special Bash convention, file descriptors can be referred to by a pathname. A path in the form of /dev/fd/n refers to file descriptor n. For example, standard output is /dev/fd/1. Using this syntax, it is possible to refer to open file descriptors when running Linux commands.

```
$ exec 4>results.out
$ printf "%s\n" "Send to fd 4 and standard out" | tee /dev/fd/4
Send to fd 4 and standard out
$ exec 4>&-
$ cat results.out
Send to fd 4 and standard out
```

Using head and tail

The Linux head command returns the first lines contained in a file. By default, head prints the first 10 lines. You can specify a specific number of lines with the —lines=n (or -n n) switch.

```
$ head —lines=5 orders.txt
Birchwood China Hutch,475.99,1,756
Bookcase Oak Veneer,205.99,1,756
```

```
Small Bookcase Oak Veneer,205.99,1,756
Reclining Chair,1599.99,1,757
Bunk Bed,705.99,1,757
```

You can abbreviate the —lines switch to a minus sign and the number of lines.

```
$ head -3 orders.txt
Birchwood China Hutch,475.99,1,756
Bookcase Oak Veneer,205.99,1,756
Small Bookcase Oak Veneer,205.99,1,756
```

The amount of lines can be followed by a c for characters, an l for lines, a k for kilobytes, or an m for megabytes. The —bytes (or -c) switch prints the number of bytes you
specify.

```
$ head -9c orders.txt
Birchwood
$ head —bytes=9 orders.txt
Birchwood
```

The Linux tail command displays the final lines contained in a file. Like head, the
amount of lines or bytes can be followed by a c for characters, an l for lines, a k for
kilobytes, or an m for megabytes.

The switches are similar to the head command. The —bytes=n (or -c) switch prints
the number of bytes you specify. The —lines=n (-n) switch prints the number of lines
you specify.

```
$ tail -3 orders.txt
Walnut TV Stand,388.99,1,756
Victorian-style Sofa,1225.99,1,757
Grandfather Clock,2045.99,1,756
```

Combining tail and head in a pipeline, you can display any line or range of lines.

```
$ head -5 orders.txt | tail -1
Bunk Bed,705.99,1,757
```

If the starting line is a plus sign instead of a minus sign, tail counts that number of
lines from the start of the file and prints the remainder. This is a feature of tail, not the
head command.

```
$ tail +17 orders.txt
Walnut TV Stand,388.99,1,756
Victorian-style Sofa,1225.99,1,757
Grandfather Clock,2045.99,1,756
```

When using head or tail on arbitrary files in a script, always check to make sure that
the file is a regular file to avoid unpleasant surprises.

File Statistics

The Linux wc (*word count*) command provides statistics about a file. By default, wc shows the size of the file in lines, words, and characters. To make wc useful in scripts, switches must be used to return a single statistic.

The —bytes (or —chars or -c) switch returns the file size, the same value as the file size returned by statftime.

```
$ wc —bytes invoices.txt
  20411 invoices.txt
```

To use wc in a script, direct the file through standard input so that the filename is suppressed.

```
$ wc —bytes < status_log.txt
  57496
```

The —lines (or -l) switch returns the number of lines in the file. That is, it counts the number of line feed characters.

```
$ wc —lines < status_log.txt
  1569
```

The max-line-length (or -L) switch returns the length of the longest line. The —words (or -w) switch counts the number of words in the file.

wc can be used with variables when their values are printed into a pipeline.

```
$ declare -r TITLE="Annual Grain Yield Report"
$ printf "%s\n" "$TITLE" | wc —words
      4
```

Cutting

The Linux cut command removes substrings from all lines contained in a file.

The —fields (or -f) switch prints a section of a line marked by a specific character. The —delimiter (or -d) switch chooses the character. To use a space as a delimiter, it must be escaped with a backslash or enclosed in quotes.

```
$ declare -r TITLE="Annual Grain Yield Report"
$ printf "%s\n" "$TITLE" | cut -d' ' -f2
Grain
```

In this example, the delimiter is a space and the second field marked by a space is Grain. When cutting with printf, always make sure a line feed character is printed; otherwise, cut will return an empty string.

Multiple fields are indicated with commas and ranges as two numbers separated by a minus sign (-).

```
$ printf "%s\n" "$TITLE" | cut -d' ' -f 2,4
Grain Report
```

You separate multiple fields using the delimiter character. To use a different delimiter character when displaying the results, use the —output-delimiter switch.

The —characters (or -c) switch prints the specified characters' positions. This is similar to the dollar sign expression substrings but any character or range of characters can be specified. The —bytes (or -b) switch works identically but is provided for future support of multi-byte international characters.

```
$ printf "%s\n" "$TITLE" | cut —characters 1,3,6-8
Anl G
```

The —only-delimited (or -s) switch ignores lines in which the delimiter character doesn't appear. This is an easy way to skip a title or other notes at the beginning of a data file.

When used on multiple lines, cut cuts each line

```
$ cut -d, -f1 < orders.txt | head -3
Birchwood China Hutch
Bookcase Oak Veneer
Small Bookcase Oak Veneer
```

The script in Listing 11.8 adds the quantity fields in orders.txt.

Listing 11.8   cut_demo.sh

```
#!/bin/bash
#
# cut_demo.sh: compute the total quantity from orders.txt

shopt -o -s nounset

declare -i QTY
declare -ix TOTAL_QTY=0

cut -d, -f3 orders.txt | {
  while read QTY ; do
    TOTAL_QTY=TOTAL_QTY+QTY
  done
  printf "The total quantity is %d\n" "$TOTAL_QTY"
}
exit 0
```

Pasting

The Linux paste command combines lines from two or more files into a single line. With two files, paste writes to standard output the first line of the first file, a Tab character, and the first line from the second file, and then continues with the second line until all the lines have been written out. If one file is shorter than the other, blank lines are used for the missing lines.

The —delimiters (-d) switch is a list of one or more delimiters to use in place of a Tab. The paste command cycles through the list if it needs more delimiters than are provided in the list, as shown in Listing 11.9.

Listing 11.9   two_columns.sh

```
#!/bin/bash
#
# two_columns.sh

shopt -s -o nounset

declare -r ORDERS="orders.txt"
declare -r COLUMN1="column1.txt"
declare -r COLUMN2="column2.txt"
declare -i LINES

LINES='wc -l < "$ORDERS"'
LINES=LINES/2

head -$LINES < "$ORDERS" > "$COLUMN1"

LINES=LINES+1
tail +$LINES < "$ORDERS" > "$COLUMN2"

paste —delimiters="|" "$COLUMN1" "$COLUMN2"

rm "$COLUMN1"
rm "$COLUMN2"
exit 0
```

Running this script, the contents of orders.txt are separated into two columns, delineated by a vertical bar.

```
$ sh two_columns.sh
Birchwood China Hutch,475.99,1,756|Bar Stool,45.99,1,756
Bookcase Oak Veneer,205.99,1,756|Lawn Chair,55.99,1,756
Small Bookcase Oak Veneer,205.99,1,756|Rocking Chair,287.99,1,757
Reclining Chair,1599.99,1,757|Cedar Armoire,825.99,1,757
Bunk Bed,705.99,1,757|Mahogany Writing Desk,463.99,1,756
Queen Bed,925.99,1,757|Garden Bench,149.99,1,757
Two-drawer Nightstand,125.99,1,756|Walnut TV Stand,388.99,1,756
Cedar Toy Chest,65.99,1,757|Victorian-style Sofa,1225.99,1,757
Six-drawer Dresser,525.99,1,757|Chair - Rocking,287.99,1,757
Pine Round Table,375.99,1,757|Grandfather Clock,2045.99,1,756
```

Suppose you had a file called `order1.txt` containing an item from `orders.txt` separated into a list of the fields on single lines.

```
Birchwood China Hutch
475.99
1
756
```

The `paste --serial` (`-s`) switch pastes all the lines of each file into a single item, as opposed to combining a single line from each file one line at a time. This switch recombines the separate fields into a single line.

```
$ paste --serial --delimiters="," order1.txt
Birchwood China Hutch,475.99,1,756
```

To merge the lines of two or more files so that the lines follow one another, use the `sort` command with the `-m` switch.

Columns

Columns created with the `paste` command aren't suitable for all applications. For pretty displays, the Linux `column` command creates fixed-width columns. The columns are fitted to the size of the screen as determined by the COLUMNS environment variable, or to a specific row width using the `-c` switch.

```
$ column < orders.txt
Birchwood China Hutch,475.99,1,756        Bar Stool,45.99,1,756
Bookcase Oak Veneer,205.99,1,756          Lawn Chair,55.99,1,756
Small Bookcase Oak Veneer,205.99,1,756    Rocking Chair,287.99,1,757
Reclining Chair,1599.99,1,757             Cedar Armoire,825.99,1,757
Bunk Bed,705.99,1,757                     Mahogany Writing Desk,463.99,1,756
Queen Bed,925.99,1,757                    Garden Bench,149.99,1,757
Two-drawer Nightstand,125.99,1,756        Walnut TV Stand,388.99,1,756
Cedar Toy Chest,65.99,1,757               Victorian-style Sofa,1225.99,1,757
Six-drawer Dresser,525.99,1,757           Chair - Rocking,287.99,1,757
Pine Round Table,375.99,1,757             Grandfather Clock,2045.99,1,756
```

The `-t` switch creates a table from items delimited by a character specified by the `-s` switch.

```
$ column -s ',' -t < orders.txt | head -5
Birchwood China Hutch      475.99   1   756
Bookcase Oak Veneer        205.99   1   756
Small Bookcase Oak Veneer  205.99   1   756
Reclining Chair            1599.99  1   757
Bunk Bed                   705.99   1   757
```

The table fill-order can be swapped with the `-x` switch.

Folding

The Linux `fold` command ensures that a line is no longer than a certain number of characters. If a line is too long, a carriage return is inserted. `fold` wraps at 80 characters by default, but the —width=*n* (or -w) switch folds at any characters. The —spaces (or -s) switch folds at the nearest space to preserve words. The —bytes (or -b) switch counts a Tab character as one character instead of expanding it.

```
$ head -3 orders.txt | cut -d, -f 1
Birchwood China Hutch
Bookcase Oak Veneer
Small Bookcase Oak Veneer
$ head -3 orders.txt | cut -d, -f 1 | fold —width=10
Birchwood
China Hutc
h
Bookcase O
ak Veneer
Small Book
case Oak V
eneer
$ head  3 orders.txt | cut -d, -f 1 | fold —width=10 —spaces
Birchwood
China
Hutch
Bookcase
Oak Veneer
Small
Bookcase
Oak Veneer
```

Joining

The Linux `join` command combines two files together. `join` examines one line at a time from each file. If a certain segment of the lines match, they are combined into one line. Only one instance of the same segment is printed. The files are assumed to be sorted in the same order.

The line segment (or field) is chosen using three switches. The -1 switch selects the field number from the first file. The -2 switch selects the field number from the second. The -t switch specifies the character that separates one field from another. If these switches aren't used, `join` separates fields by spaces and examines the first field on each line.

Suppose the data in the orders.txt file was separated into two files, one with the pricing information (orders1.txt) and one with the quantity and account information (orders2.txt).

```
$ cat orders1.txt
Birchwood China Hutch,475.99
Bookcase Oak Veneer,205.99
Small Bookcase Oak Veneer,205.99
Reclining Chair,1599.99
Bunk Bed,705.99
$ cat orders2.txt
Birchwood China Hutch,1,756
Bookcase Oak Veneer,1,756
Small Bookcase Oak Veneer,1,756
Reclining Chair,1,757
Bunk Bed,1,757
```

To join these two files together, use a comma as a field separator and compare field 1 of the first file with field 1 of the second.

```
$ join -1 1 -2 1 -t, orders1.txt orders2.txt
Birchwood China Hutch,475.99,1,756
Bookcase Oak Veneer,205.99,1,756
Small Bookcase Oak Veneer,205.99,1,756
Reclining Chair,1599.99,1,757
Bunk Bed,705.99,1,757
```

If either file contains a line with a unique field, the field is discarded. Lines are joined only if matching fields are found in both files. To print unpaired lines, use -a 1 to print the unique lines in the first file or -a 2 to print the unique lines in the second file. The lines are printed as they appear in the files.

The sense of matching can be reversed with the -v switch. -v 1 prints the unique lines in the first file and -v 2 prints the unique lines in the second file.

The tests are case-insensitive when the —ignore-case (or -i) switch is used.

The fields can be rearranged using the -o (*output*) switch. Use a comma-separated field list to order the fields. A field is specified using the file number (1 or 2), a period and the field number from that file. A zero is a short form of the join field.

```
$ join -1 1 -2 1 -t, -o "1.2,2.3,2.2,0" orders1.txt orders2.txt
475.99,756,1,Birchwood China Hutch
205.99,756,1,Bookcase Oak Veneer
205.99,756,1,Small Bookcase Oak Veneer
1599.99,757,1,Reclining Chair
705.99,757,1,Bunk Bed
```

Merging

The merge command performs a three-way file merge. This is typically used to merge changes to one file from two separate sources. The merge is performed on a line-by-line basis. If there is a conflicting modification, merge displays a warning.

For easier reading, the -L (*label*) switch can be used to specify a title for the file, instead of reporting conflicts using the filename. This switch can be repeated three times for each of the three files.

For example, suppose there are three sets of orders for ice cream. The original set of orders(file1.txt) is as follows:

```
1 quart vanilla
2 quart chocolate
```

These orders have been modified by two people. The Barrie store now has (file2.txt) the following:

```
1 quart vanilla
1 quart strawberry
2 quart chocolate
```

And the Orillia (file3.txt) is as follows:

```
1 quart vanilla
2 quart chocolate
4 quart butter almond
```

The merge command reassembles the three files into one file.

```
$ merge -L "Barrie Store" -L "Original Orders" -L "Orillia Store" file2.txt
```

file1.txt file3.txt will change file2.txt so that it contains:

```
1 quart vanilla
1 quart strawberry
2 quart chocolate
4 quart butter almond
```

However, if the butter almond and strawberry orders were both added as the third line, merge reports a conflict:

```
$ merge -L "Barrie Store" -L "Original Orders" -L "Orillia Store" file2.txt
file1.txt file3.txt
merge: warning: conflicts during merge
```

file2.txt will contain the details of the conflict:

```
<<<<<<< Barrie Store
1 quart strawberry

=======
4 quart butter almond
>>>>>>> Orillia Store
```

If there are no problems merging, merge returns a zero exit status.

The -q (*quiet*) switch suppresses conflict warnings. -p (*print*) writes the output to standard output instead of overwriting the original file. The -A switch reports conflicts in the diff3 -A format.

Reference Section

`type` Command Switches

- `-a`—Shows all locations of the command
- `-p`—Shows the pathname of the command
- `-t`—Indicates the type of command

`file` Command Switches

- `-b`—Brief mode
- `-c`—Displays magic file output
- `-f` *file*—Reads a list of files to process from *file*
- `-i`—Shows the MIME type
- `-L`—Follows symbolic links
- `-m` *list*—Colon-separated list of magic files
- `-n`—Flushes the output after each file
- `-s`—Allows block or character special files
- `-v`—Version
- `-z`—Examines compressed files

`stat` Command Switches

- `-l`—Shows information about a link
- `-f`—Shows information about the file system on which the file resides

`statftime` Command Format Codes

- `%%`—Percent character
- `%_A`—Uses file last access time
- `%_a`—Filename (no suffix)
- `%_C`—Uses file inode change time
- `%_d`—Device ID
- `%_e`—Seconds elapsed since epoch
- `%_f`—File system type
- `%_g`—Group ID (`gid`) number

- %_h—Three-digit hash code of path
- %_i—Inode number
- %_L—Uses current (local) time
- %_l—Number of hard links
- %_M—Uses file last modified time
- %_m—Type/attribute/access bits
- %_n—Filename
- %_r—Rdev ID (char/block devices)
- %_s—File size (bytes)
- %_U—Uses current (UTC) time
- %_u—User ID (uid)
- %_z—Sequence number (1,2,...)
- %A—Full weekday name
- %a—Abbreviated weekday name
- %B—Full month name
- %b—Abbreviated month name
- %C—Century number
- %c—Standard format
- %D—mm/dd/yy
- %d—Day (zero filled)
- %e—Day (space filled)
- %H—Hour (24-hr clock)
- %I—Hour (12-hr clock)
- %j—Day (1..366)
- %M—Minute
- %m—Month
- %n—Line feed (newline) character
- %P—am/pm
- %p—AM/PM
- %r—hh:mm:ss AM/PM
- %S—Second
- %T—hh:mm:ss (24-hr)
- %t—Tab character
- %U—Week number (Sunday)

- %V—Week number (Monday)
- %W—Week number (Monday)
- %w—Weekday (Sunday)
- %X—Current time
- %x—Current date
- %Y—Year
- %y–Year (two digits)
- %z—Time zone

wget **Command Switches**

- —accept *L* (or -A *list*)—Comma-separated lists of suffixes and patterns to accept
- —append-output *log* (or -a *log*)—Like —output-file, but appends instead of overwriting
- —background (or -b)—Runs in the background as if it was started with &
- —continue (or -c)—Resumes a terminated download
- —cache=*O* (or -C *O*)—Doesn't return cached Web pages when "off"
- —convert-links (or -k)—Converts document links to reflect local directory
- —cut-dirs=*N*—Ignores the first *N* directories in a URL pathname
- —delete-after—Deletes downloaded files to "preload" caching servers
- —directory-prefix=*P* (or -P *P*)—Saves files under *P* instead of current directory
- —domains *list* (or -D *list*)—Accepts only given host domains
- —dot-style=*S*—Progress information can be displayed as default, binary, computer, mega, or micro
- —exclude-directories=*list* (or -X *list*)—Directories to reject when downloading
- —exclude-domains *list*—Rejects given host domains
- —execute *cmd* (or -e *cmd*)—Runs a resource file command
- —follow-ftp—Downloads FTP links in HTML documents
- —force-directories (or -x)—Always creates directories for the hostname when saving files
- —force-html (or -F)—Treats —input-file as an HTML document even if it doesn't look like one
- —glob=*O* (or -g *O*)—Allows file globbing in FTP URL filenames when "on"
- —header=*H*—Specifies an HTTP header to send to the Web server

- −http-passwd=*P*—Specifies a password (instead of in the URL)
- −http-user=*U*—Specifies a username (instead of in the URL)
- −ignore-length—Ignores bad document lengths returned by Web servers
- −include-directories=*list* (or -I *list*)—Directories to accept when downloading
- −input-file=*F* (or -i *F*)—Reads the URLS to get from the given file; it can be an HTML document
- −level=*D* (or -l *D*)—Maximum recursion level (default is 5)
- −mirror (or -m)—Enables recursion, infinite levels, time stamping, and keeping a .listing file
- −no-clobber (or -nc)—Doesn't replace existing files
- −no-directories (or -nd)—Saves all files in the current directory
- −no-host-directories (or -nH)—Never creates directories for the hostname
- −no-host-lookup (or -nh)—Disables DNS lookup of most hosts
- −no-parent (or -np)—Only retrieves files below the parent directory
- −non-verbose (or -nv)—Shows some progress information, but not all
- −output-document=*F* (or -O *F*)—Creates one file *F* containing all files; if -, all files are written to standard output
- −output-file *log* (or -o *log*)—Records all error messages to the given file
- −passive-ftp—Uses "passive" retrieval, useful when wget is behind a firewall
- −proxy=*O* (or -Y *O*)—Turns proxy support "on" or "off"
- −proxy-passwd=*P*—Specifies a password for a proxy server
- −proxy-user=*U*—Specifies a username for a proxy server
- −quiet (or -q)—Suppresses progress information
- −quota=*Q* (or -Q *Q*)—Stops downloads when the current files exceeds Q bytes; can also specify k kilobytes or m megabytes; inf disables the quota
- −recursive (or -r)—Recursively gets
- −reject *L* (or -R *list*)—Comma-separated lists of suffixes and patterns to reject
- −relative *list* (or -L)—Ignores all absolute links
- −retr-symlinks—Treats remote symbolic links as new files
- −save-headers (or -s)—Saves the Web server headers in the document file
- −server-response (or -S)—Shows server responses
- −span-hosts (or -H)—Spans across hosts when recursively retrieving
- −spider—Checks for the presence of a file, but doesn't download it
- −timeout=*S* (or -T *S*)—Network socket timeout in seconds; 0 for none

- `—timestamping` (or `-N`)—Only gets new files
- `—tries=N` (or `-t` *N*)—Try at most N tries; if `inf`, tries forever
- `—user-agent=U` (or `-U` *U*)—Specifies a different user agent than `wget` to access servers that don't allow `wget`
- `—verbose` (or `-v`)—By default, shows all progress information
- `—wait=S` (or `-w` *s*)—Pauses *S* seconds between retrievals. Can also specify m minutes, h hours, and d days.

`ftp` Command Switches

- `-A`—Active mode `ftp` (does not try passive mode)
- `-a`—Uses an anonymous login
- `-d`—Enables debugging
- `-e`—Disables command-line editing
- `-f`—Forces a cache reload for transfers that go through proxies
- `-g`—Disables filename globbing
- `-I`—Turns off interactive prompting during multiple file transfers
- `-n`—No auto-login upon initial connection
- `-o` *file*—When auto-fetching files, saves the contents in *file*
- `-p`—Uses passive mode (the default)
- `-P` *port*—Connects to the specified port instead of the default port
- `-r` *sec*—Retries connecting every *sec* seconds
- `-R`—Restarts all non-proxied auto-fetches
- `-t`—Enables packet tracing
- `-T` *dir*, *max [,inc]*—Sets maximum bytes/second transfer rate for direction *dir*, increments by optional *inc*
- `-v`—Enables verbose messages (default for terminals)
- `-V`—Disables verbose and progresses

`csplit` Command Switches

- `—suffix-format=FMT` (or `-b` *FMT*)—Uses `printf` formatting *FMT* instead of `%d`
- `—prefix=PFX` (or `-f` *PFX*)—Uses prefix PFX instead of xx
- `—keep-files` (or `-k`)—Does not remove output files on errors
- `—digits=D` (or `-n` *D*)—Uses specified number of digits instead of two

- —quiet (or —silent or -s)—Does not print progress information
- —elide-empty-files (or -z)—Removes empty output files

expand **Command Switches**

- —initial (or -i)—Does not convert Tab characters after non-whitespace characters
- —tabs=N (or -t N)—Changes tabs to N characters apart, not eight
- —tabs=L (or -t L)—Use comma-separated list of explicit Tab positions

unexpand **Command Switches**

- —all (or -a)—Converts all whitespace, instead of initial whitespace
- —tabs=N (or -t N)—Changes Tabs to N characters apart, not eight
- —tabs=L (or -t L)—Uses comma-separated list of explicit Tab positions

mktemp **Command Switches**

- -d—Makes a directory instead of a file
- -q—Fails silently if an error occurs
- -u—Operates in "unsafe" mode; creates the file and then deletes it to allow the script to create it later

head **Command Switches**

- —bytes=B (or -c B)—Prints the first B bytes
- —lines=L (or -n L)—Prints the first L lines instead of the first 10
- —quiet (or —silent or -q)—Never prints headers with filenames

tail **Command Switches**

- —retry—Keeps trying to open a file
- —bytes=N (-c N)—Outputs the last N bytes
- —follow[=ND] (or -f ND)—Outputs appended data as the file indicated by name N or descriptor D grows
- —lines=N (or -n N)—Outputs the last N lines, instead of the last 10
- —max-unchanged-stats=N—Continues to check file up to N times (default is 5), even if the file is deleted or renamed

- –max-consecutive-size-changes=*N*—After *N* iterations (default 200) with the same size, makes sure that the filename refers to the same inode
- –pid=*PID*—Terminates after process ID *PID* dies
- -quiet (or –silent or -q)—Never outputs headers with filenames
- –sleep-interval=*S* (or -s *S*)—Sleeps *S* seconds between iterations

wc **Command Switches**

- –bytes (–chars or -c)—Prints the byte counts
- –lines (or -l)—Prints the line feed (newline) counts
- –max-line-length (or -L)—Prints the length of the longest line
- –words (or -w)—Prints the word counts

cut **Command Switches**

- –bytes=*L* (or -b *L*)—Shows only these listed bytes
- –characters=*L* (or -c *L*)—Shows only these listed characters
- –delimiter=*D* (or -d *D*)—Uses delimiter *D* instead of a Tab character for the field delimiter
- –fields=*L* (or -f *L*)—Shows only these listed fields
- –only-delimited (or -s)—Does not show lines without delimiters
- –output-delimiter=*D*—Uses delimiter *D* as the output delimiter

paste **Command Switches**

- –delimiters=*L* (or -d *L*)—Uses character list *L* instead of Tab characters
- –serial (or -s)—Pastes one file at a time instead of in parallel

join **Command Switches**

- -1 *F*—Joins on field *F* of file 1
- -2 *F*—Joins on field *F* of file 2
- -a *file*—Prints unpaired lines from *file*
- -e *s*—Replaces missing input fields with string *s*
- –ignore-case (or -i)—Ignores differences in case when comparing fields
- -o *F*—Obeys format *F* while constructing output line

- -t *C*—Uses character *C* as input and output field separator
- -v *file*—Suppresses joined output lines from *file*

merge **Command Switches**

- -A—Merges conflicts by merging all changes leading from file2 to file3 into file1
- -e—Merge conflicts are marked as ==== and ====
- -E—Merge conflicts are marked as <<<<< and >>>>>>
- -L *label*—Uses up to three times to specify labels to be used in place of the filenames
- -p—Writes to standard output
- -q—Does not warn about conflicts

12

Text File Processing

Several years ago, Dan, an old high school friend, arrived at my house with two photocopied binders and a CD-ROM. "You've got to try this," he said. "This is version 0.9 of a free operating system called Linux."

We loaded Linux onto a spare 386 computer. The distribution didn't show the current directory in the command prompt. After several minutes of searching and experimenting, Dan deleted his temporary files with `rm -f *`. After several seconds, he interrupted the command with a control-c and looked worried. "That was taking way too long. I think I was in the wrong directory."

"How bad could the damage be?" I asked, typing `ls`. The shell responded with "command not found". He had been removing files in the /bin directory.

"What are we going to do?" he asked. "The CD-ROM's still mounted, but we can't find the file to restore the `bin` directory when we can't list anything."

I didn't criticize: I had a few `rm` horror stories of my own. After a few moments, I took a chance and typed `find . type f -maxdepth 1 -print` and the files in the current directory scrolled up the screen. I smiled. "You fried `ls`, but the `find` command is still intact." We managed to replace the missing files and were back in business. The `find` command saved us from performing a complete reinstall.

This chapter contains more examples of working with text files using the `orders.txt` file introduced at the start of the last chapter.

Finding Lines

The Linux `grep` command searches a file for lines matching a pattern. On other Unix-based systems, there are two other `grep` commands called egrep (*extended grep*) and fgrep (*fixed string grep*). Linux combines these variations into one command. The `egrep` command runs `grep` with the –extended-regexp (or -E) switch, and the `fgrep` command runs `grep` with the –fixed-strings (or -F) switch.

The strange name `grep` originates in the early days of Unix, whereby one of the line-editor commands was g/re/p (globally search for a regular expression and print the matching lines). Because this editor command was used so often, a separate `grep` command was created to search files without first starting the line editor.

`grep` uses matching patterns called *regular expressions,* which are similar to the pattern matching of the extended test command ([[..]]). The basic symbols are as follows:

- -—Zero or more characters
- +—One or more characters
- ?—Follows a character, which is optional
- .—A single character (this is ? in the extended test)
- ^—The start of the line
- $—The end of the line
- [...]—A list of characters, including ranges and character classes
- {n}—Follows an item that is to appear n times
- {n, }—Follows an item that is to appear n or more times
- {n, m}—Follows an item that is to appear n to m times
- (...)—A subpattern that's used to change the order of operations

Notice that the symbols are not exactly the same as the globbing symbols used for file matching. For example, on the command line a question mark represents any character, whereas in `grep`, the period has this effect.

The characters ?, +, {, |, (, and) must appear escaped with backslashes to prevent Bash from treating them as file-matching characters.

Suppose you wanted to match all orders in the `orders.txt` file containing a W.

```
$ grep "W" orders.txt
Mahogany Writing Desk,463.99,1,756
Walnut TV Stand,388.99,1,756
```

The asterisk (*) is a placeholder representing zero or more characters.

```
$ grep "M*Desk" orders.txt
Mahogany Writing Desk,463.99,1,756
```

The —fixed-strings switch suppresses the meaning of the pattern-matching characters. When used with M*Desk, `grep` searches for the exact string, including the asterisk, which does not appear anywhere in the file.

```
$ grep —fixed-strings "M*Desk" orders.txt
$
```

The caret (^) character indicates the beginning of a line. Use the caret to check for a pattern at the start of a line.

```
$ grep "^R" orders.txt
Reclining Chair,1599.99,1,757
Rocking Chair,287.99,1,757
```

The —ignore-case (or -i) switch makes the search case insensitive. Searching for W shows all lines containing W and w.

```
$ grep —ignore-case "W" orders.txt
Birchwood China Hutch,475.99,1,756
Two-drawer Nightstand,125.99,1,756
Six-drawer Dresser,525.99,1,757
Lawn Chair,55.99,1,756
Mahogany Writing Desk,463.99,1,756
Walnut TV Stand,388.99,1,756
```

The —invert-match (or -v) switch shows the lines that do not match. Lines that match are not shown.

```
$ grep —invert-match "r" orders.txt
Bunk Bed,705.99,1,757
Queen Bed,925.99,1,757
Pine Round Table,375.99,1,757
Walnut TV Stand,388.99,1,756
```

Regular expressions can be joined together with a vertical bar (|). This has the same effect as combining the results of two separate grep commands.

```
$ grep "Stool" orders.txt
Bar Stool,45.99,1,756
$ grep "Chair" orders.txt
Reclining Chair,1599.99,1,757
Lawn Chair,55.99,1,756
Rocking Chair,287.99,1,757
Chair - Rocking,287.99,1,757
$ grep "Stool\|Chair" orders.txt
Reclining Chair,1599.99,1,757
Bar Stool,45.99,1,756
Lawn Chair,55.99,1,756
Rocking Chair,287.99,1,757
Chair - Rocking,287.99,1,757
```

To identify the matching line, the —line-number (or -n) switch displays both the line number and the line. Using cut, head, and tail, the first line number can be saved in a variable. The number of bytes into the file can be shown with —byte-offset (or -b).

```
$ grep —line-number "Chair - Rock" orders.txt
19:Chair - Rocking,287.99,1,757
$ FIRST='grep —line-number "Chair - Rock" orders.txt | cut -d: -f1 | head -1'
$ printf "First occurrence at line %d\n" "$FIRST"
First occurrence at line 19
```

The −count (or -c) switch counts the number of matches and displays the total.

```
$ CNT='grep —count "Chair" orders.txt'
$ printf "There are %d chair(s).\n" "$CNT"
There are 4 chair(s).
```

grep recognizes the standard character classes as well.

```
$ grep "[[:cntrl:]]" orders.txt
$
```

A complete list of Linux grep switches appears in the reference section at the end of the chapter.

Locating Files

The Linux locate command consults a database and returns a list of all pathnames containing a certain group of characters, much like a fixed-string grep.

```
$ locate /orders.txt
/home/kburtch/test/orders.txt
/home/kburtch/orders.txt
$ locate orders.txt
/home/kburtch/test/orders.txt
/home/kburtch/test/advocacy/old_orders.txt
/home/kburtch/orders.txt
```

Older versions of locate show any file on the system, even files you normally don't have access to. Newer versions only show files that you have permission to see.

The locate database is maintained by a command called updatedb. It is usually executed once a day by Linux distributions. For this reason, locate is very fast but useful only in finding files that are at least one day old.

Finding Files

The Linux find command searches for files that meet specific conditions such as files with a certain name or files greater than a certain size. find is similar to the following loop where MATCH is the matching criteria:

```
ls —recursive | while read FILE ; do
    # test file for a match
    if [ $MATCH ] ; then
       printf "%s\n" "$FILE"
    fi
done
```

This script recursively searches directories under the current directory, looking for a filename that matches some condition called MATCH.

`find` is much more powerful than this script fragment. Like the built-in `test` command, `find` switches create expressions describing the qualities of the files to find. There are also switches to change the overall behavior of `find` and other switches to indicate actions to perform when a match is made.

The basic matching switch is -name, which indicates the name of the file to find. Name can be a specific filename or it can contain shell path wildcard globbing characters like * and ?. If pattern matching is used, the pattern must be enclosed in quotation marks to prevent the shell from expanding it before the `find` command examines it.

```
$ find . -name "*.txt"
./orders.txt
./advocacy/linux.txt
./advocacy/old_orders.txt
```

The first parameter is the directory to start searching in. In this case, it's the current directory.

The previous `find` command matches any type of file, including files such as pipes or directories, which is not usually the intention of a user. The -type switch limits the files to a certain type of file. The -type f switch matches only regular files, the most common kind of search. The type can also be b (*block device*), c (*character device*), d (*directory*), p (*pipe*), l (*symbolic link*), or s (*socket*).

```
$ find . -name "*.txt" -type f
./orders.txt
./advocacy/linux.txt
./archive/old_orders.txt
```

The switch -name "*.txt" -type f is an example of a *find expression*. These switches match a file that meets both of these conditions (implicitly, a logical "and"). There are other operator switches for combining conditions into logical expressions, as follows:

- (expr)—Forces the switches in the parentheses to be tested first
- -not expr (or ! expr)—Ensures that the switch is not matched
- expr -and expr (or expr -a expr)—The default behavior; looks for files that match both sets of switches
- expr -or expr (or expr -o expr)—Logical "or". Looks for files that match either sets of switches
- expr , expr—Always checks both sets of switches, but uses the result of the right set to determine a match

For example, to count the number of regular files and directories, do this:

```
$ find . -type d -or -type f | wc -l
```

224

The number of files without a `.txt` suffix can be counted as well.

```
$ find . ! -name "*.txt" -type f | wc -l
    185
```

Parentheses must be escaped by a backslash or quotes to prevent Bash from interpreting them as a subshell. Using parentheses, the number of files ending in `.txt` or `.sh` can be expressed as

```
$ find . "(" -name "*.txt" -or -name "*.sh" ")" -type f | wc -l
    11
```

Some expression switches refer to measurements of time. Historically, `find` times were measured in days, but the GNU version adds `min` switches for minutes. `find` looks for an exact match.

To search for files older than an amount of time, include a plus or minus sign. If a *plus sign* (+) precedes the amount of time, `find` searches for times greater than this amount. If a *minus sign* (-) precedes the time measurement, `find` searches for times less than this amount. The plus and minus zero days designations are not the same: `+0` in days means "older than no days," or in other words, files one or more days old. Likewise, `-5` in minutes means "younger than 5 minutes" or "zero to four minutes old".

There are several switches used to test the *access time*, which is the time a file was last read or written. The `-anewer` switch checks to see whether one file was accessed more recently than a specified file. `-atime` tests the number of days ago a file was accessed. `-amin` checks the access time in minutes.

Likewise, you can check the inode change time with `-cnewer`, `-ctime`, and `-cmin`. The inode time usually, but not always, represents the time the file was created. You can check the *modified time,* which is the time a file was last written to, by using `-newer`, `-mtime`, and `-mmin`.

To find files that haven't been changed in more than one day:

```
$ find . -name "*.sh"  -type f -mtime +0
./archive/old_orders.txt
```

To find files that have been accessed in the last 10 to 60 minutes:

```
$ find . -name "*.txt"  -type f -amin +9 -amin -61
./orders.txt
./advocacy/linux.txt
```

The `-size` switch tests the size of a file. The default measurement is 512-byte blocks, which is counterintuitive to many users and a common source of errors. Unlike the time-measurement switches, which have different switches for different measurements of time, to change the unit of measurement for size you must follow the amount with a `b` (*bytes*), `c` (*characters*), `k` (*kilobytes*), or `w` (*16-bit words*). There is no `m` (*megabyte*). Like the time measurements, the amount can have a minus sign (-) to test for files smaller than the specified size, or a plus sign (+) to test for larger files.

For example, use this to find log files greater than 1MB:

```
$ find . -type f -name "*.log" -size +1024k
./logs/giant.log
```

find shows the matching paths on standard output. Historically, the -print switch had to be used. Printing the paths is now the default behavior for most Unix-like operating systems, including Linux. If compatibility is a concern, add -print to the end of the find parameters.

To perform a different action on a successful match, use -exec. The -exec switch runs a program on each matching file. This is often combined with rm to delete matching files, or grep to further test the files to see whether they contain a certain pattern. The name of the file is inserted into the command by a pair of curly braces ({}) and the command ends with an escaped semicolon. (If the semicolon is not escaped, the shell interprets it as the end of the find command instead.)

```
$ find . -type f -name "*.txt" -exec grep Table {} \;
Pine Round Table,375.99,1,757
Pine Round Table,375.99,1,757
```

More than one action can be specified. To show the filename after a grep match, include -print.

```
$ find . -type f -name "*.txt" -exec grep Table {} \; -print
Pine Round Table,375.99,1,757
./orders.txt
Pine Round Table,375.99,1,757
./archive/old_orders.txt
```

find expects {} to appear by itself (that is, surrounded by whitespace). It can't be combined with other characters, such as in an attempt to form a new pathname.

The -exec switch can be slow for a large number of files: The command must be executed for each match. When you have the option of piping the results to a second command, the execution speed is significantly faster than when using -exec. A pipe generates the results with two commands instead of hundreds or thousands of commands.

The -ok switch works the same way as -exec except that it interactively verifies whether the command should run.

```
$ find . -type f -name "*.txt" -ok rm {} \;
< rm ... ./orders.txt > ? n
< rm ... ./advocacy/linux.txt > ? n
< rm ... ./advocacy/old_orders.txt > ? n
```

The -ls action switch lists the matching files with more detail. find runs ls -dils for each matching file.

```
$ find . -type f -name "*.txt" -ls
243300    4 -rw-rw-r—   1 kburtch  kburtch      592 May 17 14:41 ./orders.txt
114683    0 -rw-rw-r—   1 kburtch  kburtch        0 May 17 14:41 ./advocacy/l
```

```
inux.txt
114684    4 -rw-rw-r—   1 kburtch  kburtch       592 May 17 14:41 ./advocacy/o
ld_orders.txt
```

The `-printf` switch makes `find` act like a searching version of the `statftime` command. The `%` format codes indicate what kind of information about the file to print. Many of these provide the same functions as `statftime`, but use a different code.

- `%a`—File's last access time in the format returned by the C `ctime` function.
- `%c`—File's last status change time in the format returned by the C `ctime` function.
- `%f`—File's name with any leading directories removed (only the last element).
- `%g`—File's group name, or numeric group ID if the group has no name.
- `%h`—Leading directories of file's name (all but the last element).
- `%i`—File's inode number (in decimal).
- `%m`—File's permission bits (in octal).
- `%p`—File's pathname.
- `%P`—File's pathname with the name of the command line argument under which it was found removed.
- `%s`—File's size in bytes.
- `%t`—File's last modification time in the format returned by the C `ctime` function.
- `%u`—File's username, or numeric user ID if the user has no name.

A complete list appears in the reference section.

The time codes also differ from `statftime`: `statftime` remembers the last type of time selected, whereas `find` requires the type of time for each time element printed.

```
$ find . -type f -name "*.txt" -printf "%f access time is %a\n"
orders.txt access time is Thu May 17 16:47:08 2001
linux.txt access time is Thu May 17 16:47:08 2001
old_orders.txt access time is Thu May 17 16:47:08 2001
$ find . -type f -name "*.txt" -printf "%f modified time as \
hours:minutes is %TH:%TM\n"
orders.txt modified time as hours:minutes is 14:41
linux.txt modified time as hours:minutes is 14:41
old_orders.txt modified time as hours:minutes is 14:41
```

A complete list of `find` switches appears in the reference section.

Sorting

The Linux `sort` command sorts a file or a set of files. A file can be named explicitly or redirected to sort on standard input. The switches for sort are completely different from commands such as `grep` or `cut`. `sort` is one of the last commands to support long versions of switches: As a result, the short switches are used here. Even so, the switches for common options are not the same as other Linux commands.

To sort a file correctly, the sort command needs to know the *sort key*, the characters on each line that determine the order of the lines. Anything that isn't in the key is ignored for sorting purposes. By default, the entire line is considered the key.

The -f (*fold character cases together*) switch performs a case-insensitive sort (doesn't use the -i switch, as many other Linux commands use).

```
$ sort -f orders.txt
Bar Stool,45.99,1,756
Birchwood China Hutch,475.99,1,756
Bookcase Oak Veneer,205.99,1,756
Bunk Bed,705.99,1,757
Cedar Armoire,825.99,1,757
Cedar Toy Chest,65.99,1,757
Chair - Rocking,287.99,1,757
Garden Bench,149.99,1,757
Grandfather Clock,2045.99,1,756
Lawn Chair,55.99,1,756
Mahogany Writing Desk,463.99,1,756
Pine Round Table,375.99,1,757
Queen Bed,925.99,1,757
Reclining Chair,1599.99,1,757
Rocking Chair,207.99,1,757
Six-drawer Dresser,525.99,1,757
Small Bookcase Oak Veneer,205.99,1,756
Two-drawer Nightstand,125.99,1,756
Victorian-style Sofa,1225.99,1,757
Walnut TV Stand,388.99,1,756
```

The -r (*reverse*) switch reverses the sorting order.

```
$ head orders.txt | sort -f -r
Two-drawer Nightstand,125.99,1,756
Small Bookcase Oak Veneer,205.99,1,756
Six-drawer Dresser,525.99,1,757
Reclining Chair,1599.99,1,757
Queen Bed,925.99,1,757
Pine Round Table,375.99,1,757
Cedar Toy Chest,65.99,1,757
Bunk Bed,705.99,1,757
Bookcase Oak Veneer,205.99,1,756
Birchwood China Hutch,475.99,1,756
```

If only part of the line is to be used as a key, the -k (*key*) switch determines which characters to use. The field delimiter is any group of space or Tab characters, but you can change this with the -t switch.

To sort the first 10 lines of the orders file on the second and subsequent fields, use this

```
$ head orders.txt | sort -f -t, -k2
Two-drawer Nightstand,125.99,1,756
Reclining Chair,1599.99,1,757
Bookcase Oak Veneer,205.99,1,756
Small Bookcase Oak Veneer,205.99,1,756
Pine Round Table,375.99,1,757
Birchwood China Hutch,475.99,1,756
Six-drawer Dresser,525.99,1,757
Cedar Toy Chest,65.99,1,757
Bunk Bed,705.99,1,757
Queen Bed,925.99,1,757
```

The key position can be followed by the ending position, separated by a comma. For example, to sort only on the second field, use a key of -k 2,2.

If the field number has a decimal part, it represents the character of the field where the key begins. The first character in the field is 1. The first field always starts at the beginning of the line. For example, to sort by ignoring the first character, indicate that the key begins with the second character of the first field.

```
$ head orders.txt | sort -f -k1.2
Reclining Chair,1599.99,1,757
Cedar Toy Chest,65.99,1,757
Pine Round Table,375.99,1,757
Birchwood China Hutch,475.99,1,756
Six-drawer Dresser,525.99,1,757
Small Bookcase Oak Veneer,205.99,1,756
Bookcase Oak Veneer,205.99,1,756
Queen Bed,925.99,1,757
Bunk Bed,705.99,1,757
Two-drawer Nightstand,125.99,1,756
```

There are many switches that affect how a key is interpreted. The -b (*blanks*) switch indicates the key is a string with leading blanks that should be ignored. The -n (*numeric*) switch treats the key as a number. This switch recognizes minus signs and decimal portions, but not plus signs. The -g (*general number*) switch treats the key as a C floating-point number notation, allowing infinities, NaNs, and scientific notation. This option is slower than -n. Number switches always imply a -b. The -d (*phone directory*) switch only uses alphanumeric characters in the sorting key, ignoring periods, hyphens, and other punctuation. The -i (*ignore unprintable*) switch only uses printable characters in the sorting key. The -M (*months*) switch sorts by month name abbreviations.

There can be more than one sorting key. The key interpretation switches can be applied to individual keys by adding the character to the end of the key amount, such as -k4,4M, which means "sort on the fourth field that contains month names". The -r and -f switches can also be used this way.

For a more complex example, the following sort command sorts on the account number, in reverse order, and then by the product name. The sort is case insensitive and skips leading blanks:

```
$ head orders.txt | sort -t, -k4,4rn -k1,1fb
Bunk Bed,705.99,1,757
Cedar Toy Chest,65.99,1,757
Pine Round Table,375.99,1,757
Queen Bed,925.99,1,757
Reclining Chair,1599.99,1,757
Six-drawer Dresser,525.99,1,757
Birchwood China Hutch,475.99,1,756
Bookcase Oak Veneer,205.99,1,756
Small Bookcase Oak Veneer,205.99,1,756
Two-drawer Nightstand,125.99,1,756
```

For long sorts, the -c (*check only*) switch checks the files to make sure they need sorting before you attempt to sort them. This switch returns a status code of 0 if the files are sorted.

A complete list of sort switches appears in the reference section.

Character Editing (tr)

The Linux tr (*translate*) command substitutes or deletes characters on standard input, writing the results to standard output.

The -d (*delete*) switch deletes a specific character.

```
$ printf "%s\n" 'The total is $234.45 US'
The total is $234.45 US
$ printf "%s\n" 'The total is $234.45 US' | tr -d '$'
The total is 234.45 US
```

Ranges of characters are represented as the first character, a minus sign, and the last character.

```
$ printf "%s\n" 'The total is $234.45 US' | tr -d 'A-Z'
he total is $234.45
```

tr supports GNU character classes.

```
$ printf "%s\n" 'The total is $234.45 US' | tr -d '[:upper:]'
he total is $234.45
```

Without any options, tr maps one set of characters to another. The first character in the first parameter is changed to the first character in the second parameter. The second character in the first parameter is changed to the second character in the second parameter. (And so on.)

```
$ printf "%s\n" "The cow jumped over the moon" | tr 'aeiou' 'AEIOU'
ThE cOw jUmpEd OvEr thE mOOn
```

tr supports character equivalence. To translate any e-like characters in a variable named FOREIGN_STRING to a plain *e*, for example, you use

```
$ printf "$FOREIGN_STRING" | tr "[=e=]" "e"
```

The –truncate-set1 (or -t) ignores any characters in the first parameter that don't have a matching character in the second parameter.

The –complement (or -c) switch reverses the sense of matching. The characters in the first parameter are not mapped into the second, but characters that aren't in the first parameter are changed to the indicated character.

```
$ printf "%s\n" "The cow jumped over the moon" | tr –complement 'aeiou' '?'
??e??o???u??e??o?e????e??oo??
```

The –squeeze-repeats (or -s) switch reduces multiple occurrences of a letter to a single character for each of the letters you specify.

```
$ printf "%s\n" "aaabbbccc" | tr –squeeze-repeats 'c'
aaabbbc
```

By far the most common use of tr is to translate MS-DOS text files to Unix text files. DOS text files have carriage returns and line feed characters, whereas Linux uses only line feeds to mark the end of a line. The extra carriage returns need to be deleted.

```
$ tr -d '\r' < dos.txt > linux.txt
```

Apple text files have carriage returns instead of line feeds. tr can take care of that as well by replacing the carriage returns.

```
$ tr '\r' '\n' < apple.txt > linux.txt
```

The other escaped characters recognized by tr are as follows:

- \o—ASCII octal value o (one to three octal digits)
- \\—Backslash
- \a—Audible beep
- \b—Backspace
- \f—Form feed
- \n—New line
- \r—Return
- \t—Horizontal tab
- \v—Vertical tab

You can perform more complicated file editing with the sed command, discussed next.

File Editing (sed)

The Linux sed (*stream editor*) command makes changes to a text file on a line-by-line basis. Although the name contains the word "editor," it's not a text editor in the usual sense. You can't use it to interactively make changes to a file. Whereas the grep command locates regular expression patterns in a file, the sed command locates patterns and then makes alterations where the patterns are found.

sed's main argument is a complex four-part string, separated by slashes.

```
$ sed "s/dog/canine/g" animals.txt
```

The first part indicates the kind of editing sed will do. The second part is the pattern of characters that sed is looking for. The third part is the pattern of characters to apply with the command. The fourth part is the range of the editing (if there are multiple occurrences of the target pattern). In this example, in the sed expression "s/dog/canine/g", the edit command is s, the pattern to match is dog, the pattern to apply is canine, and the range is g. Using this expression, sed will substitute all occurrences of the string dog with canine in the file animals.txt.

The use of quotation marks around the sed expression is very important. Many characters with a special meaning to the shell also have a special meaning to sed. To prevent the shell from interpreting these characters before sed has a chance to analyze the expression, the expression must be quoted.

Like grep, sed uses regular expressions to describe the patterns. Also, there is no limit to the line lengths that can be processed by the Linux version of sed.

Some sed commands can operate on a specific line by including a line number. A line number can also be specified with an initial line and a stepping factor. 1~2 searches all lines, starting at line 1, and stepping by 2. That is, it picks all the odd lines in a file. A range of addresses can be specified with the first line, a comma, and the last line. 1,10 searches the first 10 lines. A trailing exclamation point reverses the sense of the search. 1,10! searches all lines except the first 10. If no lines are specified, all lines are searched.

The sed s (*substitute*) command replaces any matching pattern with new text.

To replace the word Pine with Cedar in the first 10 lines of the order file, use this

```
$ head orders.txt | sed 's/Pine/Cedar/g'
Birchwood China Hutch,475.99,1,756
Bookcase Oak Veneer,205.99,1,756
Small Bookcase Oak Veneer,205.99,1,756
Reclining Chair,1599.99,1,757
Bunk Bed,705.99,1,757
Queen Bed,925.99,1,757
Two-drawer Nightstand,125.99,1,756
Cedar Toy Chest,65.99,1,757
Six-drawer Dresser,525.99,1,757
Cedar Round Table,375.99,1,757
```

Pine Round Table becomes Cedar Round Table.

If the replacement string is empty, the occurrence of the pattern is deleted.

```
$ head orders.txt | sed 's/757//g'
Birchwood China Hutch,475.99,1,756
Bookcase Oak Veneer,205.99,1,756
Small Bookcase Oak Veneer,205.99,1,756
Reclining Chair,1599.99,1,
Bunk Bed,705.99,1,
Queen Bed,925.99,1,
Two-drawer Nightstand,125.99,1,756
Cedar Toy Chest,65.99,1,
Six-drawer Dresser,525.99,1,
Pine Round Table,375.99,1,
```

The caret (^) represents the start of a line.

```
$ head orders.txt | sed 's/^Bunk/DISCONTINUED - Bunk/g'
Birchwood China Hutch,475.99,1,756
Bookcase Oak Veneer,205.99,1,756
Small Bookcase Oak Veneer,205.99,1,756
Reclining Chair,1599.99,1,757
DISCONTINUED - Bunk Bed,705.99,1,757
Queen Bed,925.99,1,757
Two-drawer Nightstand,125.99,1,756
Cedar Toy Chest,65.99,1,757
Six-drawer Dresser,525.99,1,757
Pine Round Table,375.99,1,757
```

You can perform case-insensitive tests with the I (*insensitive*) modifier.

```
$ head orders.txt | sed 's/BED/BED/Ig'
Birchwood China Hutch,475.99,1,756
Bookcase Oak Veneer,205.99,1,756
Small Bookcase Oak Veneer,205.99,1,756
Reclining Chair,1599.99,1,757
Bunk BED,705.99,1,757
Queen BED,925.99,1,757
Two-drawer Nightstand,125.99,1,756
Cedar Toy Chest,65.99,1,757
Six-drawer Dresser,525.99,1,757
Pine Round Table,375.99,1,757
```

sed supports GNU character classes. To hide the prices, replace all the digits with underscores.

```
$ head orders.txt | sed 's/[[:digit:]]/_/g'
Birchwood China Hutch,___.__,_,___
Bookcase Oak Veneer,___.__,_,___
Small Bookcase Oak Veneer,___.__,_,___
```

```
Reclining Chair,____.__,_,___
Bunk Bed,___.__,_,___
Queen Bed,___.__,_,___
Two-drawer Nightstand,___.__,_,___
Cedar Toy Chest,__.__,_,___
Six-drawer Dresser,___.__,_,___
Pine Round Table,___.__,_,___
```

The d (*delete*) command deletes a matching line. You can delete blank lines with the pattern ^$ (that is, a blank line is the start of line, end of line, with nothing between).

```
$ head orders.txt | sed '/^$/d'
```

Without a pattern, you can delete particular lines by placing the line number before the d. For example, '1d' deletes the first line.

```
$ head orders.txt | sed '1d'
Bookcase Oak Veneer,205.99,1,756
Small Bookcase Oak Veneer,205.99,1,756
Reclining Chair,1599.99,1,757
Bunk Bed,705.99,1,757
Queen Bed,925.99,1,757
Two-drawer Nightstand,125.99,1,756
Cedar Toy Chest,65.99,1,757
Six-drawer Dresser,525.99,1,757
Pine Round Table,375.99,1,757
```

A d by itself deletes all lines.

There are several line-oriented commands. The a (*append*) command inserts new text after a matching line. The i (*insert*) command inserts text before a matching line. The c (*change*) command replaces a group of lines.

To insert the title DISCOUNTED ITEMS: prior to Cedar Toy Chest, you do this

```
$ head orders.txt | sed '/Cedar Toy Chest/i\
DISCOUNTED ITEMS:'
Birchwood China Hutch,475.99,1,756
Bookcase Oak Veneer,205.99,1,756
Small Bookcase Oak Veneer,205.99,1,756
Reclining Chair,1599.99,1,757
Bunk Bed,705.99,1,757
Queen Bed,925.99,1,757
Two-drawer Nightstand,125.99,1,756
DISCOUNTED ITEMS:
Cedar Toy Chest,65.99,1,757
Six-drawer Dresser,525.99,1,757
Pine Round Table,375.99,1,757
```

To replace Bunk Bed, Queen Bed, and Two-drawer Nightstand with an Items deleted message, you can use

```
$ head orders.txt | sed '/^Bunk Bed/,/^Two-drawer/c\
<Items deleted>'
Birchwood China Hutch,475.99,1,756
Bookcase Oak Veneer,205.99,1,756
Small Bookcase Oak Veneer,205.99,1,756
Reclining Chair,1599.99,1,757
<Items deleted>
Cedar Toy Chest,65.99,1,757
Six-drawer Dresser,525.99,1,757
Pine Round Table,375.99,1,757
```

You must follow the insert, append, and change commands by an escaped end of line.

The l (*list*) command is used to display unprintable characters. It displays characters as ASCII codes or backslash sequences.

```
$ printf "%s\015\t\004\n" "ABC" | sed -n "l"
ABC\r\t\004$
```

In this case, \015 (a carriage return) is displayed as \r, a \t Tab character is displayed as \t, and a \n line feed is displayed as a $ and a line feed. The character \004, which has no backslash equivalent, is displayed as \004. A, B, and C are displayed as themselves.

The y (*transform*) command is a specialized short form for the substitution command. It performs one-to-one character replacements. It is essentially equivalent to a group of single character substitutions.

For example, y/,/;/ is the same as s/,/;/g:

```
$ head orders.txt | sed 'y/,/;/'
Birchwood China Hutch;475.99;1;756
Bookcase Oak Veneer;205.99;1;756
Small Bookcase Oak Veneer;205.99;1;756
Reclining Chair;1599.99;1;757
Bunk Bed;705.99;1;757
Queen Bed;925.99;1;757
Two-drawer Nightstand;125.99;1;756
Cedar Toy Chest;65.99;1;757
Six-drawer Dresser;525.99;1;757
Pine Round Table;375.99;1;757
```

However, with patterns of more than one character, transform replaces any occurrence of the first character with the first character in the second pattern, the second character with the second character in the second pattern, and so on. This works like the tr command.

```
$ printf "%s\n" "order code B priority 1" | sed 'y/B1/C2/'
order code C priority 2
```

Lines unaffected by sed can be hidden with the —quiet (or -n or —silent) switch.

Like the transform command, there are other sed commands that mimic Linux commands. The p (*print*) command imitates the grep command by printing a matching line. This is useful only when the —quiet switch is used. The = (*line number*) command prints the line number of matching lines. The q (*quit*) command makes sed act like the head command, displaying lines until a certain line is encountered.

```
$ head orders.txt | sed —quiet '/Bed/p'
Bunk Bed,705.99,1,757
Queen Bed,925.99,1,757
$ head orders.txt | sed —quiet '/Bed/='
5
6
```

The remaining sed commands represent specialized actions. The flow of control is handled by the n (*next*) command. Files can be read with r or written with w. N (*append next*) combines two lines into one for matching purposes. D (*multiple line delete*) deletes multiple lines. P is multiple line print. h, H, g, G, and x enable you to save lines to a temporary buffer so that you can make changes, display the results, and then restore the original text for further analysis. This works like an electronic calculator's memory. Complicated sed expressions can feature branches to labels embedded in the expressions using the b command. The t (*test*) command acts as a shell elif or switch statement, attempting a series of operations until one succeeds. Subcommands can be embedded in sed with curly brackets. More documentation on these commands can be found using info sed.

Long sed scripts can be stored in a file. You can read the sed script from a file with the —file= (or -f) switch. You can include comments with a # character, like a shell script.

sed expressions can also be specified using the —expression= (or -e) switch, or can be read from standard input when a - filename is used.

You cannot use ASCII value escape sequences in sed patterns.

Compressing Files

Most Linux programs differentiate between archiving and compression. *Archiving* is the storage of a number of files into a single file. *Compression* is a reduction of file size by encoding the file. In general, an archive file takes up more space than the original files, so most archive files are also compressed.

The Linux bzip2 (*BWH zip*) command compresses files with Burrows-Wheeler-Huffman compression. This is the most commonly used compression format. Older compression programs are available on most distributions. gzip (*GNU zip*) compresses with LZ77 compression and is used extensively on older distributions. compress is an older Lempel-Ziv compression program available on most versions of Unix. zip is the Linux version of the DOS pkzip program. hexbin decompresses certain Macintosh archives.

The Linux `tar` (*tape archive*) command is the most commonly used archiving command, and it automatically compresses while archiving when the right command-line options are used. Although the command was originally used to collect files for storage on tape drives, it can also create disk files.

Originally, the `tar` command didn't use command-line switches: A series of single characters were used. The Linux version supports command-line switches as well as the older single character syntax for backward compatibility.

To use `tar` on files, the —file *F* (or -f *F*) switch indicates the filename to act on. At least one action switch must be specified to indicate what `tar` will do with the file. Remote files can be specified with a preceding hostname and a colon.

The —create (-c) switch creates a new `tar` file.

```
$ ls -l orders.txt
-rw-rw-r—    1 kburtch  kburtch       592 May 11 14:45 orders.txt
$ tar —create —file orders.tar orders.txt
$ ls -l orders.tar
-rw-rw-r—    1 kburtch  kburtch     10240 Oct  3 12:06 orders.tar
```

The archive file is significantly larger than the original file. To apply compression, chose the type of compression using —bzip (or -I) , —gzip (or -z) , —compress (or -Z) , or —use-compress-program to specify a particular compression program.

```
$ tar —create —file orders.tbz —bzip orders.txt
$ ls -l orders.tbz
-rw-rw-r—    1 kburtch  kburtch       421 Oct  3 12:12 orders.tbz
$ tar —create —file orders.tgz —gzip orders.txt
$ ls -l orders.tgz
-rw-rw-r—    1 kburtch  kburtch       430 Oct  3 12:11 orders.tgz
```

More than one file can be archived at once.

```
$ tar —create —file orders.tbz —bzip orders.txt orders2.txt
$ ls -l orders.tbz
-rw-rw-r—    1 kburtch  kburtch       502 Oct  3 12:14 orders.tbz
```

The new archive overwrites an existing one.

To restore the original files, use the —extract switch. Use —verbose to see the filenames. `tar` cannot auto-detect the compression format; you must specify the proper compression switch to avoid an error.

```
$ tar —extract —file orders.tbz
tar: 502 garbage bytes ignored at end of archive
tar: Error exit delayed from previous errors
$ tar —extract —bzip —file orders.tbz
$ tar —extract —verbose —bzip —file orders.tbz
orders.txt
orders2.txt
```

The —extract switch also restores any subdirectories in the pathname of the file. It's important to extract the files in the same directory where they were originally compressed to ensure they are restored to their proper places.

The tar command can also append files to the archive using —concatenate (or -A), compare to archives with —compare (or —diff or -d), remove files from the archive with —delete, list the contents with —list, and replace existing files with —update. tar silently performs these functions unless —verbose is used.

A complete list of tar switches appears in the reference section.

Another archiving program, cpio (*copy in/out*) is provided for compatibility with other flavors of Unix. The rpm package manager command is based on cpio.

Reference Section

grep **Command Switches**

- —after-context=n (or -A n)—Prints n lines following the matching line
- —before-context=n (or -B n)—Prints n lines prior to a matching line
- —context[=n] (or -C [n])—Displays n lines (default is 2) around the matching line
- —basic-regexp (or -G)—Pattern is not an extended regular expression
- —binary-files=binary—Normal binary file behavior; issues a message if the pattern is somewhere in a binary file
- —binary-files=without-match (or -I)—grep assumes all binary files don't match
- —binary-files=text (or -a or —text)—Shows matches from binary files
- —byte-offset (or -b)—Prints the byte offset within the input file before each line of output
- —count (or -c)—Prints a count of matching lines for each input file
- —directories=read (or -d read)—grep uses its normal behavior, reading the directory as if it were a normal file
- —directories=skip (or -d skip or -r)—Directories are ignored
- —directories=recurse (or -d recurse or -r or —recursive)—Examines files in all subdirectories
- —extended-regexp (or -E)—Treats the expression as an egrep extended regular expression
- —file=f (or -f f)—File f is a list of grep patterns
- —files-without-match (or -L)—Prints the name of the first file that doesn't contain the pattern
- —files-with-matches (or -l)—Prints the first file that contains the pattern

- —fixed-strings (or -F)—Treats the pattern as a string, ignoring any special meaning to the characters
- —invert-match (or -v)—Selects lines that do not match the pattern
- —no-filename (or -h)—Hides the filenames with each match
- —line-number (or -n)—Shows the line number with results
- —line-regexp (or -x)—Matches only an entire line
- —mmap—Uses memory mapping to speed up search on a file that won't shrink while grep is running
- —no-messages (or -s)—Suppresses error messages about missing files
- —null (or -z)—Separates items with null characters instead of a carriage return
- —quiet (or -q)—Searches only to the first match and doesn't display it
- —regexp=p (or -e p)—Use string p as the matching pattern, useful for patterns starting with a period
- —with-filename (or -H)—Prints the filename with each match
- —word-regexp (or -w)—Only matches whole "words" separated from the rest of the line by spaces or other non-word characters

find **Command Switches**

There are a large number of find expression switches. They include the following:

- -empty—Matches an empty regular file or directory
- -false—Always fails to match
- -fstype *fs*—The file must be on a file system of type *fs*
- -gid *n*—Matches numeric group ID *n*
- -group *n*—The file must be owned by this group ID. The group ID can be a name or number
- -daystart—Measures times from the start of the day rather than 24 hours ago
- -depth—Find the contents of a directory before the directory itself (a depth-first traversal)
- -fls *file*—Writes -ls results to specified file
- -follow—Follows symbolic links. Normally, links are not followed
- -fprint *f*—Writes –print results to file *f*
- -fprint0 *f*—Writes -print0 results to file *f*
- -fprintf *f format*—Writes –printf results to file *f*
- -mindepth *n*—Descends at least *n* directories from the current directory
- -ilname *pattern*—Case-insensitive -lname

- `-iname` *pattern*—Case-insensitive -name
- `-inum` *n*—The file must have this inode number
- `-ipath` *pattern*—Case-insensitive -path
- `-iregex` *pattern*—Case-insensitive -regex
- `-links` *n*—The file must have *n* links
- `-lname` *pattern*—The file must be a symbolic link matching the specified pattern
- `-ls`—Lists the file in `ls -dils` format
- `-maxdepth` *n*—Descends at most *n* directories from the current directory
- `-noleaf`—For CD-ROMs, doesn't assume directories have . and .. entries
- `-nogroup`—The file cannot be owned by a known group
- `-nouser`—The file cannot be owned by a known user
- `-ok` *cmd*—Like -exec, but prompt the user before running the command
- `-path` *pattern*—Like -name, but matches the entire path as returned by `find`
- `-perm` *mode*—The file must have the specified permission bits. -mode requires all the set bits to be set. +mode enables any of the permission bits to be set.
- `-print`—The default action, prints the pathname to standard output
- `-print0`—Prints filenames separated with an ASCII NUL character
- `-printf` *format*—Prints the filename according to a `printf` format string
- `-prune`—With no -depth switch, doesn't descend past the current directory
- `-regex` *pattern*—Like -name, but the pattern is a regular expression
- `-true`—Always true
- `-user` *name*—The file must be owned by this user ID. The ID can be a number
- `-uid`—The file must be owned by this numeric uid
- `-xdev` (or `-mount`)—Don't examine mounted file systems other than the current one
- `-xtype`—Like -type, but checks symbolic links

`find -printf` **Formatting Codes**

- `%%`—A literal percent sign
- `%a`—File's last access time in the format returned by the C ctime function
- `%Ac`—File's last access time in the format specified by c, which is either @ (the number of seconds since Jan 1, 1970) or a statftime time directive
- `%b`—File's size in 512-byte blocks (rounded up)
- `%c`—File's last status change time in the format returned by the C ctime function

- %C*c*—File's last status change time in the format specified by *c*, which is the same as for %A
- %d—File's depth in the directory tree; 0 means the file is a command-line argument
- %f—File's name with any leading directories removed (only the last element)
- %F—Type of the file system the file is on; this value can be used for -fstype
- %g—File's group name, or numeric group ID if the group has no name
- %G—File's numeric group ID
- %h—Leading directories of file's name (all but the last element)
- %H—Command-line argument under which file was found
- %i—File's inode number (in decimal)
- %k—File's size in 1KB blocks (rounded up)
- %l—Object of symbolic link (empty string if file is not a symbolic link)
- %m—File's permission bits (in octal)
- %n—Number of hard links to file
- %p—File's pathname
- %P—File's pathname with the name of the command-line argument under which it was found removed
- %s—File's size in bytes
- %t—File's last modification time in the format returned by the C ctime function
- %T*c*—File's last modification time in the format specified by *c*, which is the same as for %A
- %u—File's username, or numeric user ID if the user has no name
- %U—File's numeric user ID

sort **Command Switches**

- -b (--ignore-leading-blanks)—Ignores leading blanks in sort fields or keys
- -c(–check)—Checks file but does not sort
- -d(–dictionary-order)—Considers only alphanumeric characters in keys
- -f (–ignore-case)—Case-insensitive sort
- -g (–general-numeric-sort)—Compares according to general numerical value (implies -b)
- -i (–ignore-nonprinting)—Ignores unprintable characters
- -k *POS1[,POS2]* (–key=*POS1[,POS2]*)—Starts a key at character position *POS1* and optionally ends it at character position *POS2*

- -m (–merge)—Merges already sorted files
- -M (–month-sort)—Compares month short forms (implies -b)
- -n (–numeric-sort)—Compares numerical values (implies -b)
- -o *f* (–output=*f*)—Writes results to file *f*
- -r (–reverse)—Reverses the sort order
- -s–(–stable)—Leaves lines with keys that sort equally in their original relative order
- -t *s*(–field-separator=*s*)—Uses separator character *s* instead of whitespace
- -T *d* (–temporary-directory=*d*)—Use directory *d* for temporary files, not $TMPDIR or /tmp
- -u (–unique)—With -c, checks for strict ordering; with -m, only outputs the first of an equal sequence
- -z (–zero-terminated)—Ends lines with the ASCII NUL byte (C strings)

tar **Command Switches**

- --absolute-paths (or -P)—Doesn't strip leading /s from filenames
- –after-date *D* (or –newer *D* or -N *D*)—Only stores files newer than the given date
- –append (or -r)— Appends files to the end of the archive
- –atime-preserve—Doesn't change access times on restored files
- –block-size *N* (-b *N*)—Block size of Nx512 bytes (default N=20)
- –checkpoint—Prints directory names while reading the archive (less verbose than –verbose)
- –compare (or –diff or -d)—Lists differences between file system and archive
- –concatenate (or –catenate or -A)—Appends archives to another archive
- –create (or -c)—Creates a new archive
- –delete—Deletes files from an archive
- –dereference (-h)—Archives the files that symbolic links point to
- –directory *D* (-C *D*)—In a list of files, changes to new directory *D*
- –exclude *F*—Excludes the given file
- –exclude-from *F* (-X *F*)— Excludes files listed in the given file
- –extract (or –get or -x)—Extracts the files in the archive
- –files-from *F* (-T *F*)—Files to extract are in the specified file
- –force-local—Treats a colon in the archive filename as part of the filename

- —info-script *F* (or —new-volume-script *F* or -F *F*)—For multi-volume archives, runs the given script at end of each volume
- —ignore-failed-read—Doesn't stop processing when a file cannot be read
- —ignore-zeros (-i)—Ignores blocks of zeros in the archive
- —incremental (-G)—Creates/lists/extracts using old GNU-format incremental backup
- —interactive (or —confirmation or -w)—User confirmation
- —keep-old-files (-k)—Doesn't overwrite existing files
- —label *N* (-V *N*)—Specifies volume label *N*
- —list (or -t)—Lists the files in the archive
- —listed-incremental (-g)—Creates/lists/extracts using new GNU-format incremental backup
- —modification-time (-m)—Doesn't change modification time on extracted files
- —multi-volume (-M)—Creates/lists/extracts multi-volume archive
- —null—With —files-from, tar expects names ending with ASCII NUL characters (that is, C strings)
- —old-archive (or —portability or -o)—Writes a Unix V7 format archive
- —one-file-system (-I)—Stays in the current file system when creating an archive
- —preserve—Same as —save-permissions and —same-order
- —read-full-blocks (-B)—Reblocks as you read (for reading 4.2BSD pipes)
- —record-number (-R)—Shows record number within archive with each message
- —remove-files—Removes files added to the archive
- —to-stdout (-O)—Prints extracted files to standard output
- —same-permissions (or —preserve-permissions or -p)—Extracts all file permissions
- —starting-file *F* (-K *F*)—Begins extracting/listing at file *F* in the archive
- —same-order (or —preserve-order or -s)—Sorts extraction names to match the archive
- —same-owner—Makes extracted files have the same owner as the owner who added them
- —sparse (-S)—Handles sparse files efficiently
- —tape-length *N* (-L)—Changes volumes after writing N*1024 bytes
- —totals—Prints total bytes saved with —create
- —update (or -u)—Adds files if they are newer than the files already in the archive
- —verify (-W)—Verifies each archive after writing it

`tr` **Command Switches**

- —complement (or -c)—Complements the first character set
- —delete (or -d)—Deletes characters in the first character set; does not translate
- —squeeze-repeats (or -s)—Replaces sequence of characters with one
- —truncate-set1 (or -t)—Truncates first character set to the length of the second set

`sed` **Command Switches**

- —quiet (or —silent or -n)—sed only produces output when p is used
- -file=*script* (or -e *script* or —expression=*script* or -f *script*)—File called *script* contains sed commands to run

`sed` **Editing Codes**

- : *label*—Labels for b and t commands
- #comment—A comment that extends until the next line feed (new line)
- { }—Nested command block
- =—Prints the current line number
- a—Appends text
- b *[label]*—Goes to (branches to) *label* or end of sed script if no label
- c—Replaces the selected lines
- d—Deletes and starts new editing cycle
- D—Deletes up to the first embedded line feed (new line) and starts new cycle
- g (or G)—Copies/appends hold space to pattern space
- h (or H)—Copies/appends pattern space to hold space
- i—Inserts text
- l—Lists the current line
- p—Prints the current pattern space
- P—Prints up to the first embedded line feed (new line) of the current pattern space
- q—Quits the sed script
- r *f*—Appends text read from file *f*
- t *[label]*—If there was a successful substitution, branches to *label* or to end of script

- x—Exchanges the contents of the hold and pattern spaces
- n (or N)—Reads/appends the next line of input into the pattern space
- s—Substitutes text
- w *f*—Writes the current pattern space to the file *f*
- y—Transliterates the characters in the pattern space

13

Console Scripting

IN ANY OF THE COMPANIES THAT I worked for, if you were given the task of writing a short utility program and, after two weeks, you returned with a beautiful-looking X Windows application, you would be called in front of the boss and be sharply criticized. In the business world, time is money and developing GUI applications is time-consuming and expensive.

Console scripts, sometimes called text-based or terminal scripts, are scripts designed to run in a text-only environment such as the Linux console, a Telnet session, or an xterm window. Console scripts are easy to design and quick to build, but they don't have to be hostile to the user. Bash and Linux both provide features for writing friendly console scripts that won't drain a department's development budget.

The Linux Console

In the early days of Unix, a computer was a number-crunching device that had neither keyboard nor monitor. To control the computer, a separate administration workstation had to be attached to the system. This dedicated workstation was known as the *console*. From its keyboard, the system administrator oversaw the startup and shutdown of the computer. All critical error messages were displayed on the console's screen or, sometimes, on its printer.

Linux, which is based on Unix, still requires a dedicated console. But from Linux's point of view, the console is not a separate device—it's the computer's keyboard and monitor. The console is the text-only display that appears when a Linux computer first starts up. When terminal windows are opened in X Windows, they are not consoles. The console is hidden "behind" the desktop.

Linux actually creates seven *virtual consoles* (also called VCs or VTs) that act much the same way as separate X Windows terminal sessions. Each one can be selected using the Alt-F1 through Alt-F7 keys.

A console acts as if it were an enhanced DEC VT-100 terminal and any program designed to run on a VT-100 (or in an xterm window) can also run on the Linux console. The text is drawn in the current console font as selected by the Linux `consolechars` command (or the obsolete `setfont` command).

To determine whether the current session is in a console, use the `tty` command. This command prints the name of the terminal you are on.

```
$ tty # not a console
/dev/pts/1
```

Each console has a unique `tty` device name, `/dev/tty1` to `/dev/tty7`. The main console, the one that appears on Linux startup, is `/dev/tty1`.

```
$ tty # the main console
/dev/tty1
```

The Linux `fgconsole` command prints the number of the console. It reports an error if you are not on a console.

```
$ fgconsole
1
```

If your distribution doesn't have `fgconsole`, check the name returned by `tty`:

```
IS_CONSOLE=
TTY='tty'
case 'tty' in
 /dev/tty*|/dev/vc/*) IS_CONSOLE="1" ;;
 *) printf "%s\n" "This is a console" ;;
esac
```

Some Linux commands work only on a console, not a text session. The error messages are not always intuitive.

```
$ showkey
Couldnt get a file descriptor referring to the console
$ setleds
KDGETLED: Invalid argument
Error reading current led setting. Maybe stdin is not a VT?
```

The Console Keyboard

A shell script can control the console keyboard's key layout, change the current input mode, and the LED lights.

The console input mode determines how the keystrokes typed by the users are pre-processed. There are four input modes:

- *Scancode* (or RAW) *mode*—Scripts read the numeric codes representing the individual keys on the keyboard. Pressing or releasing a key results in separate codes. Up to six individual scancodes can be returned for a single key press.

- *Keycode* (or MEDIUMRAW) *mode*—Scripts read the numeric codes representing the console driver's interpretation of the keys. Usually two keycodes are returned, one for pressing and another for releasing a key. Different keys have different keycodes. For example, pressing the left or right Shift key returns different keycodes.

- *ASCII* (or XLATE) *mode*—This is the normal console mode. A script reads the ASCII character codes for each keyboard character. Modifier keys like the Shift key only affect other keys.

- *UTF-8* (or UNICODE) *mode*—THE same as ASCII mode except that 16-bit Unicode characters are returned instead of ASCII. For most characters, ASCII and UTF-8 are the same. However, this mode can return as many as three bytes for a particular key instead of the usual ASCII single byte.

The Linux showkey command can demonstrate each of these modes. Use –scancodes to run the program in scancode mode, –keycodes to run the program in keycode mode, and so on. The following example shows what happens when the a key is pressed.

```
$ showkey –keycodes
kb mode was XLATE
press any key (program terminates after 10s of last keypress)...
keycode  28 release
keycode  30 press
keycode  30 release
$ showkey –scancodes
kb mode was XLATE
press any key (program terminates after 10s of last keypress)...
0x9c
0x1e
0x9e
$ showkey –keycodes
kb mode was XLATE
press any key (program terminates after 10s of last keypress)...
a ( 0x61 )
```

The kbd_mode command changes the current keyboard mode: -s (scancode), -k (keycode), -a (ASCII) or -u (UTF-8).

Scripts can safely switch between ASCII and UTF-8 mode. In both cases, the Return or Enter key is treated normally and commands such as read behave as expected.

Things are more difficult when in scancode or keycode mode. Pressing the Return key no longer returns the ASCII/UTF-8 code 13 and, as a result, read is no longer certain when to finish reading. The only solution is to use the timeout feature and have the script check for the appropriate scancode or keycode representing the Return key.

If a console has LED lights for caps lock, scroll lock, and number lock, they can be turned on and off using the setleds command. Without arguments, setleds shows the current settings.

```
$ setleds
Current default flags:  NumLock off   CapsLock off   ScrollLock off
Current flags:          NumLock off   CapsLock off   ScrollLock off
Current leds:           NumLock off   CapsLock off   ScrollLock off
```

To turn off the lights, use the following switches: -num turns off the number lock light, -caps turns off the caps lock light, and -scroll turns off the scroll lock light. Using a plus sign turns the corresponding light on.

The extent of the change is reflected with three other flags: -F (make Linux think that the light has changed when it hasn't changed), -D (change both the Linux console driver and the lights), and -L (change the lights and make Linux think the light hasn't changed).

For example, to set number lock light on tty1, you use

```
$ setleds -D +num < /dev/tty1
$ setleds
Current default flags:  NumLock on   CapsLock off   ScrollLock off
Current flags:          NumLock on   CapsLock off   ScrollLock off
Current leds:           NumLock on   CapsLock off   ScrollLock off
```

The NumLock light should now be on.

A *keymap* is a list that determines which key on a console keyboard translates into which character. Changing the keymap changes the layout of keys, typically to reflect the keyboards used in different countries.

The keymap is selected by a Linux installation program, but it can be manually changed at any time using the Linux loadkeys command. The dumpkeys command displays the current keymap.

```
$ dumpkeys | head
keymaps 0-2,4-6,8-9,12
keycode   1 = Escape
    alt     keycode   1 = Meta_Escape
    shift    alt     keycode   1 = Meta_Escape
    control    alt     keycode   1 = Meta_Escape
keycode   2 = one               exclam
    alt     keycode   2 = Meta_one
    shift    alt     keycode   2 = Meta_exclam
keycode   3 = two               at              at              nul
nul
    alt     keycode   3 = Meta_two
kb mode was XLATE
```

To determine the keycodes to use, use showkey.

The Console Display

The console's VT-100 compatible display is not controlled by Linux commands but through special sequences of characters printed to the display. The console recognizes these characters as commands to execute and the characters are not shown.

The Linux `setterm` command acts like a `printf` command, printing the appropriate characters to execute a display command. Some of the `setterm` switches use the words "on" or "off" to enable or disable features. Because `setterm` is essentially a `printf` command, you can save common commands into a variable by capturing the command's output. Doing so improves the performance of a script.

The `-reset` switch restores the terminal settings to their startup state. This is the same as using the `reset` command described in Chapter 3, "Files, Users, and Shell Customization."

There are several switches for changing the color of text. A color is one of black, red, green, yellow, blue, magenta, cyan, white, or one of these with `bright` in front of it. `default` is the default color. The `-foreground` switch sets the console normal text color. The `-background` sets the console background text color. The `-ulcolor` switch sets the console underline text color. The `-hbcolor` switch sets the console dim text color.

Different text styles can be turned on or off with the appropriate switch: `-bold`, `-half-bright`, `-blink`, `-reverse`, or `-underline`.

```
$ setterm -ulcolor bright blue
$ setterm -underline on ; printf "This is bright blue\n" ; \
setterm -underline off
This is bright blue
```

Because the Linux console cannot show underlining, underlined text is shown in the underline color you select. In this case, the color is bright blue. In an xterm window, the text is actually underlined.

The same can be done by storing the `setterm` results in variables.

```
$ UNDERON='setterm -underline on'
$ UNDEROFF='setterm -underline off'
$ printf "$UNDERON""This is underlined""$UNDEROFF""\n"
This is underlined
```

The `-inversescreen` switch reverses the console's colors. If you use it twice, `-inversescreen` can make the display flash to alert the user to an important event.

For example, to flash the screen for one second, do this

```
$ setterm -inversescreen on
$ sleep 1
$ setterm -inversescreen off
```

Other useful switches include:

- `-cursor`—Shows or hides the input cursor
- `-repeat`—Turns a console's keyboard repeating on or off
- `-appcursorkeys`—Turns cursor key application mode on or off
- `-linewrap`—Turns a console's line wrapping on or off

These can be turned on or off. For example, to hide the input cursor, type this

```
$ setterm -cursor off
```

There are other attributes to control features like power saving and Tab usage. See the reference section at the end of this chapter for a complete list of switches.

tput

You can use the `setterm` command for any terminal display, but an attempt to use a feature specific to the console is ignored. Instead, there is an old command called `tput` (*terminal put*) that works much the same as `setterm` but works with all text-only displays.

`tput` has one parameter; a screen attribute code based on the `terminfo` terminal database. These codes are different from the `setterm` switches. You can find a complete list on the `terminfo` manual page (man 5 terminfo).

```
$ tput cols # width of display
80
$ tput clear # clear the screen
```

select **Menus**

The built-in `select` command creates simple menus. `select` is a special loop. The command is followed by a list of arguments and displays them as numbered options. When the user selects an item by typing that number, the argument is assigned to the `select` variable and the commands inside the `select` statement are executed. See Listing 13.1.

Listing 13.1 `select_demo.sh`

```
#!/bin/bash
#
# select_demo.sh: a simple select menu
#
shopt -s -o nounset

declare ITEM
declare -rx SCRIPT=${0##*/}

printf "%s\n" "Select a document type:"
```

```
select ITEM in "orders" "purchase orders" "packing slips" ; do
  if [ -z "$ITEM" ] ; then
     printf "Please chose 1, 2 or 3...\n"
  else
     printf "Processing $ITEM documents...\n"
  fi
done
printf "Done\n"
```

When an item is selected that isn't in the list, the variable is assigned an empty string. The loop continues until a EOF is read (usually a Control-D).

```
Select a document type:
1) orders
2) purchase orders
3) packing slips
#? 1
Processing orders documents...
#? 4
Please chose 1, 2 or 3...
#?
1) orders
2) purchase orders
3) packing slips
#?
```

Older versions of Bash displayed the menu each time they encountered the select statement. Newer versions display the list only when the REPLY variable is empty, such as when a user presses the Return key at the select prompt.

The prompt is in the variable PS3. If PS3 isn't defined, Bash uses #? as the prompt. To change the prompt, change the value of PS3. The user's response is also saved in the variable REPLY. If the in part is missing, Bash selects from the script parameters.

Like other loops, select commands can use break and continue.

Custom Menus

Although the select command creates simple menus with very little work, it doesn't provide any features for complex user interaction. To provide a friendlier-looking communication as well as to support more complex screens, the Linux dialog command creates pop-up text screen dialog boxes.

This command works on any text-only display. There are several types of dialog boxes:

- Background text box (–textboxbg)—Monitors a command while processing others
- Calendar box (–calendar)—Selects dates

- Checklists (–checklist)—Lists of selectable items
- File select (–fselect)—Selects a file
- Gauge (–gauge)—Thermometer graphs
- Info box (–infobox)—Status messages
- Input box (–inputbox)—Requests text from the user
- Menu (–menu)—Lists alternative choices
- Message box (–msgbox)—Info box with an OK button
- Password (–passwordbox)—Requests text from the user but hide typing
- Radio list (–radiolist)—Lists of alternative items
- Tail box (–tailbox)—Monitors a command
- Time box (–timebox)—Selects time values
- Yes/No box (–yesno)—Asks a yes/no question
- Text boxes
- Yesno boxes

A *yesno* box is created with the –yesno switch. The dialog box contains a message with Yes and No buttons. The switch takes three parameters: the text, the height, and the width. All dialog boxes have these three parameters. The –defaultno switch makes the No button the default button.

For example, to create a dialog box with the message Are you sure? 70 characters wide and 7 characters high, and centered in the screen, you type the following.

```
$ dialog –yesno "Are you sure?" 7 70
```

The status code returned by dialog indicates which button was selected: 0 is Yes (or OK on other dialog boxes), and 1 is No (or Cancel on other dialog boxes). A status code of -1 indicates an error or that the user aborted the dialog box by pressing the Escape key. Figure 13.1 shows a typical yesno dialog box.

You can divide long text into separate lines by embedding line feed codes (\n) in the message.

```
$ dialog –title Testbox –yesno "Delete files.\nAre you sure?" 7 70
```

The –checklist switch creates a list of check boxes. The basic parameters are the text caption, the height, and the width of the list. After these, each checklist item is described using its name, the item text, and an indication about whether it is currently selected (on) or not (off). The selected items are printed to standard error.

```
$ dialog –checklist "Printer type:" 20 70 14 p1 "printer 1" on p2 \
"printer 2" off fax "Fax" off "p1" "fax"
$
```

In this case, printer 1 and the fax machine are selected.

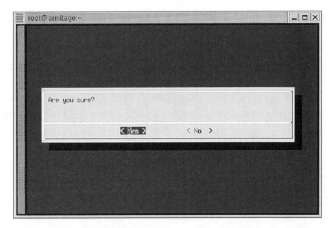

Figure 13.1 A yesno dialog box.

The results can be captured to a variable. Because standard output is used to draw the screen and the results are written to standard error, redirect standard error to a file.

```
$ declare CHOICE_FILE="/tmp/choice.$$"
$ declare CHOICE
$ dialog —checklist "Printer type:" 20 70 14 p1 "printer 1" on p2 \
"printer 2" off fax "Fax" off 2> "$CHOICE"
$ CHOICE=`cat "$CHOICE_FILE"`
```

A file select dialog box (see Figure 13.2) is created with the -fselect switch. This dialog box requires the starting directory, and a height and width.

```
$ dialog —fselect "$HOME" 10 50
```

Figure 13.2   A File Select dialog box.

A *gauge* is a thermometer bar showing the percentage progress. New percentages are read one at a time from standard input until the end of file is reached. The –gauge switch requires a text message, the height, width, and an optional starting percentage (see Listing 13.2). The percentages can be sent to the gauge by a named pipe, discussed in Chapter 11, "Text File Basics."

Suppose you would like to show a thermometer graph showing the progress of printing a series of invoice files stored in a directory called invoices. The following demo displays the invoices as they are sent another script called `print_invoice`.

Listing 13.2 `gauge_demo.sh`

```
#!/bin/bash
#
# gauge_demo.sh: a thermometer graph demo

shopt -s -o nounset

declare -rx SCRIPT=${0##*/}
declare -rx QUEUE="./status.fifo"
declare -rx INVOICES_DIR="invoices"
declare -ix TOTAL_INVOICES=0
declare -ix NUM_INVOICES=0
declare -ix PERCENT=0

# count the invoices waiting to print

TOTAL_INVOICES='ls -1 $INVOICES_DIR | wc -l'

# create the pipe

mkfifo $QUEUE
if [ $? -ne 0 ] ; then
    printf "%s\n" "$SCRIPT:$LINENO: unable to create $QUEUE" >&2
    exit 192
fi

# print the invoices in a background subshell
# print the progress to the pipe

(
  ls -1 | (
     while read INVOICE ; do
        let "NUM_INVOICES++"
        print_invoice "$INVOICE"
        PERCENT=100*$NUM_INVOICES/$TOTAL_INVOICES
        printf "%d\n" "$PERCENT"
```

```
        done
    )
) > $QUEUE &

# display the progress.  dialog will stop when nothing
# more is printed by the subshell

dialog -gauge "Printing invoices" 7 70 0 < $QUEUE

wait        # wait for the subshell to finish
rm $QUEUE   # delete the pipe
sleep 1     # make sure results can be read by user

exit 0
```

An *info box* is a status message to the user. It has no buttons and the `dialog` command completes immediately. The `-infobox` switch requires a text message, as well as a height and width.

```
$ dialog -infobox "Connecting to server" 7 70
```

An *input box* enables the user to type a response. The `-inputbox` switch requires the prompt text, the height width, and an optional default response for the user.

```
$ dialog -print-size -inputbox "Connect to which host?" 7 70 "" 2> size.txt
$ cat size.txt
Size: 7, 70
$ rm size.txt
$ dialog -print-size -no-shadow -nocancel -inputbox \
"Connect to which host?" 7 70
```

The remaining dialog boxes are similar to the ones already discussed.

A *menu* is a list of selections that the user can make a choice from. The `--menu` switch requires the menu heading text, the height, width, and the menu height. Each item is specified with a tag name and the menu item's text.

A *message box* presents a message to the user with a single OK button. The `--msgbox` switch requires the text message, as well as the height and width.

A *password box* is similar to an input box except what the user types is not shown. The `--passwordbox` requires the text message, the height and width, and an optional default password.

A *radio list* presents a list of choices of which the user can select only one item. The `--radiolist` switch requires the heading text, the height, width, and the list height. Each item is specified the same way as a checklist.

A *tail box* displays final text in a file as if the `tail -f` command were used. The `--tailbox` switch requires the filename, as well as the height and width.

A *text box* shows the contents of a text file in the dialog box. The user can browse through the file. The `--textbox` switch requires the filename, height, and width.

The *background text box* is a combination of a tail box and a text box. The text is viewed as if the "tail -f" command was used, but the user is free to browse the content. The `--textboxbg` switch requires a filename, the height, and width.

A *time box* enables the users to select a time. The `--timebox` switch requires prompt text, a height, a width, and the initial time in hours, minutes, and seconds.

A *calendar box,* shown in Figure 13.3, shows a calendar and enables the users to select a date. The `-calendar` switch requires prompt text, a height, a width, and the day, month, and year to start with.

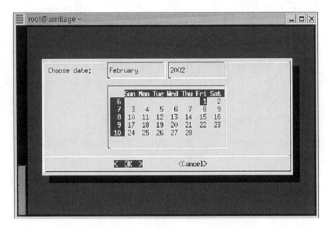

Figure 13.3 A Calendar dialog box.

You can combine consecutive dialog boxes with the –and-widget switch.

```
$ dialog –inputbox "Connect to which host?" 7 70 "" –and-widget –inputbox \
"And what TCP/IP port?" 7 70
```

You must give an input box an initial string parameter (as "" for none) or `dialog` assumes that –and-widget is the optional string.

There are a large number of switches for customizing the appearance and behavior of the boxes. These are listed in the reference section of this chapter.

Reference Section

`showkey` **Command Switches**

- `--scancodes` (or `-s`)—Scancode dump mode
- `--keycodes` (or `-k`)—Keycode dump mode (default)
- `--ascii` (or `-a`)—ASCII dump mode

`setleds` **Command Switches**

- `-caps`—Clears Caps Lock
- `+caps`—Sets Caps Lock
- `-D`—Changes both console flags and LEDs
- `-F`—Changes the console flags (default)
- `-L`—Changes the LEDs
- `-num`—Clears Num Lock
- `+num`—Sets Num Lock
- `-scroll`—Clears Scroll Lock
- `+scroll`—Sets Scroll Lock

`dumpkeys` **Command Switches**

- `--charset=c` (or `-c  c`)—Interprets character code values according to character set `c`
- `--compose-only`—Shows only compose key combinations
- `--full-table` (or `-f`)—Shows key bindings in canonical form
- `--funcs-only`—Shows function key string definitions
- `--keys-only`—Shows key bindings without string definitions
- `--long-info` (or `-l`)—Prints detailed info about the keyboard driver
- `--numeric` (or `-n`)—Shows values in hexadecimal format
- `--short-info` (or `-i`)—Prints summary info about the keyboard driver

`setterm` **Command Switches**

- `-append [ c ]`—Dumps a console screen (default is `current`) to a file, appending it if the file exists
- `-appcursorkeys [on|off]`—Sets Cursor Key Application Mode on or off
- `-background` *c*—Sets the background text color to color *c*
- `-blank [ 0-60 ]`—Number of minutes until the screen is blanked (default is 0, which is no blanking)
- `-blength [ n ]`—Console beep duration in milliseconds (default is 0)
- `-bfreq` *h*—Console beep frequency (pitch) in Hertz (default is 0)
- `-blink [on|off]`—Turns blinking text printing on or off. When not on a console, turning blinking text off also turns off all other attributes
- `-bold [on|off]`—Turns bold printing on or off. When not on a console, turning bold off also turns off all other attributes
- `-clear [ all|rest ]`—Clears the screen and homes the cursor. `rest` clears to end of screen
- `-clrtabs [ tab1 tab2 tab3 ... ]`—Clears Tab stops
- `-cursor [on|off]`—Turns the console cursor on or off
- `-defaults`—Restores rendering options to their default values
- `-dump [ c ]`—Saves a console screen (default is `current`) to a file
- `-file` *f*—Sets the `-dump` or `-append` filename
- `-foreground` *c*—Sets the foreground text color to color *c*
- `-half-bright [on|off]`—Turns dim printing on or off. When not on a console, turning dim off also turns off all other attributes
- `-hbcolor` *c*—Sets the color for half-bright characters
- `-initialize`—Restores the drawing characteristics to their default values
- `-inversescreen [on|off]`—Inverts the screen colors
- `-linewrap [on|off]`—Turns automatic line-wrapping on or off
- `-msg [on|off]`—Enables or disables `printk` kernel messages
- `-msglevel` *n*—Sets the `printk` message level to *n*
- `-powerdown [ 0-60 ]`—Number of minutes until the monitor is powered off (default is 0)
- `-powersave [ on|vsync|hsync|powerdown|off ]`—Changes the monitor's power-saving features
- `-regtabs [ n ]`—Sets Tab stops to every *n* characters (default is 8)
- `-repeat [on|off]`—Turns keyboard repeat on or off

- `-reset`—Restores the screen to its power-on state
- `-reverse [on|off]`—Turns reverse color text printing on or off. When not on a console, turning reverse color text off also turns off all other attributes
- `-softscroll [on|off]`—Turns soft keyboard scrolling on or off
- `-store`—Saves the current rendering options as the defaults
- `-tabs [tab1 tab2 tab3 ... ] ]`—Sets the Tab stop positions
- `-term terminal_name`—Uses `terminal_name` instead of value of the TERM variable
- `-ulcolor c`—Sets the color for underlined characters
- `-underline [on|off]`—Turns underline printing on or off. `ulcolor` is used if underlining is not supported

`dialog` **Command Switches**

- `--aspect r`—Line width ratio r based on the length of the prompt string to use as a guide to forcibly wrap lines that are too long relative to the dialog box (default is 9)
- `-backtitle b`—A string b to be displayed on the backdrop, at the top of the screen
- `--beep`—Beeps each time the screen is redrawn
- `--beep-after`—Beeps if input is interrupted
- `--begin y x`—The position of the upper-left corner of a dialog box, as opposed to centering
- `--clear`—Clears the screen on exit
- `--cr-wrap`—Allows embedded form feeds (new lines) in the dialog box's text
- `--create-rc f`—If runtime configuration is supported, saves a sample dialog box configuration file to file f
- `--default-item s`—Sets the default item to s in a menu box (default is `first`)
- `--no-kill`—For a `tailboxbg` box, prints the process ID to standard error. SIGHUP does not stop the command
- `--no-shadow`—No 3D shadows around the dialog box
- `--nocancel`—No Cancel button
- `--print-maxsize`—Prints the maximum size of dialog boxes to the standard error
- `--print-size`—Prints the size of each dialog box to standard error
- `--print-version`—Prints the dialog box's version to standard error
- `--separate-output`—Places checklist items on separate lines, without quote marks

- `--separate-widget` *s*—For multiple `–and-widget` dialog boxes, separates the results from different dialogs using the string *s*
- `--shadow`—Shows 3D shadows around the dialog box
- `--sleep` *s*—Delays *s* seconds after processing a dialog box
- `--stderr`—Directs messages to the standard error (the default)
- `--stdout`—Directs messages to the standard output
- `--tab-correct`—Converts each Tab character into one or more spaces
- `--tab-len` *n*—Specifies the number of spaces for a `–tab-correct` Tab (default is 8)
- `--title` *t*—Shows title *t* at the top of the dialog box

## 14

Functions and Script Execution

Once I was discussing the problem of "preacher burnout" with a minister. When people train for a life in the clergy, they are expected to master not only the concepts taught by the faith, but also accounting, counseling, writing, graphic design, and a dozen other skills. Although this guarantees that the minister has a ready background in all the areas needed to keep a congregation moving forward, it also instills in many new church leaders the feeling that they must single-handedly bear the needs of the congregation, unable or unwilling to delegate responsibilities. No human being can shoulder that many duties effectively. This burden often leads to stress, feelings of helplessness, emotional breakdowns, or even the abandonment of their chosen profession.

Shell scripting is a tool for solving simple problems quickly. When scripts become large or complex, they become difficult to maintain. Like someone suffering from "preacher burnout," they must delegate responsibilities to other scripts and coordinate with each other to get jobs done without crumbling under the load.

Running Scripts

Bash scripts are text files and not files containing executable instructions. A script cannot be executed directly; it needs an interpreter to carry out the instructions. In the case of Bash scripts, the interpreter is the Bash program. Linux must be able to find the interpreter in order to run a script.

One way is to run an interpreter explicitly starting a new Bash session. To run a script named `delayed_shipments.sh`, you supply the name to Bash as an argument.

```
$ bash delayed_shipments.sh
```

The alternative way requires a `#!` line as the first line of the script. This specifies the pathname of the interpreter needed to run the script. In this case, `#!/bin/bash` specifies the pathname of the Bash shell that's located in the `bin` directory. The script should have the permission bits set to allow the user to run the script. (Permission bits are discussed more in the next chapter.) The script can then run without explicitly starting Bash; Linux automatically starts Bash for you.

```
$ delayed_shipments.sh
```

The Linux Execution Environment

As mentioned in the later section on exporting variables, when a Linux program runs, it doesn't start with an "empty slate," but inherits any variables exported by the previous program. Exported variables are called *environment variables* because they become part of the environment in which the new program is running.

Variables are not the only things exported by the original program. The environment consists of:

- Open files
- The current working directory
- The file creation mode `umask`
- Any signal handlers set by `trap`
- Exported environment variables
- Exported shell functions
- Options enabled at invocation (either by default or with command-line arguments) or by `set`
- `shopt` shell options
- Shell aliases
- Various process IDs, including those of background jobs, the value of `$$`, and the value of `$PPID`

Subshells inherit their environment from the parent scripts. The environment of a subshell consists of:

- Open files (possibly modified by redirections to the subshell)
- The current working directory
- The `umask` value
- Shell variables marked for export
- Signal traps

Like environment variables, the process of exporting open files, the working directory, or traps is one way. If the new program decides to close standard output, it closes only its copy of the original program's standard output. The original program cannot be affected by the actions of the new program. The entire environment acts the same way.

The Source Command (.)

When one script is executed by another, all variables, aliases, and other items declared in the script are lost when the second script completes its run. Results can be returned only by files, by standard output, or by the script's status code.

Instead of running a second script, you can insert a second script into the first. The built-in `source` command (often abbreviated with a period .) copies the second script into the first script as if the programmer had typed the lines. Because the second script is treated as part of the first script, no declarations in the second script are lost when the second script finishes execution. It acts as if it were a single combined script.

For example, consider the two scripts shown in Listing 14.1.

Listing 14.1   `source1.sh`

```
#!/bin/bash
#
# source1.sh: including source fragments
#
# Source command example
shopt -s -o nounset

declare -rx SCRIPT=${0##*/}
declare -r source2="source2.sh"

if test ! -r "$source2" ; then
    printf "SCRIPT: the command $source2 is not available\n" >&2
    exit 1
fi

source $source2
printf "The variable YEAR is %s\n" "$YEAR"
exit 0



# source2.sh: this will be inserted into source1.sh

declare -r YEAR='date '+%Y''
```

When the script runs, the content of `source2.sh` is inserted into the original script at the point of the `source` command. When the variable YEAR is declared, it is effectively being declared in the original script.

$ bash source1.sh
The variable YEAR is 2003

The variable YEAR exists at the point of the `printf` command; there is no error.

Notice that the sourced script is a fragment and not a standalone script; it doesn't contain an `exit` command or a `#!` line.

The `source` command can be used to define commonly declared items shared among several scripts. This saves a programmer from having to type the same definitions over and over again into several different scripts. Placing the declared items in a single place also makes scripts easier to maintain. See Listing 14.2.

Listing 14.2 `common.sh`

```
# common.sh
#
# This script contains fragment global definitions and should be executed
# with the source command (.).

# Common constants

declare -rx SCRIPT=${0##*/}
declare -r ORDERS_DIR="/usr/local/orders"
declare -r ARCHIVE_DIR="$ORDERS_DIR/archive"
declare -r START_DATE='date'
```

Parameters in script fragments refer to the parameters included in the `source` command, not the original script. If there are no parameters included with source, the original script parameters are used.

You can end source script fragments prematurely with the `return` command. This command has the same format as the `exit` command. If you use `exit`, the entire script stops.

Because source script fragments aren't executed like a program, they do not need to have execute permissions to run; they simply need read permissions so that Bash can load them.

Switching Scripts with `exec`

A third way to run a script is with the built-in `exec` command. When running another script or inserting a script fragment with source, control always resumes at the next line in the original script. The `exec` command instead provides an unconditional change to a new script. Bash discards the original script entirely, never to return. See Listings 14.3 and 14.4.

Listing 14.3 `exec1.sh`

```
#!/bin/bash
#
# exec1.sh
#
# Source command example
shopt -s -o nounset

declare -rx SCRIPT=${0##*/}
declare -r exec2="./exec2.sh"
if test ! -x "$exec2" ; then
   printf "$SCRIPT:$LINENO: the script $exec2 is not available\n" >&2
   exit 192
```

```
fi

printf "$SCRIPT: Transferring control to $exec2, never to return...\n"
exec "$exec2"

printf "$SCRIPT:$LINENO: exec failed!\n" >&2
exit 1
```

Listing 14.4   `exec2.sh`

```
#!/bin/bash
#
# exec2.sh

declare -rx SCRIPT=${0##*/}

printf "$SCRIPT: now running exec2.sh"
exit 0
```

After the exec command is performed in `exec1.sh`, the script is discarded and Bash begins executing `exec2.sh` instead. When `exec2.sh` is finished, `exec1.sh` doesn't resume.

```
$ bash exec1.sh
exec1.sh: Transferring control to exec2.sh, never to return...
exec2.sh: now running exec2.sh
```

You can use the `exec` command to run other programs, not just other shell scripts. If the `-c` switch is used, `exec` destroys all variables before running the new program. The `-l` switch runs the program as if it were the first program being run when a user logs in (by putting a minus sign in parameter `$0`). The `-a` switch can specify a specific name for `$0`.

The exec never returns unless you set the `execfail` option. If it is not set and the script cannot run the new program, the script simply exits.

A specialized command, exec is used primarily for scripts that are a "front end" to a series of other scripts. For example, a script can examine a file sent by a customer, categorize it, and then run an appropriate script to process it using `exec`. Because there's no reason to return to the original script, exec is the appropriate command to use.

Writing Recurring Scripts

There are several Linux commands for scheduling recurring jobs. The main scheduling program is called `cron` (as in *chronological*). The cron program runs continually in the background, starting up scripts or other programs at specific times.

The `crontab` (*chronological table*) command maintains a list of jobs for `cron` to execute. Each user has his or her own `crontab` table. The `-l` (*list*) switch lists currently scheduled tasks. Linux reports an error if you don't have permission to use `cron`. Because jobs are added or removed from the `crontab` table as a group, always start with the `-l` switch, saving the current table to a file.

```
$ crontab -l > cron.txt
```

After the current table is saved, the file can be edited. There are five columns for specifying the times when a program is to run: The minute, hour, day, month, and the day of the week. Unused columns are marked with an asterisk, indicating any appropriate time.

Times are represented in a variety of formats: Individually (1), comma-separated lists (1,15), ranges (0-6, 9-17), and ranges with step values (1-31/2). Names can be used for months or days of the week.

The final column contains the name of the command to execute. The following line runs a script called `cleanup.sh` at 1:00 AM every morning.

```
*      1      *      *      *        /home/kburtch/cleanup.sh
```

Environment variables can also be initialized in the `crontab`. When a shell script is started by `cron`, it is not started from a login session and none of the profile files are executed. Only a handful of variables are defined: `PWD`, `HOSTNAME`, `MACHTYPE`, `LOGNAME`, `SHLVL`, `SHELL`, `HOSTTYPE`, `OSTYPE`, `HOME`, `TERM`, and `PATH`. You have to explicitly set any other values in the script or in the `crontab` list.

`PATH` is defined as only `/usr/bin:/bin`. Other paths are normally added by profile files and so are unavailable.

Because a script running under cron is not in a login session, there is no screen to write standard output to. Anything that is normally written to standard output is instead captured by `cron` and mailed to the account owning the `cron` script. The mail has the unhelpful subject line of `cron`. Even printing a blank line results in a seemingly empty email being sent. For this reason, scripts designed to run under `cron` should either write their output to a log file, or should create and forward their own email with a meaningful subject line. It is common practice to write a wrapper script to capture the output from the script doing the actual work.

The example in Listing 14.6 shows a wrapper script that runs the script in Listing 14.5 called `show_users.sh`.

Listing 14.5 `show_users.sh`

```
#!/bin/bash
#
# show_users.sh: show all users in the database table "users"

shopt -s -o nounset

declare -rx SCRIPT=${0##*/}
```

```
declare -r SQL_CMDS="sort_inventory.sql"
declare -rx ON_ERROR_STOP

if [ ! -r "$SQL_CMDS" ] ; then
   printf "$SCRIPT: the SQL script $SQL_CMDS doesn't exist or is not \
 readable" >&2
   exit 192
fi

RESULTS=`psql —user gordon —dbname custinfo  -quiet —no-align —tuples-only \
 —field-separator "," —file "$SQL_CMDS"`
if [ $? -ne 0 ] ; then
   printf "$SCRIPT: SQL statements failed." >&2
   exit 192
fi
```

Listing 14.6 `show_users_wrapper.sh`

```
#!/bin/bash
# show_users_wrapper.sh - show_users.sh wrapper script

shopt -s -o nounset

declare -rx SCRIPT=${0##*/}
declare -rx USER="kburtch"
declare -rx mail="/bin/mail"
declare -rx OUTPUT='mktemp /tmp/script_out.XXXXXX'
declare -rx SCRIPT2RUN="./show_users.sh"

# sanity checks

if test ! -x "$mail" ; then
   printf "$SCRIPT:$LINENO: the command $mail is not available — aborting" >&2
   exit 1
fi

if test ! -x "$SCRIPT2RUN" ; then
   printf "$SCRIPT: $LINENO: the command $SCRIPT2RUN is not available\
 — aborting" >&2
   exit 1
fi

# record the date for any errors, and create the OUTPUT file

date > $OUTPUT
```

Listing 14.6 **Continued**

```
# run the script

$SCRIPT2RUN 2>&1 > "$OUTPUT"

# mail errors to USER

if [ $? -ne 0 ] ; then
    $mail -s "$SCRIPT2RUN failed" "$USER" < "$OUTPUT"
fi

# cleanup

rm "$OUTPUT"
exit 0
```

Writing Continually Executing Scripts

A *daemon* is a program that runs independently of a shell session, continually performing some task. Server software, for example, is almost always a daemon because it runs continually, waiting for clients to request services.

The Linux nohup (*no hang up*) command runs a program so that it will not quit after a session has disconnected. You need this command if you want to start daemons interactively from the command line. nohup reduces the priority of a program slightly and, if standard output is open, redirects it to a file called nohup.out because, the moment the shell session terminates, there will no longer be a standard output to write to.

Generally speaking, a front-end script is necessary to set up and start the daemon script. To avoid the nohup.out file, it's good design practice to close standard output or redirect it using exec with a front-end script to the daemon script. Also, nohup does not automatically place a command in the background. The front-end script has to do this with an &.

For example, Listings 14.7 and 14.8 show a pair of scripts that check files coming into a directory called ftp_incoming.

Listing 14.7 ftp_daemon.sh

```
#!/bin/bash
#
# ftp_daemon.sh: a script fragment for the wrapper.

shopt -s -o nounset

declare -rx SCRIPT=${0##*/}
declare -rx INCOMING_FTP_DIR="/home/ftp/ftp_incoming"
```

```
cd $INCOMING_FTP_DIR
while true; do
    # do something to files in the incoming directory here
done
```

Listing 14.8 shows a wrapper script to daemonize `ftp_daemon.sh`.

Listing 14.8   `ftp_daemon_wrapper.sh`

```
#!/bin/bash
#
# ftp_daemon_wrapper.sh - start our sample daemon
#
shopt -s -o nounset

declare -rx SCRIPT=${0##*/}
declare -rx DAEMON="ftp_daemon.sh"
declare -rx DAEMON_LOG="ftp_daemon.log"

if test -f "$DAEMON_LOG" ; then
    if test ! -w "$DAEMON_LOG" ; then
        printf "%s\n" "$SCRIPT:$LINENO: unable to write to the log file\
—aborted" >&2
        exit 1
    fi
fi

# Standard Output is now the log file
# Redirect Standard Error there as well

exec 1>$DAEMON_LOG
exec 2>&1

# Start the daemon in the background

nohup bash ftp_daemon.sh &
echo "Daemon $DAEMON started"
exit 0
```

The daemon itself is a script with an infinite loop. There are two methods of checking for a task to do. In the first, *polling*, the daemon checks to see whether there is work for it to do. If there is no work, it puts itself to sleep for a few seconds, freeing up CPU time for other tasks, before checking again.

The script shown in Listing 14.9 checks every 30 seconds for files arriving in a directory called `ftp_incoming`. If the files are more than 30 minutes unchanged, their names are time-stamped and the files are moved to a new directory called `processing`.

Listing 14.9   `polling.sh`

```bash
#!/bin/bash
#
# polling.sh: a daemon using polling to check for new files

shopt -s -o nounset

declare -rx SCRIPT=${0##*/}
declare -rx INCOMING_FTP_DIR="/home/ftp/ftp_incoming"
declare -rx PROCESSING_DIR="/home/ftp/processing"
declare -rx statftime="/usr/bin/statftime"
declare FILE
declare FILES
declare NEW_FILE

printf "$SCRIPT started at %s\n" "'date'"

# Sanity checks

if test ! -r "$INCOMING_FTP_DIR" ; then
  printf "%s\n" "$SCRIPT:$LINENO: unable to read the incoming directory\
—aborted" >&1
  exit 1
fi
if test ! -r "$PROCESSING_DIR" ; then
  printf "%s\n" "$SCRIPT:$LINENO: unable to read the incoming directory\
—aborted" >&1
  exit 1
fi
if test ! -r "$statftime" ; then
  printf "%s\n" "$SCRIPT:$LINENO: unable to find or execute $statftime\
—aborted" >&1
  exit 1
fi

# Poll for new FTP files

cd $INCOMING_FTP_DIR
while true; do

  # Check for new files more than 30 minutes unchanged
```

```
    FILES='find . -type f -mmin +30 -print'

    # If new files exist, move them to the processing directory

    if [ ! -z "$FILES" ] ; then
        printf "$SCRIPT: new files have arrived at %s\n" "`date`"
        printf "%s\n" "$FILES" | {
            while read FILE ; do
                # Remove leading "./"
                FILE="${FILE##*/}"
                # Rename the file with the current time
                NEW_FILE='$statftime -f "%_L%_a_%T.dat" "$FILE"'
                if [ -z "$NEW_FILE" ] ; then
                    printf "%s\n" "$SCRIPT:$LINENO: statftime failed to\
 create a new filename—skipping"
                else
                    # Move the file to the processing directory
                    printf "%s\n" "$SCRIPT: moved $FILE to \
$PROCESSING_DIR/$NEW_FILE"
                    mv "$FILE" "$PROCESSING_DIR/$NEW_FILE"
                fi
            done
        }
    fi
    sleep 30
done

printf "$SCRIPT finished unexpectedly at %s\n" "`date`"
exit 1
```

The script can use *blocking* instead of polling. By replacing the `sleep` command with a suspend command, the script will sleep indefinitely until it wakes up with the `kill -SIGCONT` command. This is useful when one script relies upon another.

A daemon script runs until it's suspended or stopped with the `kill` command. It can be started so that it runs in the background and automatically restarts itself:

```
$ { { while true ; do nohup bash polling.sh ; done ; } \
>/dev/null 2>&1 </dev/null & } &
```

This command line creates two processes. The outer process redirects standard input, output, and error to /dev/null because they no longer apply. The inner process repeats the bash script in the `while` loop. When the command prompt returns, use the `ps` command to see that the `polling.sh` script is running. (It is possible to get rid of one of the command groupings by using `exec` to close standard input, output, and error before the `while` loop.)

Shell Functions

Functions are a way of embedding small subscripts into a Bash script without saving them in a separate file. Because they are embedded in a script, they do not have to be loaded in order to be used. This, in turn, makes them run faster than separate scripts. Like separate scripts, functions can be used to break up a complex script into separate, named, tasks to improve readability.

Shell functions differ from functions in other programming languages in that they return a status code instead of a return value. Without a return value, they cannot be used in expressions.

Like variables, functions must be declared before they can be used. Instead of the `declare` command, functions are declared using the `function` command. Each function has a name and the statements composing the function are enclosed in curly brackets. See Listing 14.10.

Listing 14.10   `function.sh`

```
#!/bin/bash
#
# function.sh - A simple function example

declare -rx SCRIPT=${0##*/}
declare -rx TMP="/tmp/temp.$$"
declare -rx TRASH_DIR="$HOME/trash"

# TRASH TMP
#
# Move the TMP file to the trash directory

function trash_tmp {

        if test ! -d "$TRASH_DIR" ; then
                printf "%s\n" "$SCRIPT:$FUNCNAME:$LINENO: trash directory \
$TRASH_DIR is missing" >&2
                exit 1
        fi
        if test -f "$TMP" ; then
                mv $TMP "$TRASH_DIR""/"
        fi

}
readonly -f trash_tmp
declare -t trash_tmp

printf "This is a function test\n" > $TMP
trash_tmp

exit 0
```

The function `trash_tmp` moves the `TMP` file to a directory called `trash` in the user's home directory. The function is created by the `function` command but it doesn't execute until it is explicitly named in the program.

The `readonly` command prevents a function from being redefined. The command is discussed in detail later in this chapter.

Normally, the `DEBUG` trap is not executed by functions. `declare -t` turns on debug trap execution in functions.

Like scripts, functions can have parameters. Although parameter `$0` remains the pathname of the script, the other parameters are parameters supplied to the functions, with `$#` indicating the number of parameters. When the function completes, the parameter variables are restored to their previous values.

The `FUNCNAME` variable contains the name of a function while the function is executing. Using `$SCRIPT: $FUNCNAME:` when reporting errors identifies the script and the function where the error occurred.

Because functions are not subscripts, functions return status codes and declare variables differently.

In a script, the `exit` command returns a status code. In a function, the `exit` command exits the script containing the function. To return a status code without exiting a script, functions use a `return` command instead. The `return` statement is used the same way as an `exit` statement.

Local Variables

Variables declared inside a function exist only for the duration of the function. These are called *local variables*. When the function completes, the variables are discarded, the same way variables are discarded by subscripts. See Listing 14.11.

Listing 14.11 `function2.sh`

```
#!/bin/bash
#
# function2.sh: A simple function example with local variables
#
shopt -s -o nounset

declare -rx SCRIPT=${0##*/}
declare -rx TMP="/tmp/temp.$$"

# TRASH FILE
#
# Move the specified file to the trash directory
# The first parameter is the file to move

function trash_file {
```

Listing 14.11   **Continued**

```
        declare -r TRASH_DIR="$HOME/trash"

        if test ! -d "$TRASH_DIR" ; then
                printf "%s\n" "$SCRIPT:$FUNCNAME:$LINENO: trash \
directory $TRASH_DIR is missing" >&2
                return 1
        fi
        if test -f "$1" ; then
                mv $1 "$TRASH_DIR""/"
        fi
        return 0

}
readonly -f trash_file
declare -t trash_file

printf "This is a function test\n" > $TMP
trash_file $TMP
if [ $? -ne 0 ] ; then
    printf "%s\n" "$SCRIPT:$LINENO: unable to trash $TMP—aborting" >&2
    exit 1
fi

exit 0
```

In `function2.sh`, the variable TRASH_DIR exists only within the function
trash_file. Instead of exiting the script when an error occurs, the function returns a
status code to indicate whether it succeeded, allowing the main script to decide whether
it should exit.

The `local` command can also declare local variables inside functions and assign initial
values. However, `local` lacks the other switches used by the `declare` command.
Therefore, it's best to use the `declare` command instead.

If new variables are not explicitly declared, they are not discarded when the function
completes. This behavior is for backward compatibility with the Bourne shell but can
cause variables to linger around unexpectedly.

```
$ function f { COMPANY="NightLight Inc." ; }
$ f
$ printf "%s\n" "$COMPANY"
NightLight Inc.
```

In this example, the variable COMPANY is not discarded when the tiny f function ends because it is not formally declared inside f.

```
$ function f { declare COMPANY="Nightlight Inc." ; }
$ f
$ printf "%s\n" "$COMPANY"
$
```

Recursion and Nested Functions

Functions can be nested or used recursively in Bash. Local variables are shared with the nested functions. See Listing 14.12.

Listing 14.12 `factorial.sh`

```
#!/bin/bash
#
# factorial.sh: A recursive function example
#
shopt -s -o nounset

declare -rx SCRIPT=${0##*/}
declare -i REPLY

# FACTORIAL : compute a factorial
#
# $1 is the number to compute the factorial for

function factorial {
   declare -i RESULT=1              # shared with factorial1

   function factorial1 {
     declare -i FACT=$1             # the current number
     let "FACT-"                    # deduct one
     if [ $FACT -gt 1 ] ; then      # greater than 1?
        factorial1 $FACT            # repeat
        let "RESULT=RESULT*FACT"    # and multiply in result
     else                           # otherwise
        RESULT=1                    # factorial of 1 is 1
     fi
     return                         # leave function
   }
```

Listing 14.12   **Continued**

```
    factorial1 $1                      # start with param 1
    printf "%d\n" $RESULT
}
readonly -f factorial
declare -t factorial

printf "Factorial of what number? —> "
read REPLY
factorial $REPLY
exit 0
```

Unexpected recursions can occur when the name of a function is the same as a built-in command. When functions override built-in commands, use the built-in `command` command to execute a command instead of the function.

```
function ls {
  command ls -CFp $*
}
readonly -f ls
declare -t ls
```

Without the `command` command, this function would begin a never-ending recursion.

Function Attributes

Like variables, functions have attributes. Because functions are not declared with the `declare` command, different commands are used to change function attributes.

Functions can be shared with subscripts using the `export` command with the `-f` (*function*) switch.

```
export -f trash_file
```

Exported functions created inside a user's start-up profile act as more powerful versions of shell aliases.

Because functions are declared with a command, functions can be redefined "on the fly" or discarded at will using `unset -f`. In a script, this is a dangerous practice because deleting or redefining functions makes your scripts difficult to debug. It can be hard to know which version of a function was defined when a script stops unexpectedly because of an error.

Well-structured scripts create functions near the top of the script and set the read-only attribute with the `readonly` command.

```
readonly -f trash_file
```

Read-only functions cannot be unset or redefined.

The current functions are listed with `declare` and with the `-F` (*function*) switch. You can list the complete functions, along with all variables, with the `-p` switch.

Functions can also be created using the older Bourne shell syntax of omitting the word "function" and adding an empty pair of parentheses after the function name.

Reference Section

exec Command Switches

- `-c`—Makes exec destroy all variables before running the new program
- `-l`—Runs the program as if it were the first program being run when a user logs in
- `-a` *n*—Specifies a different program name *n* for $0

crontab Command Switches

- `-u` *user*—Lists the name of a different user whose crontab is to be modified
- `-l`—Lists the current crontab
- `-r`—Deletes the current crontab
- `-e`—Edits the current crontab using the default editor

15

Shell Security

SYSTEM SECURITY CAN OFTEN BE A TWO-EDGED SWORD. Many companies spend large sums of money on system administration tools; often then inadequately train their admin staff. The first word of system resource shortages invariably comes from the programmers themselves.

At one company I worked for, the official policy was to prevent the programmers on the system from accessing the performance monitoring utilities. When head of administration discovered the tools were accessible, he ordered them to be made secure. After a couple of weeks, the staff silently enabled the utilities again because disabling them bottled up the company's first line of defense.

Security in a shell script, like system security, is a matter not of tightening everything to the point that the script barely functions, but of ensuring that the script doesn't make any unnecessary assumptions that make porting to a new system or debugging a difficult problem worse later. It involves making your scripts crash-proof in case of an emergency or during the malicious sabotage of a coworker. Like using the `nounset` shell option, more security means less maintenance.

The Basic Linux Security Model

All files on Linux are owned by an owner and a group. But who owns a file? Each file is assigned the user ID number of a particular login. Users are further divided into groups, and each user is assigned a group number. Originally, Unix assigned users to a single group, called the primary `gid`. BSD 4.3 introduced additional supplemental groups. In terms of files, a user must have a primary or supplemental group that matches the file GID in order to qualify for group access.

Each Linux user has a *uid* (a user id number) and every file on a Linux system has a uid number that indicates who owns that file.

The `–numeric-uid-gid` `ls` switch shows the octal numbers instead of the names of the file's `uid` and `gid` owners.

```
$ id
uid=500(ken) gid=100(users) groups=100(users),14(uucp),16(dialout)
$ ls —numeric-uid-gid -l
total 11068
drwx——    2 500        100             4096 Dec  5  2000 Mail
drwxr-xr-x 11 500        100             4096 Jan 23 00:52 archive
-rw-r—r—  1 500        100              267 Nov 30 09:33 script.sh
-rw-r—r—  1 500        100               36 Feb 12 11:51 company.txt
-rw-r—r—  1 499        100              309 Feb 12 15:45 eval_example.sh
```

Most of the files are owned by user 500 (ken) and primary group 100 (users). Because my login is ken, I qualify for owner's access rights on all files except the last one. Because eval_example.sh is owned by someone else but is in one of my groups, group access rights apply if I try to access the file.

Only the owner of a file can delete it.

Each file has a file access permissions number that indicates which users can access it. Each bit in the file permissions represents the right to perform certain kinds of actions such as reading the file, writing the file, or executing a program.

The file permissions are grouped into sets of three bits. Each set represents access rights for a particular kind of user. Because three bits form one octal (base 8) digit, permissions are often written as four octal digits. The right-most digit represents the access rights for users not in any other category: These are commonly called "other" or "world" permissions. The second digit from the right represents the access rights for users in the same group as the file. The third digit represents the access rights for the file's owner. For example, the /tmp directory has user permission numbers of 777, which indicate full rights to any user.

For directories, read access indicates the capability to read the directory's contents. Write access enables a user to create new files in the directory, effectively "writing" a new directory entry. Because directories can never be executed, the execute permission enables a program to search the contents of the directory. Without execution permissions, users can run a program in a directory only if they know the name.

The meaning of the bits within each set of three is partially determined by the kind of file. The left bit indicates the capability to read a file. The middle bit enables writing. The right bit enables the file to be executed, or in the case of a directory, the capability to move the current directory to that directory. A common user permission number of 755 indicates a file can be read or executed by anyone, but only the file's owner can make changes.

The following is a complete breakdown of the bits.

- 1 (octal 1)—Others execute
- 2 (octal 2)—Others write
- 4 (octal 4)—Others read
- 8 (octal 10)—Group execute

- `16` (octal 20)—Group write
- `32` (octal 40)—Group read
- `64` (octal 100)—User execute
- `128` (octal 200)—User write
- `256` (octal 400)—User read
- `512` (octal 1000)—Sticky bit
- `1024` (octal 2000)—Set `gid`
- `2048` (octal 4000)—Set `uid`

The `ls` command doesn't display the octal digits. Instead, it displays the list of bits, `-rwxrwxrwx`. When the letter appears, the corresponding bit is on. A minus sign indicates that the access right is turned off.

The actual Linux security model is much more complex with more types of ID numbers, but these don't affect shell scripting. The fourth and left-most permissions digit represents access rights for special programs and directories. These are covered in the section on `chmod`, later in this chapter. Normally, this digit is a zero.

The superuser, root, or `uid` 0 always has full access to all files.

Knowing Who You Are (`id`)

The Linux `id` command identifies your login name and group and any supplementary groups you belong to. The command displays both the names and the corresponding numbers.

```
$ id
uid=503(kburtch) gid=503(kburtch) groups=503(kburtch)
```

Any files created under the current session are owned by the `uid` and belong to the group `gid`.

```
$ touch temp.txt
$ ls -l temp.txt
-rw-rw-r—    1 kburtch  kburtch        0 Jun 25 11:45 temp.txt
```

The various ID switches hide parts of the information. The —user (or -u) switch prints only the `uid` information. The —group (or -g) switch prints only the group information. The —groups (or -G) switch prints only the supplementary groups information. The —real (or -r) switch displays real, instead of effective, `uid`s or `gid`s. The —name (or -n) switch displays only names, not the numeric values.

```
$ id —user —real —name
kburtch
```

Transferring Ownership (`chown`/`chgrp`)

The Linux `chown` (*change owner*) command changes the owner of a file. To use `chown`, you must be the owner of the file. Only root can use `chown` to change ownership. An ordinary user can use it to change the group, as long as the user is also a member of the target group.

The owner can either be a numeric `uid` or a name.

```
$ chown order_sys orders.txt
```

The `--reference` switch can copy the ownership from another file.

```
$ chown --reference=last_orders.txt orders.txt
```

For additional security in switches, the `--from` switch can verify the old owner before changing it to a new owner. The `--reference` and `--from` switches can't be combined in a single `chown`.

```
$ chown --from="kburtch" order_sys orders.txt
```

When a colon and a group name follow the owner, `chown` changes both the owner and the group. If the group part is missing, the group is set to the owner's group. If the owner part is missing, only the owner is changed. A group can also be specified in the `--from` switch using a colon.

```
$ chown order_sys:nogroup orders.txt
```

The `--recursive` (or `-R`) switch recursively changes files in subdirectories. The `--changes` (or `-c`) switch announces each change. The `--verbose` (or `-v`) switch provides even more information. The `--quiet` (or `--silent` or `-f`) switch hides error messages. The `--dereference` switch dereference symbolic links.

Use `chown` to determine who can access a script and its related files, minimizing the problems a hidden script problem can cause.

Avoid running scripts under the superuser login. A script running under the superuser login can change the owner of any file. However, if you find that you have to use the superuser login for a script that performs a task other than system administration, it is an indication that the ownership of the files is wrong. Change the owner of the files, or even create a new fictitious user to own the files, instead of running under the superuser login. Mistakes in a superuser script can be wide-ranging, very dangerous, and difficult to track down.

The Linux `chgrp` (*change group*) command is a short form for `chown :group`. `chgrp` changes only the ownership group.

Changing Access Rights (`chmod`)

Like `chown` to change file ownership, the Linux `chmod` (*change mode*) command changes a file's permissions. The name comes from the Linux term *file mode*, a number consisting of the permission bits and some other file information. Although the name suggests that the command can change any file mode settings, this command changes just the access rights.

The permissions can be expressed in two ways.

First, they can be represented by the four-digit octal permissions number.

```
$ touch orders.txt
$ ls -l orders.txt
-rw-r—r—   1 ken        users          0 May  9 12:48 orders.txt
$ chmod 0755 orders.txt
$ ls -l orders.txt
-rwxr-xr-x   1 ken        users          0 May  9 12:48 orders.txt
```

For those who are not used to octal numbers, permissions can be added with a plus sign, or removed with a minus sign. Permissions are grouped by user (u), group (g), others (o), or all (a) and can have read (r), write (w), or execute (x) permissions. Therefore, to add read permissions for the user and the file's group, you do this

```
$ chmod 0000 orders.txt
$ ls -l orders.txt
————   1 ken        users          0 May  9 12:48 orders.txt
$ chmod ug+r orders.txt
$ ls -l orders.txt
-r—r——   1 ken        users          0 May  9 12:48 orders.txt
```

To remove write permission from users who don't own the file and aren't in the same group, do this

```
$ chmod a+rwx orders.txt
$ ls -l orders.txt
-rwxrwxrwx   1 ken        users          0 May  9 12:48 orders.txt
$ chmod o-w orders.txt
$ ls -l orders.txt
-rwxrwxr-x   1 ken        users          0 May  9 12:48 orders.txt
```

An equals sign causes the permissions to be set to the specified values, rather than adding or subtracting them from the existing set. The letters u, g, and o refer to the current values of the user, group, and other access bits respectively. For example, g=u assigns the group permissions the same value as the user permissions.

```
$ chmod 0755 orders.txt
$ ls -l orders.txt
-rwxr-xr-x   1 ken        users          0 May  9 12:48 orders.txt
$ chmod g=u orders.txt
$ ls -l orders.txt
-rwxrwxr-x   1 ken        users          0 May  9 12:48 orders.txt
```

Another shorthand, the x symbol, assigns execute permissions only if the file is a directory or already has execute permissions for some user.

Besides r, w, and x, there are three special access bits that can be changed. These are all found in the left-most octal digit of the file permissions number: set uid or set gid (s), or the so-called "save program text on swap device" bit (t).

The t permission, commonly called the *sticky bit*, is used primarily for temporary file directories. Normally, only the owner of a file can delete a file. With the sticky bit set, the owner of the file or the owner of the directory the file is in can delete the file, making it easier to write temporary file clean-up scripts. Anyone can add files to a directory with the sticky bit set. The sticky bit has no meaning for other kinds of files; even though it can be set, it is ignored. On some other versions of Unix, the sticky bit has other meanings.

The effect of setting the setuid/setgid bits is described in the next section. These bits have no effect on shell scripts.

chmod does not change symbolic links. Linux ignores the permissions on a symbolic link and they always appear as 0777 permissions. The only access rights that matter are the permissions of the file that the symbolic link points to. If a file cannot be accessed, it also won't be accessed through a symbolic link.

The chmod switches are the same as the chown command, except there is no –from switch to verify old permissions.

If no g, o, or a appears, the permission is applied as if a was typed, except that only reasonable changes are allowed. What is a reasonable change? This is determined by the umask command.

Use chmod to qualify how the users with the right to access a file can change the file. The correct permissions should reflect how the file is to be used. If a file is infrequently updated, remove the write permission to protect against accidental changes. If a file is maintained by its owner and only read by its group, remove the group's permission to write. Files with 777 permissions are a sign of a sloppy programmer or the hasty work of a busy consultant.

In most cases, you don't want other users to have any access to the file; remove all access rights for other users. If you can't remove all access rights for other users, consider changing the file ownership.

Users who run a script should always be able to read it. Unlike a normal program, execute permission does not allow a user to run a script. Because Bash must load a script in order to execute it, scripts must be read. If you want a user to be able to run a script directly, without referring to the Bash program, include both execute and read rights.

Don't depend on the access rights of a directory to protect a file. There is always a chance that the file will move in the future; moving the file should not change the access to the data it contains.

Default Access Rights (umask)

Bash determines the default access rights to a file using the built-in umask command. The umask, or *user file creation mask*, is a number indicating which access rights are normally disallowed. Running umask by itself shows the current umask value as an octal number, and the -s switch shows which bits the umask allows.

```
$ touch newfile.txt
$ ls -l newfile.txt
-rw-rw-r—    1 kburtch  kburtch           0 May 22 11:34 newfile.txt
$ umask
0002
$ umask -S
u=rwx,g=rwx,o=rx
```

In this example, the umask is set to 2, meaning bit 2 (others can write to the file) should normally be off. The touch command gave all users read and write access except for other users who are not allowed to write.

You can create new umask values by specifying either an octal number or a permission string.

```
$ umask 0
$ rm newfile.txt
$ touch newfile.txt
$ ls -l newfile.txt
-rw-rw-rw-    1 kburtch  kburtch           0 May 22 11:40 newfile.txt
```

With a umask of 0 (everything allowed), the touch command created a file that can be written or read by anybody.

Honoring the umask command is strictly up to an individual script or command. There is nothing built into Bash that forces programs to check the umask value. In a script, applying umask is cumbersome because the umask and the permissions are in octal notation, but it can be done, as shown in Listing 15.1.

Listing 15.1 calculate_mode.sh

```
#!/bin/bash
#
# calculate_mode.sh: fragment showing how to honor the umask

DESIRED_MODE="$1"
# Convert from octal to decimal
DESIRED_MODE_DECIMAL=`printf "%d" 0"$DESIRED_MODE"`
# Get umask and convert to decimal
UMASK_DECIMAL=`printf "%d" \`umask\``
# Invert the bits in the umask so set bits are the allowed bits
let "UMASK_INVERT=~$UMASK_DECIMAL"
# Only allow bits that are allowed by the umask
```

Listing 15.1   **Continued**

```
let "EFFECTIVE_MODE=DESIRED_MODE_DECIMAL & UMASK_INVERT"
# Convert back to octal
MODE=`printf "%o" "$EFFECTIVE_MODE"`

printf "Desired mode = %s\n" "$DESIRED_MODE"
printf "Umask is = %s\n" `umask`
printf "Effective mode = %s\n" "$MODE"
```

The results for reading and writing by everyone with a umask of 2 is:

```
$ sh calculate_mode.sh 666
Desired mode = 666
Umask is = 0002
Effective mode = 664
```

If the umask -p switch is used, the umask prints the umask command needed to restore the current umask value.

setuid/setgid **and Scripts**

Sometimes a program has to perform actions on behalf of a number of people. For example, the Linux lp command prints files on behalf of the users on a computer. Rather than running the program under a particular user's ownership, the program can run under its own permissions, the permissions of its creator. To accomplish this, Linux provides setuid and setgid permissions. When these permissions are set, the program temporarily runs with the permissions of its creator instead of the person running it.

setuid and setgid permissions are necessary under certain circumstances, but they also introduce security loopholes. If there is a bug in the program, it can allow users to perform actions that bypass the normal system security. This is especially dangerous when a setuid or setgid program acts on behalf of the superuser.

In the case of Bash scripts, Bash ignores the setuid and setgid bits on a script. Scripts always run with the ownership of the user running the script. After all, a script is data, not a compiled program that runs as a certain owner.

If a script absolutely must run with setuid or setgid, you can create a short C language "wrapper" program to run the script, and then set setuid or setgid on the C program. When the wrapper program runs, it runs as the owner of the wrapper and then runs the Bash script.

There are two drawbacks to using wrapper programs. First, it is risky from a security viewpoint. Unless the script is serving the needs of a large number of users, setuid probably opens up access to too many people. It's easy to forget either the wrapper or the script when changing permissions. Scripts also are more sensitive than compiled programs to environment and PATH changes. For an alterative to a wrapper program, consider using the Linux sudo command.

Secondly, wrappers place extra load on the machine, because two programs must run instead of one. It's good practice to avoid wrappers unless they are absolutely necessary and apply as many security checks as possible.

The `chroot` Command

The Linux `chroot` command is available only to superuser scripts. `chroot` changes the apparent location of the root directory `/`. By moving the root directory, you can isolate the files a script can access to a particular branch of the file system.

`chroot` can be applied to a command. The command to be run must appear within the new directory structure, and the path should be relative to the new root directory.

```
$ chroot /home/kburtch ls /
```

In this example, `ls` refers to `/home/kburtch/ls`: `ls` must be in the `kburtch` directory.

It is now impossible for `ls` to access files outside of `/home/kburtch`. When the `/` is altered, there's no way to undo a `chroot` except by ending the session using the new root directory.

Without a command, `chroot` assumes there's a command called `/bin/sh` (usually a link to Bash) under the new root directory and attempts to start a new shell session. For example, this command

```
$ chroot /home/kburtch/
```

starts a new shell session by running `/home/kburtch/bin/sh`. The directory `/` now refers to `/home/kburtch/`. A reference to `/orders.txt` now refers to `/home/kburtch/orders.txt`.

`chroot` provides a measure of security for superuser scripts by limiting the directories that can be accessed. However, use care with `chroot`. In the previous examples, a script cannot access any Linux commands in `/usr/bin` because that directory can no longer be "seen." Any Linux commands required by the script have to be linked to a directory visible to the `chroot`-using script.

Resource Limits (`ulimit`)

The built-in `ulimit` command places limits on the resource usage of a script. Like `chroot`, this command places boundaries on the environment that a script is operating in. Resources refer to operating system limits such as the number of files that are allowed to be open or the maximum amount of memory a program can request.

The word `unlimited` indicates that there is no limit imposed. The `-a` switch displays a list of all resource limits.

```
$ ulimit -a
core file size          (blocks, -c) 0
data seg size           (kbytes, -d) unlimited
file size               (blocks, -f) unlimited
```

```
max locked memory      (kbytes, -l) unlimited
max memory size        (kbytes, -m) unlimited
open files                    (-n) 1024
pipe size          (512 bytes, -p) 8
stack size             (kbytes, -s) unlimited
cpu time              (seconds, -t) unlimited
max user processes            (-u) 1024
virtual memory         (kbytes, -v) unlimited
```

Individual switches specify specific resources:

- -c—Maximum size of core files
- -d—Maximum size of a process's data segment
- -f—Maximum size of shell-created files
- -l—Maximum amount of memory that can be locked
- -m—Maximum resident set size
- -n—Maximum number of open file descriptors
- -p—Pipe size (cannot be set)
- -s—Maximum stack size
- -t—Maximum CPU time
- -u—Maximum number of processes for a single user
- -v—Maximum amount of virtual memory available to the shell

Each resource has both a maximum *hard limit,* and a current *soft limit*, which can be any amount up to the maximum. For example, the stack size can have both a hard and soft limit. You can check these limits with the -H (*hard limit*) and -S (*soft limit*) switches.

```
$ ulimit -H -s
unlimited
$ ulimit -S -s
8192
```

The stack size here is limited to 8K, but it can be changed to any number of bytes. To change a limit, supply a new value to the ulimit command

```
$ ulimit -S -s 16384
$ ulimit -S -s
16384
```

The special values, hard and soft, refer to the current hard or soft limit. Use them to copy one limit to the other limit.

```
$ ulimit -H -s soft
$ ulimit -H -s
16384
```

Restricted Shells

Bash enters restricted mode when it starts with the name rbash or when the -r option is supplied when Bash runs. A restricted shell prevents a script or user from creating or accessing files outside of the current directory. In particular, a restricted shell has the following restrictions:

- No changing directories with cd
- No setting or unsetting the values of SHELL, PATH, ENV, or BASH_ENV
- No specifying command names containing /
- No specifying a filename containing a / (slash) as an argument to the built-in command
- No specifying a filename containing a slash as an argument to the -p option to the hash built-in command
- No parsing the value of SHELLOPTS from the shell environment at startup
- No redirecting output using the >, >|, <>, >&, &>, and >> redirection operators
- No using the exec built-in command to replace the shell with another command
- No adding or deleting built-in commands with the -f and -d options to the enable built-in command
- No specifying the p option to the built-in command
- No turning off restricted mode with set +r or set +o restricted
- No exporting of shell functions

Otherwise, a restricted Bash shell operates the same as a normal shell. These restrictions are enforced after any start-up files are read, so the profile files can set up the user's environment without restrictions. The only exception is that function definitions can't be imported at startup.

```
$ bash -r
$ cd ..
bash: cd: restricted
$ echo $DATE > temp.txt
bash: temp.txt: restricted: cannot redirect output
$ NOW=`date`
$ printf "%s\n" "$NOW"
Thu Jul  5 16:59:28 EDT 2001
$ exit
exit
```

Restricted shells are very confining but provide a high level of security. When used in script programming, redirect standard output and standard error prior to running the restricted script because the script itself cannot redirect standard output.

Secure File Deletion (`wipe`)

The `rm` command removes a file by deleting the directory entry, but the old information is still available on the disk until a new file overwrites it. Normally, this information is not accessible except at the device driver level. However, for critical information that must never be read, this might not be acceptable.

The `wipe` utility first overwrites all the information in a file with random data and then deletes the file like the `rm` command does. Nothing remains on the disk that can be read by an unscrupulous person.

```
$ ls
logins.txt
$ wipe logins.txt
$ ls
$
```

The `-s` switch wipes quietly (not the usual `-q`). `-r` wipes all subdirectories. `-D` wipes the data but keeps the file. For faster wiping, `-z` fills the file with zeros instead of random data. `-b` overwrites the file using a specific character. There are a few other `wipe` switches, primarily related to how the random data is generated.

Use `wipe` with caution. If a device file, such as a hard disk partition, is specified instead of a file, `wipe` attempts to erase the entire partition.

All shell script programmers need to pay careful attention to security concerns. They not only keep important programs and data safe, but they limit the amount of damage a script mistake can cause.

Reference Section

`id` **Command Switches**

- —`group` (or `-g`)—Prints only the group ID
- —`groups` (or `-G`)—Prints only the supplementary groups
- —`name` (or `-n`)—Prints a name instead of a number; for `-ugG`
- —`real` (or `-r`)—Prints the real ID instead of the effective ID; for `-ugG`
- —`user` (or `-u`)—Prints only the user ID

`chown` **Command Switches**

- —`changes` (or `-c`)—Is verbose whenever changes occur
- —`dereference`—Follows symbolic links
- —`no-dereference` (or `-h`)—Affects symbolic links instead of any referenced file

- —quiet (or -f or —silent)—Suppresses most error messages
- —reference=*f*—Uses the owner and group of file *f*
- —recursive (or -R)—Operates on files and directories recursively

chmod **Command Switches**

- —changes (or -c)—Like verbose, but reports only when a change is made
- —quiet (or -f or —silent)—Suppresses most error messages
- —recursive (or -R)—Changes files and directories recursively
- —reference=*f*—Uses file *f* for mode values
- —verbose (or -v)—Outputs a diagnostic for every file processed

ulimit **Command Switches**

- -c—Maximum size of core files
- -d—Maximum size of a process's data segment
- -t—Maximum size of shell-created files
- -l—Maximum amount of memory that can be locked
- -m—Maximum resident set size
- -n—Maximum number of open file descriptors
- -p—Pipe size (cannot be set)
- -s—Maximum stack size
- t—Maximum CPU time
- -u—Maximum number of processes for a single user
- -v—Maximum amount of virtual memory available to the shell

wipe **Command Switches**

- -B*size*—Overridesblock device sector count
- -b—Custom byte; overwrites once with a specific byte
- -D—Keeps after wiping
- -d—Keeps after wiping
- -E—Uses the random char device; disables tiger hash
- -e—Uses the tiger hash function
- -f—Forces file wiping and suppresses permission warnings

- -I—Disables interaction
- -i—Prompts whether to remove each file
- -L—Sets wipe secure level to 0
- -p *cnt*—Performs wipe sequence *cnt* times, including random passes
- -r (or -R)—Repeats process for all files in any subdirectories
- -S*size*—Sets byte size for block device sector size (defaults to 512)
- -s—Disables percent reporting and some warnings
- -V—Shows percentage if file size is above a certain limit
- -v—Always shows percentage
- -T*size*—Block device buffer size (defaults to 4096)
- -t*size*—Sets tiger hash input buffer size
- -x*cnt*—Enables random passes and (optionally) number of passes to perform
- -X—Disables random passes
- -Z—Overrides -z
- -z—Zeros out the file (fills it with zeros)
- -l*num* (*vertical bar*)—Sets generic security level to *num*

16

Network Programming

"SO YOU'RE KEN BURTCH?" he said with a smile that wasn't pleasant. The Sun computer dealer shook my hand.

At the time, a friend and I were running the first Internet news and email service in the Niagara Falls region. Looking for a secondary Usenet feed, we approached the Sun dealer to see whether they would let us network with their computers. We emailed several times but received no response. The mystery was solved as the dealer explained that he had set up a Usenet feed and emailed us the connection information. Unfortunately, he didn't realize that his emails were being routed along with the news, awaiting our computer to connect, and so we never received his messages. A simple communication's oversight left him with a bad impression.

Networking is a very complex issue because, by its nature, it requires intricate communications over uncertain channels. Fortunately, Bash takes care of most of the details, thus making enterprise-wide scripts easy to write and use.

Sockets

To communicate over a network, two programs must follow a communications protocol. The protocol defines how to respond new connections, how to acknowledge the safe arrival of the data over the network, what to do when a connection is unexpectedly terminated, and so forth. Sending files across a network is a much more unreliable procedure than saving files to a hard drive.

Each computer on a network is designated an IP number and one or more hostnames. Hostnames can often be aliases for the same machine. You can look up the IP number of the machine a hostname refers to by using the host command.

```
$ host www.vaxxine.com
www.vaxxine.com is a nickname for alpha.vaxxine.com
alpha.vaxxine.com has address 209.5.212.5
alpha.vaxxine.com has address 209.5.212.5
```

The -v switch produces a copy of the domain master file. Specific information can be requested by the -t switch—there are many options for t.

localhost is an alias in Linux for the current computer on all Linux systems.

Connections between machines are referred to as *sockets*. The name dates back to the early 1980s when they were first used with BSD Unix. The term symbolizes two imaginary connectors on separate computers. When a connection is established (picture a cable connected to the sockets), the two computers can communicate.

The primary protocol of the Internet and many local area networks (LANs) is *TCP/IP* (Transport Control Protocol/Internet Protocol). You can open network TCP/IP sockets in Bash using a special /dev/tcp pathname. This is not the location of an actual file: Bash interprets this pathname as a request to open a socket.

Bash can also create UDP (User Datagram Protocol) sockets using /dev/udp pathnames. However, UDP is used to send short messages that might not arrive at their destination and isn't covered in this chapter.

In addition to the protocol, sockets require a *port*. Ports are numbers used to identify different services on the remote computer. Different programs listen to different port numbers, waiting for new connections. Although there's no requirement that a particular service be available on a particular port, some services are given traditional port numbers. Web servers, for example, are usually assigned to port number 80. This is the port Web browsers connect to by default.

Bash takes care of most of the details of opening and maintaining sockets. To a Bash script, a socket is a regular file with an unusual pathname. Sockets act like named pipes, blocking until there is new information to read. When a socket is closed, the read command indicates that the end of the file has been reached. Unlike pipes, sockets are always both readable and writable.

Client–Server and Peer-to-Peer

Although the networking protocol sets up the rules for communication, they impose no strictures on the messages exchanged between two computers. If a socket is opened between two computers and both wait for the other to send the first message, the programs will wait indefinitely. To resolve this problem, there are two common networking strategies—client-server and peer-to-peer.

The most common strategy is *client-server*. One program is designated the *server*. It "serves up" data upon request. The other program is the *client,* and it makes the requests. Web servers and browsers are an example of a client-server pair. The Web browser always initiates the conversation with the server.

Alternatively, the *peer-to-peer* (or P2P) strategy has both a client and a server integrated into a single program, typically by assigning the client and server functions to separate ports. Each program can receive requests or make them. Because all programs are considered equal (or "peers") and there is no single server acting as overseer to the data being shared, this strategy is useful for sharing a large task or data across several computers operating in parallel.

Client–server is the most common method of networking because of its simplicity. The server, like a Bash function, hides all the complexity of finding and processing the data returned to the client.

Bash scripts can only be written as clients because there is no way to configure Bash to listen for incoming connections on a given port.

Network Clients

Network connections are always opened as readable and writable files (<>). The pathnames beginning with /dev/tcp open TCP/IP connections. Follow the pathname with the host and port numbers. For example, to open a connection to the Web server on the current computer, do this

```
$ exec 3<> /dev/tcp/localhost/80
```

Suppose a Web server is running on the current computer on port 8080. (Port 8080 is the standard port for running a Web server under a personal account.) A connection can be opened for read and write with exec and the default Web page retrieved, as shown in Listing 16.1.

Listing 16.1 getpage.sh

```
#!/bin/bash
#
# getpage.sh - get a web page
#
shopt -o -s nounset

declare LINE
declare -rx SCRIPT=${0##*/}

# Open an HTML socket to the localhost
# For both read and write

printf "Connecting to host\n"
exec 3<> /dev/tcp/localhost/8080

# Send the HTTP request to retrieve the default page

printf "Sending request to host\n"
printf "%s HTTP/1.0\r\n" "GET /" >&3
printf "Accept: text/html, text/plain\r\n" >&3
printf "Accept-Language: en\r\n" >&3
printf "User-Agent: %s (Bash Script)\r\n" "$SCRIPT" >&3
printf "\r\n" >&3
```

Listing 16.1 **Continued**

```
# Read the response and display it on the screen

printf "Receiving page\n"
printf "%s\n" "——————————"
while read LINE <&3 ; do
   printf "%s\n" "$LINE"
done

exit 0
```

Running this script retrieves and displays the Web page.

```
$ bash getpage.sh
Connecting to host
Sending request to host
Receiving page
——————————
HTTP/1.0 200 Document follows
Date: Wed, 04 Jul 2001 18:26:27 GMT
Server: NCSA/1.5.2
Last-modified: Tue, 22 Aug 2000 18:33:31 GMT
Content-type: text/html
Content-length: 108

<html>
<head>
<title>Test Page</title>
<body>
This is the home page for Widgits Inc.
</body>
</html>
```

Other network services such as Telnet and SMTP can be accessed the same way.

CGI Scripting

CGI (Common Gateway Interface) scripts are programs run by a Web server. Information is given to the script through environment variables and standard input and the script responds by returning a Web page or document to standard output.

CGI scripts must be placed in a special directory (usually called cgi-bin). Having a standard directory keeps all the scripts in a central location and prevents unauthorized people from posting scripts as well as Web pages. Your Web server has to be configured to allow CGI scripts if it is not so already. The script files end with .cgi instead of .sh or .bash to differentiate them from general-purpose scripts.

A CGI script must write a proper HTTP Web server response (or header) before returning any information. The shortest header is a content line describing the kind of data being returned to the Web browser, followed by a blank line. The content is either text/plain for pure text or text/html for a Web page. For example, to return simple text, use this

```
printf "Content-type: text/plain \r\n"
printf "\r\n"
```

Like the HTTP client example, Web servers expect all lines to end in a carriage return and line feed rather than a simple line feed. Data appearing after the header doesn't have to be formatted with the extra carriage return character.

Listing 16.2 shows a short CGI script that runs the env command and returns a list of environment variables to a Web browser.

Listing 16.2   env.cgi

```
#!/bin/bash
#
# env.cgi - display the environment variables available to a CGI program
#
shopt -s -o nounset

declare -rx SCRIPT=${0##*/}
declare GATEWAY_INTERFACE

if [ -z "GATEWAY_INTERFACE" ] ; then
   printf "%s\n" "$SCRIPT: this script should be run by a web browser" >&2
   exit 192
fi

# Write Response Header

printf "Content-type: text/plain\r\n"
printf "\r\n"

# Generate text message to Return

env

exit 0
```

Because CGI scripts run under a unique environment, it is difficult to test them from the command line. Instead, store them in the cgi-bin directory and attempt to run the script through the Web browser. The most common errors are listed here:

- 403 Forbidden—The script permissions are wrong or the script is not in a CGI directory
- 404 Not Found—The CGI script was missing or the wrong URL was used.
- 500 Internal Server Error—The script didn't return a proper CGI header.

The server error is the most common error. This occurs when the script stops with an error before it is able to write the HTTP header. Any messages written to standard error appear in the Web server's error log. If a Web page returned has missing or incorrect information, check the Web server log for errors.

Because it's inconvenient to check the Web server error log, the CGI script should attempt to capture any errors and display them through standard output on the Web page.

To return a Web page instead, change the content to text/html. When displaying errors using a Web page, make sure the font and colors are set to reasonable values so that the errors are clearly visible. In Listing 16.3, errors are displayed in a white box with black print at the bottom of the page.

Listing 16.3 html_env.cgi

```
#!/bin/bash
#
# html_env.cgi - display the environment variables given to a CGI program

shopt -s -o nounset

# Declarations

declare -rx SCRIPT=${0##*/}
declare GATEWAY_INTERFACE
if [ -z "GATEWAY_INTERFACE" ] ; then
    printf "%s\n" "$SCRIPT: this script should be run by a web browser" >&2
    exit 192
fi
declare -rx ERRORS=`mktemp /tmp/env_errors.XXXXXX`
if [ -z "$ERRORS" ] ; then
    ERRORS="/tmp/env_errors.$$"
    printf "%s\n" "mktemp failed" 2> "$ERRORS"
fi

# Write Response Header

printf "Content-type: text/html\r\n"
```

```
printf "\r\n"

# Write HTML Header

printf "<html>"
printf "<head>"
printf "<title>$SCRIPT results</title>"
printf "</head>"
printf "<body>"
printf "<h1>$SCRIPT results</h1>"

# Generate Web Page to Return

printf "<pre>"
env 2> $ERRORS

printf "</pre>"

# Display any errors

if test -s "$ERRORS" ; then
  printf " <br />"
  printf "<table border=\"1\" summary=\"error\">"
  printf "<tr bgcolor=\"white\"><td>"
  printf "<font color=\"black\" size=\"3\">"
  printf "<p><b>Error(s)</b>:<br />"
  printf "<pre>"
  cat "$ERRORS"
  printf "</pre>"
  printf " <br />"
  printf "<i>If the problem persists, contact tech support.</i></p>"
  printf "</font></td></tr></table>"
  rm -f "$ERRORS"
fi

# Write HTML Trailer

printf " <br /><h6>"
printf "Host %s - Script %s - Time " "$HOSTNAME" "$SCRIPT"
date
printf "</h6>"
printf "</body>"
printf "</html>"

exit 0
```

CGI Environment Variables

CGI programs have additional environment variables assigned by the Web server. Different Web servers include different variables. Here is a list of some common variables:

- `AUTH_TYPE`—Authorization type if pages are password protected
- `CONTENT_LENGTH`—Number of bytes being written to standard input (for `POST` forms)
- `CONTENT_TYPE`—The form's content type
- `DOCUMENT_ROOT`—The root directory of the Web server's document tree
- `GATEWAY_INTERFACE`—The version of the CGI standard being used by the Web server
- `HTTP_ACCEPT`—Types of data acceptable to the browser (for example, `text/html`)
- `HTTP_ACCEPT_CHARSET`—Character set requested by the Web browser
- `HTTP_ACCEPT_ENCODING`—Compression methods allowed by the Web browser (for example, `gzip`)
- `HTTP_ACCEPT_LANGUAGE`—Language requested by the Web browser (for example, `en for English`)
- `HTTP_USER_AGENT`—The browser used by the user
- `HTTP_HOST`—The URL's hostname
- `HTTP_REFERER`—The Web page executing this CGI program
- `PATH_INFO`—Extra information included in the URL
- `PATH_TRANSLATED`—`PATH_INFO`, as a file/directory under the root of the document tree
- `QUERY_STRING`—For `GET` forms, the variables on the form
- `REMOTE_ADDR`—IP of the user's computer
- `REMOTE_HOST`—Hostname of the user's computer
- `REMOTE_USER`—Username used when accessing password-protected pages
- `REQUEST_METHOD`—Usually `GET` or `POST`
- `SCRIPT_NAME`—Pathname of the script being executed
- `SCRIPT_FILENAME`—The absolute pathname of the script being executed
- `SERVER_ADDR`—IP address of the Web server
- `SERVER_ADMIN`—Email address to email messages to the person in charge of the Web server
- `SERVER_NAME`—Domain name of the Web server

- `SERVER_PORT`—The TCP/IP port used to connect to the Web server
- `SERVER_PROTOCOL`—Version of HTTP used by the server
- `SERVER_SOFTWARE`—Description of the Web server

Processing Forms

The HTML equivalent of environment variables is the form. Each form contains a set of variables. For example, the form input tag

```
<input type 'hidden" name="user" value="bsmith">
```

is the HTML equivalent of

```
declare user="bsmith"
```

Other nonhidden input tags represent variables whose values can be changed by the user through items on the form. Such items include buttons, menus, and text boxes. In all these cases, the choices made by the user are saved as new values of the variable before the form is sent to a CGI script.

Because the CGI script doesn't receive a copy of the Web page, how then does it know the values of the input tags? There are two methods. The older GET method stores the HTML variables in an environment variable called QUERY_STRING. Consider the following form.

```
<html>
<head>
<title>Form Test</title>
</head>
<body>
<form action="http://localhost/cgi-bin/form.cgi>
<input type="hidden" name="user" value="bsmith">
<input type="submit" name="submit" value="Click Me!">
</form>
</body>
</html>
```

The query string contains the names and values of the two variables.

```
user=bsmith&submit=Click+Me%21
```

One of the reasons forms are difficult to work with is that the information is encoded. The standard form encoding (x-www-form-urlencoded) converts spaces to plus signs and non-alphanumeric characters to ASCII hexadecimal numbers with leading percent signs. In this case, the exclamation point is converted to hexadecimal 21.

The POST method writes the variables to standard input, eliminating the risk of a buffer overflow in the Web server if the list of variables becomes very long. It also keeps the variables off of the Web page URL. If a script reads the variables in a while loop, the final line is not executed in the while because the line doesn't end in a line feed.

```
while read LINE ; do
  echo "$LINE<br />"
done
echo "$LINE<br />"
```

This displays the same encoded information that appears in QUERY_STRING when the GET method is used.

```
user=bsmith&submit=Click+Me%21
```

The form.cgi script shown in Listing 16.4 decodes and displays the form variables.

Listing 16.4   form.cgi
_____

```
#!/ /bin/bash

#
# form.cgi - decode and display all variables in a form

shopt -s -o nounset

# DECODE: decode all variables in $1 and display them

function decode {
  declare VARIABLES="$1"       # the list of variables to process
  declare VAR                  # variable to decode
  declare NAME                 # variable name
  declare VALUE                # value of variable
  declare LAST                 # last decoded variable
  declare -i CNT=1             # running total of variables processed
  declare PART1                # part before % hex code
  declare PART2                # part after a % hex code
  declare TMP
  declare REMAINING            # remaining variables to process
  declare HEX                  # ASCII code as hexadecimal
  declare OCT                  # ASCII code as octal

  # Replace '+' with ' '

  VARIABLES="${VARIABLES//+/ }"

  # Hex code replacement

  while true ; do
    LAST="$VAR"                              # remember last variable
    VAR="${VARIABLES##*\&}"                  # extract next variable
    REMAINING="${VARIABLES%\&*}"             # variables left to process
    NAME="${VAR%=*}"                         # variable's name is before =
```

```
       VALUE="${VAR##*=}"                     # variable's encoded value is after =

     # Process any hex values

     while true ; do
       PART1="${VALUE%\%*}"               # value before last %
       if [ "$PART1" = "$VALUE" ] ; then  # same as whole value?
          break                           # then no % left
       fi
       TMP="${VALUE##*\%}"                # value after last %
       HEX="${TMP:0:2}"                   # extract two digit hex code
       PART2="${TMP:2}"                   # value after the hex code
       VALUE="$PART1"`printf "\x$HEX"`"$PART2"  # combine, replacing hex code
     done
     printf "Var %d %s is '%s'\n" "$CNT" "$NAME" "$VALUE" # display variable
     if [ "$REMAINING" = "$VARIABLES" ] ; then      # remaining same as last?
        printf "%s\n" "<br />"                       # all variables done
        printf "%s\n" "End of CGI variables<br />" # display end message
        break
     fi
     VARIABLES="$REMAINING"                # do remaining variables
     CNT=CNT+1                             # increment count
  done

} # end of decode
readonly -f decode
declare -t decode

# Declarations

declare -rx SCRIPT=${0##*/}
declare GATEWAY_INTERFACE
if [ -z "GATEWAY_INTERFACE" ] ; then
   printf "%s\n" "$SCRIPT: this script should be run by a web browser" >&2
   exit 192
fi
declare -rx ERRORS=`mktemp /tmp/env_errors.XXXXXX`
if [ -z "$ERRORS" ] ; then
   ERRORS="/tmp/env_errors.$$"
   printf "%s\n" "mktemp failed" 2> "$ERRORS"
fi
declare QUERY_STRING              # ensure QUERY_STRING exists
declare REQUEST_METHOD            # ensure REQUEST_METHOD exists

# Write Response Header
```

Listing 16.4   **Continued**

```
printf "Content-type: text/html\r\n"
printf "\r\n"

# Write HTML Header

printf "<html>"
printf "<head>"
printf "<title>$SCRIPT results</title>"
printf "</head>"
printf "<body>"
printf "<h1>$SCRIPT results</h1>"

# For POST, read the data into QUERY_STRING
# Otherwise, variables are already in QUERY_STRING

if [ "$REQUEST_METHOD" = "POST" ] ; then
   while read LINE ; do
      QUERY_STRING="$QUERY_STRING""$LINE"
   done
   QUERY_STRING="$QUERY_STRING""$LINE"
fi

# Generate Web Page to Return

# Display original, encoded variables

echo "Processing: $QUERY_STRING<br />"

printf "<pre>"

decode "$QUERY_STRING" 2> "$ERRORS"

printf "</pre>"

# Display any errors

if test -s "$ERRORS" ; then
  printf " <br />"
  printf "<table border=\"1\" summary=\"error\">"
  printf "<tr bgcolor=\"white\"><td>"
  printf "<font color=\"black\" size=\"3\">"
  printf "<p><b>Error(s)</b>:<br />"
  printf "<pre>"
  cat "$ERRORS"
  printf "</pre>"
```

```
  printf " <br />"
  printf "<i>If the problem persists, contact tech support.</i></p>"
  printf "</font></td></tr></table>"
  rm -f "$ERRORS"
fi

# Write HTML Trailer

printf " <br /><h6>"
printf "Host %s - Script %s - Time " "$HOSTNAME" "$SCRIPT"
date
printf "</h6>"
printf "</body>"
printf "</html>\n"

exit 0
```

Run `form.cgi` with the form in Listing 16.5 to see a list of variables from the form and the decoded values.

Suppose you had a form to send a message to the tech support department.

Listing 16.5   `form.html`

```
<html>
<head>
<title>Form Test</title>
</head>
<body>
<h1>Ask Tech Support Question</h1>
<form action="http://localhost/cgi-bin/form.cgi>
<input type="submit" name="submit" value="Send Question">
<input type="textarea" name="message" value="" maxlength="80">
<input type="text" name="name" value="" maxlen="80">
</form>
</body>
</html>
```

When the form is submitted to `form.cgi`, the `decode` function reports:

```
Var 1 submit is 'Send Question'
Var 2 message is 'When will the email system
upgrade occur?

`

Var 3 name is 'Alice Q. Walters'

End of CGI variables
```

The script works for both GET and POST forms. Figure 16.1 shows a picture of the tech support example.

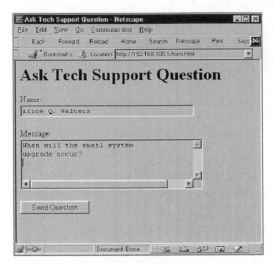

Figure 16.1   The Ask Tech Support form.

Basic Web Page Stripping (lynx)

Vast amounts of information are available in Web pages on the Internet. Headlines can be pulled from news sites. Prices can be stripped from competitor's sites. Much of this information is publicly available and accessible from shell scripts.

The easiest way to access this information is through lynx, the text Web browser available on most Linux distributions. lynx has two modes for retrieving data for script processing. The -source switch returns the HTML source code for the Web page just as if you used the View Source option on a graphical Web browser.

```
$ lynx -source http://www.pegasoft.ca | head -10
<?xml version="1.0"?>
<!DOCTYPE html PUBLIC "-//W3C//DTD XHTML 1.0 Transitional//EN"
    "http://www.w3.org/TR/xhtml1/DTD/xhtml1-transitional.dtd">
<html xmlns="http://www.w3.org/1999/xhtml">
<head>
<meta name="generator" content="HTML Tidy, see www.w3.org" />
<meta http-equiv="Content-Type"
content="text/html; charset=iso-8859-1" />
<meta name="description" content="Linux Software Solutions" />
<meta name="keywords"
```

You can get the same effect by opening a socket with Bash and sending the appropriate HTTP commands. However, the browser can take care of Web server issues like cookies and Web site aliases for you.

The -source switch is useful when a Web page contains many kinds of information. For example, you can search HTML tags and identify headlines on a news site by looking for the fonts and styles of headline text.

The -dump switch returns a rendered version of the Web page. On Web pages with simple content, this switch hides the HTML tags, thus making the page easier to work with. Normally, lynx footnotes all the links on a Web page, but you can hide these with the —no-list switch.

```
$  lynx -dump —no-list http://www.pegasoft.ca
   REFRESH(10 sec): http://www.pegasoft.ca/frames.html


                       PegaSoft Canada

           Your computer takes flight with PegaSoft


                            —-



   PegaSoft Home  Welcome to the PegaSoft's home
    Most people click here
   Basic Site  Same Site, Less Filling
    No music or Java
   Pegasoft Portal  The Start Page for Linux Professionals
    News, weather, categories, more


                    Please select a site
                  Veuillez choisir un site
                Wählen Sie bitte eine Site aus
                 Seleccione por favor un sitio


   The full site will automatically be chosen after a few seconds
   _____


   PegaSoft logo  Copyright © 1998-2003 PegaSoft Canada. All Rights
                            Reserved.
```

Using the -source option, you can check the official time on the National Research Council of Canada's (NRCC) Web site. The time is the first line on the Web page containing UTC.

```
$  lynx -dump http://time5.nrc.ca/webclock_e.shtml | grep UTC | head -1
                            15:45:55 UTC
```

The script shown in Listing 16.6 strips the official time from the NRCC and compares it to the time on the local computer.

Listing 16.6 `compare_time.sh`

```
#!/bin/bash
#
# compare_time.sh: compare our time against National Research
# Council of Canada's atomic clock.

shopt -s -o nounset

# Global declarations

declare -rx SCRIPT=${0##*/}          # name of our script
declare -rx lynx="/usr/bin/lynx"     # lynx command
declare -rx date="/bin/date"         # data command

declare   OUR_TIME                   # our time as reported by date(1)
declare   TIME_PAGE                  # the content of the NRCC web page
declare   TIME_LINE                  # the page line with the time on it
declare   OFFICIAL_TIME              # the correct time from the line

declare -rx NRCC="time5.nrc.ca/webclock_e.shtml"  # NRCC web site

# Sanity Check

if test ! -x "$date" ; then
  printf "$SCRIPT: the command $date is not available — aborting\n" >&1
  exit 192
fi
if test ! -x "$lynx" ; then
  printf "$SCRIPT: the command $lynx is not available — aborting\n" >&1
  exit 192
fi

# Get the Time

OUR_TIME=`$date —universal '+%H:%M:%S'`
TIME_PAGE=`$lynx -dump -nolist "http://$NRCC"`
if [ -z "$TIME_PAGE" ] ; then
  printf "$SCRIPT: the web page $NRCC has moved — aborting\n" >&1
  exit 192
fi
TIME_LINE=`printf "%s\n" "$TIME_PAGE" | grep UTC | head -1`
if [ -z "$TIME_PAGE" ] ; then
  printf "$SCRIPT: the format of the web page $NRCC has changed —\
```

```
  aborting\n" >&1
    exit 192
fi
OFFICIAL_TIME=`printf "%s\n" "$TIME_LINE" | sed 's/\ //g;s/UTC//g'`

# Display time

printf "Note: This script doesn't take into account Internet delays\n"
printf "Our computer time = %s UTC\n" "$OUR_TIME"
printf "Official UTC time = %s UTC\n" "$OFFICIAL_TIME"

exit 0
```

The content and addresses of Web pages are prone to change. When stripping Web pages, take care to verify that the page hasn't moved and the content hasn't changed. The compare_time.sh script checks both that lynx retrieved the Web page and that the timeline containing the time was actually found by grep. If the Web page has changed location, you can find it again using a search engine such as Google.

Running the script shows a side-by-side comparison between the NRCC time and the time on your local computer.

```
$ bash compare_time.sh
Note: This script doesn't take into account Internet delays
Our computer time = 14:55:56 UTC
Official UTC time = 14:56:51 UTC
```

For more information on lynx, visit http://lynx.browser.org.

Reference Section

host **Command Switches**

- -a—Equivalent to -v -t *
- -c—Class to look for non-Internet data
- -d—Turns on debugging
- -l—Turns on list mode
- -r—Disables recursive processing
- -s—Recursively chases a signature found in answers
- -t *q*—Query type *q* to look for a specific type of information
- -v—Verbose output
- -w—Waits forever until reply

Common CGI Variables

- `AUTH_TYPE`—Authorization type if pages are password-protected
- `CONTENT_LENGTH`—Number of bytes being written to standard input (for POST forms)
- `CONTENT_TYPE`—The form's content type
- `DOCUMENT_ROOT`—The root directory of the Web server's document tree
- `GATEWAY_INTERFACE`—The version of the CGI standard being used by the Web server
- `HTTP_ACCEPT`—Types of data acceptable to the browser (for example, `text/html`)
- `HTTP_ACCEPT_CHARSET`—Character set requested by the Web browser
- `HTTP_ACCEPT_ENCODING`—Compression methods allowed by the Web browser (for example, `gzip`)
- `HTTP_ACCEPT_LANGUAGE`—Language requested by the Web browser (for example, `en` for English)
- `HTTP_USER_AGENT`—The browser used by the user
- `HTTP_HOST`—The URL's hostname
- `HTTP_REFERER`—The Web page executing this CGI program
- `PATH_INFO`—Extra information included in the URL
- `PATH_TRANSLATED`—`PATH_INFO`, as a file/directory under the root of the document tree
- `QUERY_STRING`—For GET forms, the variables on the form
- `REMOTE_ADDR`—IP of the user's computer
- `REMOTE_HOST`—Hostname of the user's computer
- `REMOTE_USER`—Username used when accessing password-protected pages
- `REQUEST_METHOD`—Usually GET or POST
- `SCRIPT_NAME`—Pathname of the script being executed
- `SCRIPT_FILENAME`—The absolute pathname of the script being executed
- `SERVER_ADDR`—IP address of the Web server
- `SERVER_ADMIN`—Email address to email messages to the person in charge of the Web server
- `SERVER_NAME`—Domain name of the Web server
- `SERVER_PORT`—The TCP/IP port used to connect to the Web server
- `SERVER_PROTOCOL`—Version of HTTP used by the server
- `SERVER_SOFTWARE`—Description of the Web server

`lynx` **Page-Stripping Switches**

- `-auth=id:pw`—Authenticates protected documents with login `id` and password `pw`
- `-base`—Prefixes a BASE tag to output for `-source` dumps
- `-buried_news`—Searches for other article references in news articles (default is on)
- `-cmd_script=f`—Input comes from file `f`
- `-connect_timeout=n`—Seconds to timeout connection (default is 18000)
- `-crawl`—Outputs each page to a file (with `-dump`) or formats output to `stdout`
- `-dont_wrap_pre`—Inhibits wrapping of text in `<pre>` (the default is off)
- `-dump`—Dumps the file to `stdout` and exits
- `-get_data`—User data for GET forms, read from `stdin`, and terminated by `--` on a line
- `-image_links`—Toggles inclusion of links for all images (default is off)
- `-link=n`—Starting cfile name for `-crawl` `lnk.dat` files (default is 0)
- `-mime_header`—Includes MIME headers and forces source dump
- `-nolist`—Disables the link list feature in dumps (default is off)
- `-noredir`—Doesn't follow Web server Location: redirection (default is off)
- `-pauth=id:pw`—Like `-auth` but for proxy Web servers
- `-post_data`—User data for POST forms, read from `stdin`, and terminated by `--` on a line
- `-reload`—Clears the cache on a proxy server (default is off)
- `-source`—Dumps the source of the file to `stdout` and exits
- `-stdin`—Reads the start file from standard input
- `-tlog`—Toggles use of a `lynx` trace log for the current session (default is on)
- `-trace`—Turns on `lynx` trace mode (default is off)
- `-traversal`—Traverses all HTTP links derived from the start file
- `-useragent=b`—Masquerades as browser `b`
- `-width=n`—Screen width for formatting of dumps (default is 80)
- `-with_backspaces`—Emits backspaces in output if `-dumping` or `-crawling` (default is off)

17

Data Structures and Databases

I ALWAYS SAID THAT I WOULD RATHER die than work in a tiny, windowless office with a green monochrome terminal. Of course, the first job I had after university featured just that, except the monochrome terminal was amber instead of green.

While I was pondering a taxation problem in the custom-built BASIC software that company used, I got a buzz on my phone and the president asked me to come to his office. His office, of course, had windows. The president had written much of the software in his early days and he motioned me to come over to his terminal. "Look at this," he said. "Here is an array of nine numbers. I turned it into a two-dimensional 3x3 array by multiplying one index by three and adding a second index! Pretty slick, huh?"

Having graduated from university with straight A's, I suppressed a yawn and said, "Oh, yes, sir. You are very clever."

It was my first introduction to the fact that most software in that company and every other company I ever worked at was written at a high school programming level. Hash tables and binary trees are considered dangerously elaborate and unnecessarily risky, even though they save time and money. Multimillion dollar corporations rely on flat files and simple arrays—things that the boss will understand and are, therefore, safe. If the software is slow and clunky, the corporation can always requisition the newest hardware to improve performance.

Working in a small company can put a premium on programming skills. This chapter demonstrates how to do some of these "dangerous" things, if you're lucky enough that you won't be reprimanded for programming above a junior level.

Associative Arrays Using Bash Arrays

Associative arrays (also called "lookup tables" or what the Perl language calls "hashes") are tables containing pairs of values. The first item is the *key*, the known value being looked up. The second item is the value associated with the key. For a table of phone numbers, the key might be the names of employees and the associated value is the phone number extension for each employee.

Associative arrays can be created quite easily using Bash arrays. Pairs of items can be combined into a single item using a special separator character. The character should be a seldom-used character, such as a tilde.

```
TABLE[$NEXTITEM]="$1""$SEPARATOR""$2"          # add the pair to the table
printf "%s\n" "Added $1 / $2 at $NEXTITEM"
let "NEXTITEM++"
```

If NEXTITEM is an integer variable containing the next free position in the TABLE array, the pair is added to the table and NEXTITEM is advanced to the next free position. If NEXTITEM starts at zero, the pair is added at position zero and NEXTITEM is incremented to one.

To find an item, the table must be searched until the item is found or until the end of the table is reached.

```
while [ $ITEM -lt $NEXTITEM ] ; do          # reached end of table?
   KEY="${TABLE[$ITEM]}"                     # if not, get the pair
   KEY="${KEY%$SEPARATOR*}"                  # extract the key part
   if [ "$KEY" = "$KEY2FIND" ] ; then        # is it the key we want?
      break                                  # good, it matches
   else                                      # otherwise
      let "ITEM=ITEM+1"                      # move to the next item
   fi
done
```

If ITEM is the position in the table, when the loop completes, ITEM will either be the table position containing the correct pair or ITEM will be equal to NEXTITEM; one position past the end of the table.

Listing 17.1 contains a complete script for creating an associative array and searching item pairs within it.

Listing 17.1 `lookup.sh`

```
#!/bin/bash
#
# lookup.sh
#
# create a lookup table and look up items
#
# Ken O. Burtch
# CVS: $Header$
shopt -s -o nounset

declare -ax TABLE                       # the lookup table
declare -ix NEXTITEM=0                   # next free spot in table
declare -x  SEPARATOR="~"                # delimiter for key/value
declare -rx SCRIPT=${0##*/}              # name of the script
```

Listing 17.1 Continued

```
# add_table: add a key/value pair to the lookup table
#           (doesn't check for uniqueness)
#
#   parameter 1: the key
#   parameter 2: the associated value

function add_table {
  declare TEMP

  # Check the number of parameters

  if [ $# -ne 2 ] ; then
    printf "%s\n" "$SCRIPT: $FUNCNAME: Expected two parameters" >&2
    return
  fi

  # Make sure the separator isn't in the key or value

  TEMP="${1/$SEPARATOR/_}"                  # remove separator (if any)
  if [ "$1" != "$TEMP" ] ; then            # from key.  Found any?
     printf "%s\n" "$SCRIPT: $FUNCNAME: Key $1 must not contain $SEPARATOR" >&2
    return
  fi
  TEMP="${2/$SEPARATOR/_}"                  # remove separator (if any)
  if [ "$2" != "$TEMP" ] ; then            # from value. Found any?
    printf "%s\n" "$SCRIPT: $FUNCNAME: Value $2 must not contain $SEPARATOR" >&2
    return
  fi

  TABLE[$NEXTITEM]="$1""$SEPARATOR""$2"        # add the pair to the table
  printf "%s\n" "Added $1 / $2 at $NEXTITEM"
  let "NEXTITEM++"
}
readonly -f add_table

# lookup_table: search for and display item matching key in the lookup table
#
function lookup_table {
  declare -i ITEM=0                         # position in array
  declare KEY
  declare VALUE

  # The key must not contain the separator

  TEMP="${1/$SEPARATOR/_}"                  # remove separator (if any)
```

Listing 17.1   Continued

```
  if [ "$1" != "$TEMP" ] ; then              # from key.  Found any?
    printf "%s\n" "$SCRIPT: $FUNCNAME: Key must not contain $SEPARATOR" >&2
    return
  fi

  while [ $ITEM -lt $NEXTITEM ] ; do      # reached end of table?
    KEY="${TABLE[$ITEM]}"                 # if not, get the pair
    KEY="${KEY%$SEPARATOR*}"              # extract the key part
    if [ "$KEY" = "$1" ] ; then           # is it the key we want?
        break                             # good, it matches
    else                                  # otherwise
        let "ITEM=ITEM+1"                 # move to the next item
    fi
  done

  # Display search results

  if [ $ITEM -eq $NEXTITEM ] ; then
      printf "%s\n" "$1 is not in the table"
  else
      VALUE="${TABLE[$ITEM]}"
      VALUE="${VALUE#*$SEPARATOR}"
      printf "%s\n" "$1 has the value $VALUE"
  fi
}
readonly -f lookup_table

# Main script begins

printf "Building the lookup table...\n\n"

add_table "4324" "Hazel's Ladies Wear"
add_table "1879" "Crowther Insurance Brokers Limited"
add_table "3048" "Clarke Plumbing"
add_table "4267" "Shakur LLP"
add_table "9433" "Scott Furniture Ltd"
add_table "2018" "Zap Electric"
add_table "2250" "Sommer Water"

printf "\nLooking up some items...\n\n"

lookup_table "1879"
lookup_table "2250"
lookup_table "0000"

exit 0
```

The add_table function adds a pair of items to the associative array. The two items are combined into a single value separated by the separator character (in this case, a tilde). The pair is added to the end of the table and NEXTITEM, the next free position in the table, is increased by 1.

The lookup_table function searches the table for a key and returns the associated value. The table is searched for the key. If the key is found, the company name is displayed. Otherwise, the script announces that the ID number is not in the table.

The script creates a sample lookup table containing ID numbers and associated company names.

```
$ lookup.sh
Building the lookup table...

Added 4324 / Hazel's Ladies Wear at 0
Added 1879 / Crowther Insurance Brokers Limited at 1
Added 3048 / Clarke Plumbing at 2
Added 4267 / Shakur LLP at 3
Added 9433 / Scott Furniture Ltd at 4
Added 2018 / Zap Electric at 5
Added 2250 / Sommer Water at 6

Looking up some items...

1879 has the value Crowther Insurance Brokers Limited
2250 has the value Sommer Water
0000 is not in the table
```

Hash Tables Using Bash Arrays

Hash tables store single items in a way that makes them quick to find again. Hash tables rely on a *hash*, or mathematical formula, which converts the item being stored into a single number. This number is used to determine where in the hash table the item is stored. A good hash algorithm scatters items as evenly as possible throughout the table.

It is possible to write your own hash formula, but for the purposes here, the Linux MD5 checksum function works quite nicely and creates a unique number. You can use this as your hash formula.

```
HEXCODE=`echo "$1" | $MD5SUM`              # compute the hash value (hex)
HEXCODE="${HEXCODE:0:4}"                    # take first 4 hex digits
CODE=`printf "%d\n" 0x"$HEXCODE"`          # covert to 0...65535
printf "%d\n" "$((CODE%TABLE_SIZE))"      # restrict to table size
```

This routine takes the first four hexadecimal digits computed by md5sum and converts these to a number between 0 and 65535. The number is then constrained to the size of the table. If the table size is 100, the hash code is between 0 and 99, the positions in an array of 100 items.

It is possible for two items to generate the same hash value. This is called a *collision* and the item has to be stored in a different table position.

Like associative arrays, hash tables can be stored in Bash arrays, as shown in Listing 17.2.

Listing 17.2   `hash.sh`

```bash
#!/bin/bash
#
# hash.sh
#
# Create a hash table and look up items
#
# Ken O. Burtch
# CVS: $Header$
shopt -s -o nounset

declare -ax TABLE                        # the hash table
declare -ix TABLE_SIZE=100               # size of the hash table
declare -rx SCRIPT=${0##*/}              # name of the script
declare -rx MD5SUM='/usr/bin/md5sum'     # used for hash generation

# hash_of: generate a table position from a string
#
function hash_of {
   declare HEXCODE                       # 4 hex digits of MD5 signature
   declare -i CODE                       # the hex digits in decimal

   HEXCODE=`echo "$1" | $MD5SUM`         # compute the hash value (hex)
   HEXCODE="${HEXCODE:0:4}"              # take first 4 hex digits
   CODE=`printf "%d\n" 0x"$HEXCODE"`     # covert to 0...65535
   printf "%d\n" "$((CODE%TABLE_SIZE))"  # restrict to table size
}
readonly -f hash_of

# add_hash: add item to the hash table
#
function add_hash {
   declare -i ITEM=0                      # current position in table

   # Empty strings are used for empty table positions

   if [ -z "$1" ] ; then
      printf "%s\n" "$SCRIPT: $FUNCNAME: Cannot add empty items" >&2
      return
   fi

   # Search for a free position
```

Listing 17.2   Continued

```
    ITEM=`hash_of "$1"`                        # search starts here

    shopt -u -o nounset                        # empty spots will cause error
    while [ -n "${TABLE[$ITEM]}" ] ; do        # free position yet
       printf "%s\n" "Position $ITEM for $1 in use, moving forward..."
       let "ITEM=ITEM+1"                        # if not, keep looking
    done
    shopt -s -o nounset                        # safe to use now
    TABLE[$ITEM]="$1"                          # add the item to the table
    printf "%s\n" "Added $1 at $ITEM"
}
readonly -f add_hash

# lookup_hash: search and display items in the hash table
#
function lookup_hash {
    declare -i ITEM=0                          # position in array

    # Empty items used for empty hash table positions

    if [ -z "$1" ] ; then
       printf "%s\n" "$SCRIPT: $FUNCNAME: Cannot lookup empty items" >&2
       return
    fi

    # Find the item or arrive at an empty spot

    ITEM=`hash_of "$1"`                        # search starts here

    shopt -u -o nounset                        # empty spots will cause errors
    while [ -n "${TABLE[$ITEM]}" ] ; do        # reached an empty spot?
       if [ "${TABLE[$ITEM]}" = "$1" ] ; then  # if not, check the item
          break                                 # good, it matches
       else                                     # may be inserted after
          let "ITEM=ITEM+1"                     # move to the next item
       fi
    done

    # Display search results

    if [ -z "${TABLE[$ITEM]}" ] ; then
       printf "%s\n" "$1 is not in the table"
    else
       printf "%s\n" "$1 is in the table at $ITEM"
    fi
```

Listing 17.2   Continued

```
}
readonly -f lookup_hash

# Main script begins

if [ ! -x "$MD5SUM" ] ; then
    printf "Unable to run command %s\n" "$MD5SUM" >&2
    exit 129
fi
printf "Building the hash table...\n\n"

add_hash "Hazel's Ladies Wear"
add_hash "Crowther Insurance Brokers Limited"
add_hash "Clarke Plumbing"
add_hash "Shakur LLP"
add_hash "Scott Furniture Ltd"
add_hash "Zap Electric"
add_hash "Sommer Water"

printf "\nLooking up some items...\n\n"

lookup_hash "Hazel's Ladies Wear"
lookup_hash "Sommer Water"
lookup_hash "Bogus test data"

exit 0
```

The `add_hash` function adds items to the hash table. If a collision occurs, `add_hash` tries to add the item at the following position in the table. It keeps moving through the table until it finds an empty position.

The `lookup_hash` function searches the hash table for an item. If the item is not found at the expected position, it moves through the table until it encounters an empty position. It reports the location of the item or otherwise announces that the item cannot be found.

```
$ bash hash.sh
Building the hash table...

Added Hazel's Ladies Wear at 34
Added Crowther Insurance Brokers Limited at 29
Added Clarke Plumbing at 19 Added Shakur LLP at 70
Added Scott Furniture Ltd at 86
Added Zap Electric at 49
Position 70 for Sommer Water in use, moving forward...
Added Sommer Water at 71
```

```
Looking up some items...

Hazel's Ladies Wear is in the table at 34
Sommer Water is in the table at 71
Bogus test data is not in the table
```

Hash tables can be combined with associative arrays to create Perl-style hashes with fast lookup times.

Binary Trees Using Bash Arrays

Hashes chose apparently random positions to store items. Because the items are scattered, it is difficult to sort them.

Binary trees provide a compromise: They are slower than hashes, but the items they contain are sorted and can be displayed in sorted order. A *binary tree* is a family tree whereby each parent has two children. The children are sorted according to the parent. Usually children that are alphabetically before the parent are stored to the left, and children that are alphabetically after the parent are stored to the right.

A common problem with binary trees are *degenerate trees*. If the items being added to the binary tree are sorted under the same conditions that the tree is sorted, the tree is a single long list. If necessary, randomize the items before adding them to the tree.

Binary trees can be represented in a Bash array. The size of each tier of the tree is known. The first item, or the *root* of the tree, is always a single item. The next row of the tree has two items, the two children of the root. The next row has four items, and so forth. So if the root of the tree is position zero in the Bash array, the second row is in positions 1 and 2, and the third row is in positions 3, 4, 5, and 6.

```
if [ "${TREE[$ITEM]}" \> "$1" ] ; then      # sort alphabetically
    let "ITEM=ITEM*2+1"                      # lesser items to left child
else
    let "ITEM=ITEM*2+2"                      # greater items to right child
fi
```

You can use this simple mathematical formula to store the tree in the array. For example, the left child of the item at position 1 in the tree is stored at position 1*2+1, or position 3. The right child is located at position 4, the following position. The items are sorted alphabetically (or, at least, according to their ASCII values) .

Because new items are added at empty positions in the TREE array, the nounset shell option has to be temporarily turned off while checking for empty positions. Empty positions are technically "unset" and cause an error if this option is left on.

Listing 17.2 shows a script that stores a binary tree in a Bash array.

Listing 17.3 `binary.sh`

```
#!/bin/bash
#
# binary.sh
```

Listing 17.3   Continued

```
#
# create a binary tree and look up items
#
# Ken O. Burtch
# CVS: $Header$
shopt -s -o nounset

declare -ax TREE                          # the binary tree
declare -rx SCRIPT=${0##*/}               # name of the script

# add_tree: add item to the binary tree
#
function add_tree {
   declare -i ITEM=0                      # current position in array

   # Empty strings are used for the tree leaves

   if [ -z "$1" ] ; then
      printf "%s\n" "$SCRIPT: $FUNCNAME: Cannot add empty items" >&2
      return
   fi

   # Search for a free leaf

   shopt -u -o nounset                    # leaves will cause an error
   while [ -n "${TREE[$ITEM]}" ] ; do     # at a leaf yet?
      if [ "${TREE[$ITEM]}" \> "$1" ] ; then   # sort alphabetically
         let "ITEM=ITEM*2+1"              # lesser items to left child
      else
         let "ITEM=ITEM*2+2"             # greater items to right child
      fi
   done
   shopt -s -o nounset                    # safe to use now
   TREE[$ITEM]="$1"                       # add the item to the tree
   printf "%s\n" "Added $1 at $ITEM"
}
readonly -f add_tree

# dump_tree: display items in tree in alphabetical order
#
function dump_tree {
  declare -i ITEM                         # current position
  declare -i NEW_ITEM                     # child positions

  if [ $# -gt 0 ] ; then                  # an item number?
```

Listing 17.3   Continued

```
    ITEM="$1"                              # check it
  else                                     # otherwise user invoked
    ITEM=0                                 # and we start at the top
  fi
  shopt -u -o nounset                      # leaves will cause an error
  if [ -n "${TREE[$ITEM]}" ] ; then        # leaf? then nothing to do
    let "NEW_ITEM=ITEM*2+1"                # otherwise go to left child
    dump_tree "$NEW_ITEM"                  # display the left child
    printf "%s\n" "$ITEM = ${TREE[$ITEM]}" # display this item
    let "NEW_ITEM=ITEM*2+2"                # go to right child
    dump_tree "$NEW_ITEM"                  # display the right child
  fi
  shopt -s -o nounset                      # safe to use
}
readonly -f dump_tree

# lookup_tree: search and display items in the binary tree
#
function lookup_tree {
  declare -i ITEM=0                        # position in array

  # Empty items used for the leaves

  if [ -z "$1" ] ; then
    printf "%s\n" "$SCRIPT: $FUNCNAME: Cannot lookup empty items" >&2
    return
  fi

  # Find the item or arrive at an empty leaf

  shopt -u -o nounset                      # leaves will cause an error
  while [ -n "${TREE[$ITEM]}" ] ; do       # reached a leaf? not found
    if [ "${TREE[$ITEM]}" = "$1" ] ; then  # otherwise the item?
      break                                # good
    elif [ "${TREE[$ITEM]}" \> "$1" ] ; then # continue search
      let "ITEM=ITEM*2+1"                  # lesser items to left child
    else
      let "ITEM=ITEM*2+2"                  # greater items to right child
    fi
  done

  # Display search results

  if [ -z "${TREE[$ITEM]}" ] ; then
    printf "%s\n" "$1 is not in the tree"
```

Listing 17.3   Continued

```
    else
        printf "%s\n" "$1 is in the tree at $ITEM"
    fi
}
readonly -f lookup_tree

# Main script begins

printf "Building the tree...\n\n"

add_tree "Hazel's Ladies Wear"
add_tree "Crowther Insurance Brokers Limited"
add_tree "Clarke Plumbing"
add_tree "Shakur LLP"
add_tree "Scott Furniture Ltd"
add_tree "Zap Electric"

printf "\nThe tree contains...\n\n"

dump_tree

printf "\nLooking up some items...\n\n"

lookup_tree "Zap Electric"
lookup_tree "Clarke Plumbing"
lookup_tree "Bogus test data"

exit 0
```

The add_tree function adds items to the tree, sorted alphabetically.

The lookup_tree function searches the tree for items. If the function reaches an unset position in the array, it knows that the item doesn't exist.

The dump_tree function traverses the tree, touching every item in sorted order and displaying the item.

```
$ bash binary.sh
Building the tree...

Added Hazel's Ladies Wear at 0
Added Crowther Insurance Brokers Limited at 1
Added Clarke Plumbing at 3
Added Shakur LLP at 2
Added Scott Furniture Ltd at 5
Added Zap Electric at 6
```

```
The tree contains...

3 = Clarke Plumbing
1 = Crowther Insurance Brokers Limited
0 = Hazel's Ladies Wear
5 = Scott Furniture Ltd
2 = Shakur LLP
6 = Zap Electric

Looking up some items...

Zap Electric is in the tree at 6
Clarke Plumbing is in the tree at 3
Bogus test data is not in the tree
```

Because of their sorted nature, binary trees can also be used as a simple sort. However, the Linux sort command is almost always faster.

Working with PostgreSQL Databases (psql)

Text files and Bash arrays are fast and convenient for small quantities of data. If you are going to work with hundreds of thousands of pieces of information, you need to use a database to manage your information.

Most databases (including Oracle, MySQL, and PostgreSQL) come with console client applications. These applications are sometimes referred to as "monitors" or "console monitors." Console clients look and operate much as a shell but they have a different command prompt and expect SQL commands instead of Linux or Bash commands. With the proper options, console clients can run database commands on behalf of a Bash script.

The PostgreSQL database is available with most Linux distributions but it might not be installed by default depending on your installation settings. For example, a "desktop" or "workstation" installation might not include PostgreSQL. The PostgreSQL database has a console client called psql. If psql is not installed, see if it is available on your distribution disks. The remainder of this section assumes that you have PostgreSQL installed and the database server is up and running.

To log into PostgreSQL, use psql with the --user *username* (or -U *username*) switch. The --list (or -l) switch lists all available databases.

```
$ psql --user gordon --list
        List of databases
   Name    |  Owner   | Encoding
-----------+----------+-----------
 custinfo  | postgres | SQL_ASCII
 template0 | postgres | SQL_ASCII
 template1 | postgres | SQL_ASCII
(3 rows)
```

Select a starting database with the --dbname db (or -d db) switch. You can run short queries with the --command *sqlcmd* (or -c *sqlcmd*) switch. This is similar to Bash's -e switch. There is also a --file switch to run commands contained in a separate file.

```
$ psql --user gordon --dbname custinfo --command "SELECT COUNT(*) FROM USER"
 count
-------
    3
(1 row)
```

psql can be used from a script to access databases. SQL commands can be redirected to psql through standard input. You can use --file='-' switch to provide special features for scripts such as line numbers on errors. A here file can be used to place the SQL commands immediately after invoking psql.

```
psql --user gordon --dbname custinfo --file='-'  <<!
select count(*) from products
!
```

This script fragment counts the number of products in the products table.

```
 count
-------
   165
(1 row)
```

Shell variables can be included in the here file to customize your SQL commands.

```
declare ID=5
psql --user gordon --dbname custinfo --file='-'  <<!
select product_name from products where product_id = $ID
!
```

The query results are placed on standard output. They can be captured using backquotes or by redirecting standard output.

```
RESULT=`psql --user gordon --dbname custinfo --file='-'   <<!
select product_name from products where product_id = $ID
!`
```

or even

```
RESULT=`printf "%s" "select product_name from products where product_id = $ID" | \
    psql --user gordon --dbname custinfo --file='-' `
```

psql displays the results of commands with column headings, borders, and totals. Although these are attractive for interactive sessions, they create more work for scripts. These formatting features can be turned off using the appropriate switches.

```
psql --user gordon --dbname custinfo --file='-' -quiet --no-align --tuples-only \
    --field-separator "," --file '-' <<!
```

```
select * from products
!
```

The results are displayed in CSV (comma-separated value) format. --no-align (or -A) removes the whitespace padding between the columns. --field-separator "," (or -F ",") separates columns with a particular character; in this case, they are separated with commas. --tuples_only (or -t) removes the headings and totals. Finally, progress information is suppressed with --quiet (or -q).

PostgreSQL has an unusual set of status codes. It returns a status code of 0 on success or a 1 if an internal error occurred (for example, unable to allocate memory), 2 if the client was disconnected, or 3 if the SQL commands were aborted because of an error. The 3 code occurs only if you declare a variable called ON_ERROR_STOP: Unless this variable exists, PostgreSQL ignores the error and continues with the next database command; it does not report a problem.

Because of this status code scheme, if the script looks for a SQL command file with the --file switch and the file doesn't exist, psql returns a successful status. It's very important to check all files prior to executing psql.

Listing 17.4 shows a complete example that executes a set of SQL commands stored in a separate file.

Listing 17.4   show_users.sh

```bash
#!/bin/bash
#
# show_users.sh: show all users in the database table "users"

shopt -s -o nounset

declare -rx SCRIPT=${0##*/}
declare -r SQL_CMDS="sort_inventory.sql"
declare -rx ON_ERROR_STOP

if [ ! -r "$SQL_CMDS" ] ; then
   printf "$SCRIPT: the SQL script $SQL_CMDS doesn't exist or is not \
 readable" >&2
   exit 192
fi

RESULTS=`psql --user gordon --dbname custinfo  -quiet --no-align --tuples-only \
 --field-separator "," --file "$SQL_CMDS"`
if [ $? -ne 0 ] ; then
   printf "$SCRIPT: SQL statements failed." >&2
   exit 192
fi
```

Instead of capturing the results with backquotes, you can redirect the results to a file using `--output` *fname* (or `-o` *fname*).

Working with MySQL Databases

The MySQL database is available with most Linux distributions, but it might not be installed by default depending on your installation settings. The MySQL database has a console client called, appropriately, `mysql`. The remainder of this section assumes that you have MySQL installed and the database server is up and running.

To log into MySQL, use `mysql` with the `--user=`*username* (or `-u` *username*) and `--password=`*pswd* (or `-p` *pswd*)) switches. If you omit a password with `--password`, MySQL prompts you for one.

Type `quit` (or `\q`) to quit the client.

```
$ mysql --user gordon --password=tifbig198
mysql> quit
$
```

You can run short queries with the `--exec=`*sqlcmd* (or `-e` *sqlcmd* execute command) switch. This is similar to Bash's `-e` switch.

```
$ mysql --user gordon --password=tifbig198 --exec="SHOW DATABASES"
+----------+
| Database |
+----------+
| bashtest |
| mysql    |
| test     |
+----------+
$
```

MySQL returns a status code of zero (0) on success or one (1) for an error. You can check the status code the usual way with the `$?` variable, as shown in Listing 17.5.

Listing 17.5 `show_mysqldb.sh`

```
#!/bin/bash
#
# show_mysqldb.sh
#
# Show all databases

shopt -s -o nounset

declare -rx SCRIPT=${0##*/}

$ mysql --user=gordon --password=tifbig198 --exec="SHOW DATABASES"
if [ $? -ne 0 ] ; then
```

Listing 17.5   Continued

```
    printf "$SCRIPT: SQL statement failed." >&2
    exit 192
fi
```

You can load a group of SQL commands from a file by redirecting input, as shown in Listing 17.6.

Listing 17.6 showusers.bush

```
#!/bin/bash
#
# showusers.bush: Show users in the bushtest/user table

shopt -s -o nounset

declare -rx SCRIPT=${0##*/}
$ mysql -user-gordon -password=tifbig198 <<HERE
USE bushtest
select * from user
QUIT
HERE
if [ $? -ne 0 ] ; then
    printf "$SCRIPT: SQL statement failed." >&2
    exit 192
fi
```

If the bashtest database has a table called user, the script returns a list like this:

```
$ sh showusers.bash
name
Sally
Jane
Britney
```

QUIT is not required at the end of the here file.
MySQL automatically removes the borders and titles to make the information easier to handle by scripts.

Reference Section

psql **Command Switches**

- --echo-all (or -a)—Traces SQL commands
- --no-align (or -A)—No output alignment
- --command *q* (or -c *q*)—Runs SQL query *q*

- `--dbname` *d* (or `-d` *d*)—Uses database d
- `--echo-queries` (or `-e`)—Prints SQL commands (but not backslash commands)
- `--echo-hidden` (or `-E`)—Prints SQL commands caused by backslash commands
- `--file` *f* (or `-f` *f*)—Runs SQL commands in file *f*
- `--field-separator` *c* (or `-F` *c*)—Uses character *c* to separate columns
- `--host` *h* (or `-h` *h*)—Computer h has the database
- `--html` (or `-H`)—Uses simple HTML output
- `--list` (or `-l`)—Lists available databases
- `--output` *f* (or `-o` *f*)—Saves query results in file f
- `--port` *p* (or `-p` *p*)—Uses TCP/IP port p
- `--pset` *s* (or `-P` *s*)—Executes \pset commands s
- `--quiet` (or `-q`)—Hides status information
- `--record-separator` *s* (or `-R` *s*)—Uses character s as the row separator
- `--single-step` (or `-s`)—Prompts before executing SQL commands
- `--tuples-only` (or `-t`)—Doesn't print column names or totals
- `--table-attr` *o* (or `-T` *o*)—HTML table options for --html
- `--username` *u* (or `-u` *u*)—Logs in to database as user u
- `--variable` *s* (or `-v` *s*)—Assigns \set values
- `--password` (or `-W`)—Prompts for password
- `--expanded` (or `-x`)—Uses expanded row format
- `--no-psqlrc` (or `-X`)—Doesn't execute instructions in startup file

`mysql` Command Switches

- `--batch` (or `-B`)—Prints results in Tab separated format
- `--exec=`*c* (or `-e` *c*)—Runs SQL commands c
- `--force` (or `-f`)—Continues after an error occurs
- `--host=`*h* (or `-h` *h*)—Computer h has the database
- `--unbuffered` (or `-n`)—Doesn't buffer query results
- `--password=`*p* (or `-p` *p*)—Supplies a login password
- `--port=`*p* (or `-P` *p*)—Uses TCP/IP port p
- `--quick` (or `-q`)—Doesn't cache the results
- `--raw` (or `-r`)—With --batch, doesn't convert results
- `--silent` (or `-s`)—Hides status information
- `--socket=`*f* (or `-S` *f*)—Uses Unix domain socket file f
- `--user=`*u* (or `-u` *u*)—Logs in to database as user *u*
- `--wait` (or `-w`)—Tries to connect again if the database is down

18

Final Topics

THE ARCANE AND THE OBSCURE. The obsolete and the advanced. This final chapter contains a mix of subjects suitable for those who need to know every last detail about the Bash shell.

The echo Command

The built-in echo command is an older form of printf. Bash provides it for compatibility with the Bourne shell. echo does not use a format string: It displays all variables as if "%s\n" formatting was used. It can sometimes be used as a shortcut when you don't need the full features of printf.

```
$ echo "$BASH_VERSION"
2.05a.0(1)-release
```

A line feed is automatically added after the string is displayed. It can be suppressed with the -n (*no new line*) switch.

```
$ echo -n "This is " ; echo "one line."
This is one line
```

If the -e (*escape*) switch is used, echo interprets certain escape sequences as special characters.

- \a—A beep ("alert")
- \b—A backspace
- \c—Suppresses the next character; at the end of the string, suppresses the trailing line feed
- \E—The escape character
- \f—A form feed
- \n—A line feed (new line)
- \r—A carriage return
- \t—A horizontal tab

- \v—A vertical tab
- \\—A backslash
- \num—The octal ASCII code for a character

```
$ echo "\101"
\101
$ echo -e "\101"
A
```

The -E switch turns off escape sequence interpretation. This is the default setting.

More Uses for set

The built-in set command is used to turn on or off certain shell options. However, set has other uses as well.

When set has arguments, the arguments are assigned to the position parameters. This is the only way to change the value of positional parameters.

```
$ printf "%s %s %s\n" "$1" "$2" "$3"

$ set "first" "second" "third"
$ printf "%s %s %s\n" "$1" "$2" "$3"
first second third
```

When set is used by itself, it acts like the env command, displaying all variables. It also displays all functions.

Date Conversions

The Linux date command returns the current date in a variety of formats. date with the -d switch converts an arbitrary text date and displays it in different formats.

```
$ date -d 'may 1 10am'
Tue May  1 09:00:00 2001
$ date -d '8pm 01/03/02'
Thu Jan  3 19:00:00 2002
```

On some older Linux distributions, the convdate command is provided and performs a similar function.

```
$ convdate '8pm 01/03/02'
```

Thu Jan 3 19:00:00 2002

The -n (*number*) switch returns the seconds since January 1, 1970 (the epoch). The -c switch returns a date string for the seconds from the epoch.

```
$ convdate -n 'may 1 10am'
988722000
$ convdate -c 988722000
Tue May  1 10:00:00 2001
```

Completions

Completions occur when Bash makes a guess about what a user is typing. With filename completion, a user presses the Tab key (or Esc in vi mode) to determine whether Bash recognizes the filename being typed based on the first few characters. This completion mechanism is available to shell scripts through the use of two built-in commands.

The `compgen` (*generate completions*) command generates a list of possible completions. In order to use `compgen`, you need to indicate the type of completion with the `-A` (*action*) switch:

- `-A alias` (or `-a`)—Alias names
- `-A arrayvar`—Array variable names
- `-A binding`—Bind command key binding names
- `-A builtin` (or `-b`)—Built-in shell commands
- `-A command` (or `-c`)—Linux commands
- `-A directory` (or `-d`)—Directory names
- `-A disabled`—Names of disabled built-in shell commands
- `-A enabled`—Names of enabled built-in shell commands
- `-A export` (or `-e`)—Exported shell variables
- `-A group` (or `-g`)—Group name completion
- `-A file` (or `-f`)—Filenames
- `-A functions`—Shell function names
- `-A helptopic`—Subjects recognized by the shell `help` command
- `-A hostname`—Hostnames in the file indicated by HOSTFILE variable
- `-A job` (or `-j`)—The names of jobs in the job table
- `-A keyword` (or `-k`)—Shell reserved words
- `-A running`—The names of running jobs
- `-A service` (or `-s`)—Complete a networking service name
- `-A setopt`—The names of shopt -o options
- `-A shopt`—The names of shopt options (not the -o options)
- `-A signal`—The names of signals
- `-A stopped`—The names of stopped jobs
- `-A user` (or `-u`)—Usernames
- `-A variable` (or `-v`)—Shell variable names

To find all the directories beginning with *t*, use

```
$ compgen -A directory t
tia
test
texttools
```

The completion process is more complicated than you might think.

A script can run functions or programs specified with the -F (*function*) switch or run commands with the -C (*command*) switch to create the initial list of possible completions. The arguments include the name of the command being completed ($1), the shell word being completed ($2), and the word before the word being completed ($3).

```
$ function info { printf "%s\n" "Cmd=$1 Word=$2 Prev=$3" ; }
$ compgen -A directory -F info t
bash: warning: compgen: -F option may not work as you expect
Cmd= Word=t Prev=
temp
tia
texttools
```

In this case, *t* is the word being completed, and there is no command or word prior to *t*.

Acceptable matches are returned in the COMPREPLY variable (or to standard output for -C). Assigning trucking_reports to COMPREPLY adds trucking_reports to the list of possible matches.

```
$ function info { printf "%s\n" "Cmd=$1 Word=$2 Prev=$3" ; \
  COMPREPLY="trucking_reports" ;}
$ compgen -A directory -F info t
bash: warning: compgen: -F option may not work as you expect
Cmd= Word=t Prev=
temp
tia
texttools
trucking_reports
```

Several variables provide additional information when completing functions and commands. COMP_LINE is the command being completed. COMP_POINT is the cursor position relative to the start of the command. COMP_WORDS is an array of the words in the command. COMP_CWORD is the cursor position as an index into the COMP_WORDS array.

Bash contains profiles for many commands so that it knows the kind of completion that is necessary. These are called *completion specifications*. If the -G switch is used, the process takes a filename pattern and creates additional matches. After a list of possible solutions is found, any items found in the shell variable FIGNORE are discarded. The -W (*words*) switch is used to narrow the list.

After the user's custom filtering, the -X (*exclude*) switch applies a pathname pattern match to further reduce the list. An ampersand represents the text of the word being replaced. Any suffix provided by the -s switch or prefix provided by the -p switch are added to all surviving items. This is the final list.

```
$ compgen -A directory -X tia t
test
texttools
$ compgen -A directory -S '.txt' -X tia t
test.txt
texttools.txt
```

The `complete` command sets the default completion behavior when completing a certain command. It uses the same options as `compgen`, but saves them for future use with the command. You can also assign completion commands and functions this way.

```
$ compgen -A directory t
temp
tia
texttools
$ complete -A directory -X tia ls
$ ls t
temp        texttools
$ complete -A directory -F info ls
$ ls t Cmd=ls Word=t Prev=ls
```

The -p (*print*) switch lists the currently defined completion for a command.

```
$ complete -p ls
complete -d -F info ls
```

The -r (*remove*) command removes the defined completion.

The -o (*option*) switch sets various options. -o `dirnames` attempts to match directories if no other matches exist. -o `filenames` allows the word to be altered (such as dropping a trailing slash) to help identify matches. -o `default` is the default, providing no special handling when a match fails. Newer versions of Bash also support -o `nospace`, which prevents a space from being appended to the end of a completed word.

The completion commands can be combined with functions to create powerful new command-line utilities.

Locales

Under Linux, the language and culture of a user is represented by his or her "locale." The locale information is stored in environment variables. Some of the standard ones are:

- LC_CTYPE—The character classes and case conversion
- LC_COLLATE—The collating sequence for the character set
- LC_NUMERIC—The radix character (character used to separate number from base) and thousands separator
- LC_MONETARY—Like LC_NUMERIC, but for formatting money

- LC_MESSAGES—The formatting of diagnostic messages and user dialogue
- LC_TIME—The local month spellings and other aspects of date formatting

Each of these variables contains a locale category name to use. The categories are stored in a locale database located in /usr/lib/locale. The database is updated with the Linux localedef command.

The locale command displays the current locale settings. en_US is the category for United States English, en_CA is Canadian English, fr_CA is Canadian French, and so forth.

```
$ locale
LANG=en_US
LC_CTYPE="en_US"
LC_NUMERIC="en_US"
LC_TIME="en_US"
LC_COLLATE="en_US"
LC_MONETARY="en_US"
LC_MESSAGES="en_US"
LC_PAPER="en_US"
LC_NAME="en_US"
LC_ADDRESS="en_US"
LC_TELEPHONE="en_US"
LC_MEASUREMENT="en_US"
LC_IDENTIFICATION="en_US"
LC_ALL=
```

locale -a (*all*) displays a list of all locale categories. The -m (*map*) switch displays a list of all character mappings.

Locales are usually selected by the user during the Linux installation process. To change the locale, assign new values to an LC variable.

```
$ LC_NUMERIC="fr_CA" # use French Canadian number conventions
```

Certain Bash and Linux commands are affected by the settings. For example, dollar double quote substitution converts a string to the preferred character set for the current locale. The value of LC_COLLATE affects the order in which pathnames are pattern matched by Bash as well as the sorting order of the Linux sort command.

The du Command

The Linux du (*disk usage*) command shows the amount of disk space used by a directory and all subdirectories within it. The --summarize (or -s) switch displays only the grand total. The --human-readable (or -h) switch converts the total to the nearest megabytes or gigabytes.

```
$ pwd
/home/kburtch
```

```
$ du --summarize --human-readable
36M     .
$ du --summarize --human-readable . archive
36M     .
28M     archive
```

For scripts, there are a number of switches controlling how the results are grouped and what units are used. The space totals can be in `--bytes` (or `-b`) , `--kilobytes` (or `-k`) , `--megabytes` (or `-m`) , or blocks of `--blocksize=b` bytes. The default units are kilobytes. The `--si` (or `-H`) switch uses units of 1000 instead of 1024. You can determine a `--total` (or `-c`) for all files on the command line, as well as totals for `--all` (or `-a`) all files within directories. `--separate-dirs` (or `-S`) shows the totals for subdirectories, the default behavior.

The amounts and the filenames are separated by a Tab character. To extract one column or the other, use the `cut` command.

```
$ TAB='printf "\t"'
$ du --all --kilobytes incoming_orders | cut -d"$TAB"  -f1
20
12
40
56
132
```

Other switches affect the way files are searched. The `--dereference-args` (or `-D`) switch dereferences paths that are symbolic links. The `--count-links` (`-l`) switch counts each hard link to the same file as separate files. The `--one-file-system` (`-x`) switch constrains the search to the current file system. The search can be constrained to `--max-depth=n` levels of subdirectories, or can exclude any files with `--exclude=f` or a list of files in a file f with `--exclude-from=f` (or `-X f`) .

Memory Usage

The Linux `free` command reports the memory usage on the system.

```
$ free
                total       used       free     shared    buffers     cached
Mem:            61792      58756       3036      10116      36152       8988
-/+ buffers/cache:         13616      48176
Swap:          514072       8180     505892
```

The total, used, and free columns are the total amount of memory, the amount of memory currently used by the Linux kernel, and the amount of free memory, respectively. The free and used columns always add up to the total. The last three columns show how the used memory is allocated; within shared memory, buffers, or caches. The final line shows the swap space allocated, used, and free on disk.

The -t switch displays an additional total line.

```
$ free -t
             total      used      free    shared   buffers    cached
Mem:         61792     58760      3032     10116     36152      8988
-/+ buffers/cache:     13620     48172
Swap:       514072      8180    505892
Total:      575864     66940    508924
```

By default, the display is in kilobytes. The -b switch displays bytes, and the -m switch displays megabytes.

free is not script-friendly. To get the information you need, you have to use cut and grep. The columns are separated by spaces, which must be compressed for use with cut.

```
$ free | grep "^Mem"
Mem:         61792     58880      2912     10120     36156      9068
$ free | grep "^Mem" | tr -s ' '
Mem: 61792 58876 2916 10120 36156 9068
$ free | grep "^Mem" | tr -s ' ' | cut -d\  -f2
61792
```

noclobber **and Forced Overwriting**

Normally, when standard output is redirected using >, an existing file with the same name is overwritten.

```
$ printf "First line\n" > temp.txt
$ printf "Second line\n" > temp.txt
$ cat temp.txt
Second line
```

To provide a safety measure against overwriting an important file, the noclobber shell option prevents a file from being overwritten by a redirection.

```
$ shopt -s -o noclobber
$ printf "First line\n" > temp.txt
$ printf "Second line\n" > temp.txt
bash: temp.txt: cannot overwrite existing file
```

A file can be forcibly overwritten using >| instead of >.

```
$ printf "Second line\n" >| temp.txt
$ cat temp.txt
Second line
```

The noclobber option is primarily intended for interactive sessions whereby a user might type the wrong filename. However, it can also be used as a debugging tool in scripts, identifying places where > is used instead of >> or where files are not cleaned up between script runs.

For example, in the following script fragment, a log is created, but the date is missing from the log. Using `noclobber`, Bash displays an error for the line overwriting the date.

```
#!/bin/bash

shopt -s -o nounset
shopt -s -o noclobber

declare -rx LOG="log.txt"

date > $LOG
printf "Results of night batch run:\n" > $LOG

# etc.
```

The `printf` should use a `>>` redirection.

`>|` shouldn't be used in a script because it defeats the purpose of using `noclobber`.

The `fc` Command

The built-in `fc` (*fix command*) command lists and edits the command history. This command has been largely superceded by the `history` and `!` history recall commands.

`fc` starts the default editor to alter the last command executed. When you leave the editor, the command executes. Instead of the entire command, only the first characters of a command are needed to make a match. Alternatively, you can specify a range of lines to edit. If the lines begin with a minus sign, the lines are counted from the end of the history (with `-1` being the most recent command).

With the `-s` (*substitute*) switch, instead of starting the editor, `fc` substitutes all occurrences of a word that you specify before executing the command for another word. For example, to edit a file with pico and then compile the file with the gcc compiler, use `-s` `"pico=gcc"` to substitute gcc for pico.

```
$ pico project.c
$ fc -s "pico=gcc" p
gcc project.c
```

The `-l` (*list*) switch lists the most recent items in the history, and you can specify the first line, or the first and last lines, to display. The `-n` (*no line numbers*) switch suppresses the line numbers in the history, and `-r` (*reverse*) reverses the order in which they are printed.

! Word Designators and Modifiers

The basic features of the `!` history recall command were discussed in Chapter 3. In fact, `!` has a number of features that enable you to select which command is recalled and determine whether or not new information should be substituted into the command before executing it.

! recognizes *word designators,* which recall a different word than the command. The term "word" is a word in the shell sense; a string separated by whitespace. The word designator is separated from the rest of the history recall command with a colon.

A :n selects the *n*th word on the history line. Word zero is the command.

```
$ printf "%s\n" "`date`"
Thu Jul  5 14:34:41 EDT 2001
$ NOW=!!:2
NOW="`date`"
$ printf "%s\n" "$NOW"
Thu Jul  5 14:34:55 EDT 2001
```

A :^ indicates the first word after the command, the same as :1. A :$ indicates the last word. A :* represents :^ through :$.

```
$ touch temp.txt
$ rm !!:^
rm temp.txt
```

Other designators include :% (the last word matched by a history search), :*x-y* (words x through y, inclusive), :*x** (word x through to the end), :*x-* (word x through to the end, not including the last word) .

```
$ printf "%s and %s\n" "apples" "oranges"
apples and oranges
$ printf "Two fruits are %s and %s\n" !!:2*
printf "Two fruits are %s and %s\n" "apples" "oranges"
Two fruits are apples and oranges
```

After a word designator, you can include a series of command modifiers, each proceeded by a colon:

- :e—Indicates the suffix of a pathname
- :g—Makes the changes "global" over the entire command line
- :h—Indicates the path of a pathname
- :p—Prints but doesn't execute
- :r—Shows the pathname without the filename
- :s/old/new—Substitutes the first occurrence of the string old with new (essentially the same as :^)
- :t—Shows the filename of a pathname
- :q—Quotes the words substituted
- :x—Quotes the words after breaking them into individual words
- :&—Repeats the last :s

Here are a few examples.

```
$ touch /home/kburtch/temp.txt
$ ls -l /home/kburtch/temp.txt
```

```
-rw-rw-r--    1 kburtch  kburtch           0 Jul  5 14:48 /home/kburtch/temp.txt
$ ls -l !!:2:t
ls -l temp.txt
-rw-rw-r--    1 kburtch  kburtch           0 Jul  5 14:48 temp.txt
$ ls -l *!-2:2:e
ls -l *.txt
-rw-rw-r--    1 kburtch  kburtch           0 Jun 25 12:02 last_orders.txt
-rw-rw-r--    1 kburtch  kburtch         592 May 11 14:45 orders.txt
-rw-rw-r--    1 kburtch  kburtch           0 Jul  5 14:48 temp.txt
-rw-rw-r--    1 kburtch  kburtch          33 Jul  4 14:48 test.txt
$ ls -l !-3:2:s/temp/orders
ls -l /home/kburtch/orders.txt
-rw-rw-r--    1 kburtch  kburtch         592 May 11 14:45 /home/kburtch/orders.txt
```

Running Scripts from C

Scripts are often combined with high-level languages like C to provide customizations without having to recompile and link a large project. Although scripting languages such as Guile and Scheme are popular choices, Bash itself is a scripting language, perhaps the quintessential scripting language under Linux.

The C function system starts a shell and runs a command in the shell. The command's parameter is a string that's executed as if a user typed in the command in an interactive session. system returns the shell's exit status, or a −1 if there was a problem starting the shell.

The C program shown in Listing 18.1 runs an ls command.

Listing 18.1 c_system.c

```
/* c_system.c: run a shell command from C using system */

#include <stdio.h>
#include <stdlib.h>

int main() {
  int result;

  result = system ( "ls -l *.sh" );
  return 0;
}
```

When the program runs, the shell command is executed.

```
$ c_system
company.txt
log.txt
orders.txt
temp.txt
```

When using system to run a script, two shell sessions are created; one for system and another to run the script (unless the script is started with exec). To run scripts instead of shell commands, the C popen function is a less cumbersome method. popen runs a program and attaches a pipe to or from the program, as if the shell pipe operator | was used. The command has two parameters: the program to run and its arguments, and an r if the C program reads the standard output of the script, or a w if the program writes to the standard input of the script. When the program is finished, close the pipe with the pclose command.

In the case of shell scripts, the program popen runs is Bash. You can rewrite the c_system.c program using popen, as shown in Listing 18.2.

Listing 18.2   c_popen.c

```
/* c_popen.c: run a Bash command from C using popen */

#include <stdio.h>
#include <stdlib.h>

int main() {

  FILE *f = NULL;                              /* the pipe file */
  char s[ 255 ] = "";                          /* a string buffer */

  f = popen( "/bin/bash -c 'ls -1 *.txt'", "r" ); /* open the pipe */
  while ( ! feof( f ) ) {                       /* while more output */
    fgets( s, 255, f );                        /* get the next line */
    printf( "%s", s );                         /* print the results */
  }
  pclose( f );                                 /* close the pipe */

  return 0;                                    /* successful status */
}
```

The results are the same.

```
$ ./c_popen
company.txt
log.txt
orders.txt
temp.txt
temp.txt
```

If C variables are to be shared with a Bash script, they must be exported to the shell's environment. The C putenv function declares or changes an environment variable. The declaration should be in the same form as a Bash variable assignment. Because putenv increases the size of the environment, there is a chance it might fail. The command returns a zero if the assignment was successfully carried out.

One common mistake when using putenv is reusing the string assigned to the environment. The command actually creates a pointer to the string being assigned; it does not copy the string into the environment. Running a command such as putenv(s) means that the string s must be untouched until it is removed from the environment.

For a simple variable sharing example, suppose you created a script called c_script.sh to multiply a variable called COUNT by the first script argument, as shown in Listing 18.3.

Listing 18.3 c_script.sh

```
#!/bin/bash
#
# c_script.sh: an example of exporting a C variable to a script

shopt -s -o nounset

let "COUNT=COUNT*$1"
echo "$COUNT"

exit 0
```

The script assumes the variable COUNT exists.

```
$ declare -ix COUNT=4
$ bash c_script.sh 3
12
```

Using putenv and popen, a C variable can be copied to the environment, and a new value for the variable can be read from the pipe, as shown in Listing 18.4.

Listing 18.4 c_script.c

```
/* c_script.c: run a script from C using popen */

#include <stdio.h>
#include <stdlib.h>

int main() {

  FILE *f = NULL;                        /* the pipe file */
  char env_count[ 255 ] = "";            /* string buffer for COUNT */
  int count = 5;                         /* C variable count */

  /* Declare COUNT in the environment */

  sprintf( env_count, "COUNT=%d", count );   /* declare env var */
  putenv( env_count );                       /* export it */
```

Listing 18.4 Continued

```
f = popen( "/bin/bash c_script.sh 2", "r" ); /* open the pipe */
fscanf( f, "%d", &count );                   /* read new count */
pclose( f );                                 /* close the pipe */
printf( "count is %d\n", count );            /* print result */

   return 0;
}
```

When the program is executed, the C variable count is assigned the value 10.

```
$ c_script
count is 10
```

Journey's End

When I began this book, I received a lot of comments like "What's to know about the Bash shell. I've used the Bourne shell for 20 years." And I would say to them, "Did you know Bash can open network sockets?" They would stare at me and ask, "Really?"

Bash is more than a successor to the Bourne shell or a popular alternative to the Korn shell. It's a full-featured shell with a powerful scripting language and dozens of built-in commands and functions. It is also open source, and it makes a worthy tool to be bundled with Linux.

Reference Section

echo **Command Switches**

- -E—Doesn't interpret the escape codes
- -e—Interprets escape codes
- -n—The trailing form feed (new line) is suppressed

echo **Escape Codes**

- \a—A beep ("alert")
- \b—A backspace
- \c—Suppresses next character; at the end of string, suppress the trailing line feed
- \E—The escape character
- \f—A form feed
- \n—A line feed (new line)

- \r—A carriage return
- \t—A horizontal tab
- \v—A vertical tab
- \\—A backslash
- \num—The octal ASCII code for a character

compgen **Command Switches**

- -A action—Selects type of completion
- -C command—Runs command and uses results as possible completions
- -F func—Gets a list of possible completions from shell function func
- -G globpat—Uses filename globbing pattern globpat to generate completions
- -P prefix—Adds a prefix to each possible completion
- -o option—Specifies how compspecs are interpreted (default, filenames, or dirnames)
- -S suffix—Adds a suffix to each possible completion
- -W list—Specifies a list of possible completions
- -X filterpat—Filters the completion list using filterpat

compgen **Action Types**

- -A alias (or -a)—Alias names
- -A arrayvar—Array variable names
- -A binding—Binds command key binding names
- -A builtin (or -b)—Built-in shell commands
- -A command (or -c)—Linux commands
- -A directory (or -d)—Directory names
- -A disabled—Names of disabled built-in shell commands
- -A enabled—Names of enabled built-in shell commands
- -A export (or -e)—Exported shell variables
- -A group (or -g)—Group name completion
- -A file (or -f)—Filenames
- -A functions—Shell function names
- -A helptopic—Subjects recognized by the shell help command
- -A hostname—Hostnames in the file indicated by HOSTFILE variable

- `-A job` (or `-j`)—The names of jobs in the job table
- `-A keyword` (or `-k`)—Shell reserved words
- `-A running`—The names of running jobs
- `-A setopt`—The names of `shopt -o` options
- `-A shopt`—The names of `shopt` options (not the `-o` options)
- `-A signal`—The names of signals
- `-A stopped`—The names of stopped jobs
- `-A user` (or `-u`)—Usernames
- `-A variable` (or `-v`)—Shell variable names

`complete` Command Switches

- `-A action`—Selects type of completion
- `-C command`—Runs `command` and uses the results as possible completions
- `-F func`—Gets a list of possible completions from shell function `func`
- `-G globpat`—Uses filename globbing pattern `globpat` to generate completions
- `-P prefix`—Adds a prefix to each possible completion
- `-p`—Lists completions
- `-o option`—Specifies how `compspecs` are interpreted (default, filenames, or dirnames)
- `-r`—Removes completion
- `-S suffix`—Adds a suffix to each possible completion
- `-W list`—Specifies a list of possible completions
- `-X filterpat`—Filters the completion list using `filterpat`

`du` Command Switches

- `--all` (or `-a`)—Writes counts for all files, not just directories
- `--block-size=size`—Uses blocks of `size` bytes
- `--bytes` (or `-b`)—Prints size in bytes
- `--total` (or `-c`)—Produces a grand total
- `--dereference-args` (or `-D`)—Dereferences symbolic links in arguments
- `--human-readable` (or `-h`)—Prints sizes rounded to any easy to understand value
- `--si` (or `-H`)—Like `--human-readable`, but uses powers of 1000, not 1024
- `--kilobytes` (or `-k`)—Prints sizes in kilobytes

- `--count-links` (or `-l`)—Counts sizes each time if the files are hard linked
- `--dereference` (or `-L`)—Dereferences all symbolic links
- `--megabytes` (or `-m`)—Like `--block-size=1048576`
- `--separate-dirs` (or `-S`)—Does not include size of subdirectories
- `--summarize` (or `-s`)—Displays only a total for each argument
- `--one-file-system` (or `-x`)—Skips directories located on different mounted file systems
- `--exclude-from=f` (or `-X f`)—Excludes files that match globbing patterns listed in file f
- `--exclude=PAT`—Excludes files that match globbing pattern PAT
- `--max-depth=N`—Prints directory (or file, with `--all`) totals when N or fewer levels below the root du directory

! Word Modifiers

- `:e`—Indicates the suffix of a pathname
- `:g`—Makes the changes "global" over the entire command line
- `:h`—Indicates the path of a pathname
- `:p`—Prints but doesn't execute
- `:r`—Indicates the pathname without the filename
- `:s/old/new`—Substitutes the first occurrence of the string old with new (essentially the same as `:^`)
- `:t`—Indicates the filename of a pathname
- `:q`—Quotes the words substituted
- `:x`—Quotes the words after breaking them into individual words
- `:&`—Repeats the last `:s`

A Complete Example

PEEK IS A FUN AND USEFUL EXAMPLE OF WHAT SHELL scripts can do. A resource monitoring and troubleshoot script, peek sleeps for 20 or 30 seconds. Upon waking, it checks (or "peeks at") system statistics using commands such as free and vmstat, and draws graphs representing the computer activity. Across the top of the display is the time of the last update, and the actual CPU and memory usage. Below the graphs, warnings appear about potential problems or bottlenecks.

Because the format of commands such as vmstat changes over time, the script might have to be modified for certain distributions. This version was designed for Red Hat 7.3. Figure A.1 shows peek in action.

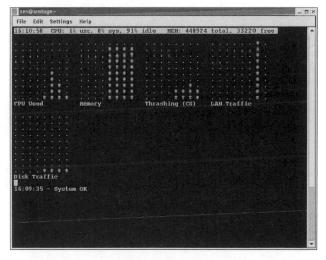

Figure A.1   peek.sh.

The full source code appears in Listing A.1.

Listing A.1   **The Full Source Code for** peek.sh

```bash
#!/bin/bash
#
# peek.sh
#
# Show system resource usage graphs.  Record and display alarms messages
# for important conditions
#
# by Ken O. Burtch
#
# CVS: $Id$
# ─────────────────────────────────────
shopt -s -o nounset
shopt -s -o noclobber


# Bash Variables
#
# Bash may not declare these.  Declare them before we test their values.
# ─────────────────────────────────────

declare -ri COLUMNS                           # BASH COLUMNS variable
declare -ri LINES                             # BASH LINES variable


# Global Declarations
# ─────────────────────────────────────

declare -rx SCRIPT=${0##*/}                   # script name

# Commands paths
#
# Change these paths as required for your system

declare -rx ping="/bin/ping"                  # check network connections
declare -rx vmstat="/usr/bin/vmstat"          # check resource usage
declare -rx df="/bin/df"                      # check disk space
declare -rx free="/usr/bin/free"              # check free memory
declare -rx hostname="/bin/hostname"          # name of computer

# Settings
#
# How long vmstat tests and delay between screen updates. These values should
# be good for most systems.
```

```
declare -rix INTERVAL=4          # vmstat interval (seconds)
declare -rix SLEEP=23            # sleep time between updates (seconds)

# Alarm Settings
#
# These determine when an alarm is announced.  Changes these to suit your
# system.

declare -rix THRASHING=8000      # context switch limit before warning (faults)
declare -rix DISK_LIMIT=2500     # disk bottleneck limit before warning (faults)
declare -rix CPU_LIMIT=90        # CPU busy limit before warning (percent)
declare -rix NET_LIMIT=9         # LAN ping limit before warning (mseconds)
declare -rix MEM_LIMIT=95        # Virtual memory warning limit (percent)
declare -rx  LAN_HOST=hitomi     # Computer to ping over LAN (hostname)
declare -rix DISK_GRAPH_TOP=100  # disk interrupt limit (interrupts)

# Graph bar values
#
# All bars start at zero for each of the seven columns

declare  i CPU1=0 CPU2=0 CPU3=0 CPU4=0 CPU5=0 CPU6=0 CPU7=0 CPU8=0
declare -i MEM1=0 MEM2=0 MEM3=0 MEM4=0 MEM5=0 MEM6=0 MEM7=0 MEM8=0
declare -i PAG1=0 PAG2=0 PAG3=0 PAG4=0 PAG5=0 PAG6=0 PAG7=0 PAG8=0
declare -i NET1=0 NET2=0 NET3=0 NET4=0 NET5=0 NET6=0 NET7=0 NET8=0
declare -i DSK1=0 DSK2=0 DSK3=0 DSK4=0 DSK5=0 DSK6=0 DSK7=0 DSK8=0

# Alarm Log
#
# The alarm log holds no more than 8 entries

declare LOG1 LOG2 LOG3 LOG4 LOG5 LOG6 LOG7 LOG8

declare LASTLOG=                 # last alarm message
declare SYSTEM_OK=               # cleared if there was an alarm
declare LOG_UPDATED=             # set if the log has changed

# Global constants
#
# Put tput values in variables for speed

declare -rx HOME_CURSOR=`tput home`   # cursor to top-left corner
declare -rx UP=`tput cuu1`            # move cursor up
declare -rx DOWN=`tput cud1`          # move cursor down
#declare -rx DOWN=`echo -e "\e[B"`
declare -rx LEFT=`tput cub1`          # move cursor left
declare -rx RIGHT=`tput cuf1`         # move cursor right
```

Listing A.1 **Continued**

```
declare -rx CEOL=`tput el`              # clear to end of the line
declare -rx INVERSE=`tput smso`         # reverse video on
declare -rx INVERSE_OFF=`tput rmso`     # reverse video off
declare -rx UP10="$UP$UP$UP$UP$UP$UP$UP$UP$UP$UP"
declare -rx DOWN10="$DOWN$DOWN$DOWN$DOWN$DOWN$DOWN$DOWN$DOWN$DOWN"

# VMSTAT fields

declare -ix PROC_R=                     # Ready processes
declare -ix PROC_B=                     # Blocked processes
declare -ix PROC_W=                     # Swapped out processes
declare -ix MEM_SWPD=                   # Active virtual mem (KB)
declare -ix MEM_FREE=                   # Free virtual mem (KB)
declare -ix MEM_BUF=                    # Buffer space (KB)
declare -ix MEM_CACHE=                  # Disk cache (KB)
declare -ix SWAP_SI=                    # Swapped in processes
declare -ix SWAP_SO=                    # Swapped out processes
declare -ix IO_BLKI=                    # Blocks sent to IO devices
declare -ix IO_BLKO=                    # Blocks received from IO devices
declare -ix SYS_SI=                     # interrupts (incl. the clock)
declare -ix SYS_CS=                     # Context switches
declare -ix CPU_US=                     # User CPU usage
declare -ix CPU_SY=                     # System CPU usage
declare -ix IDLE=                       # CPU idle time

# Misc Global Variables

declare TIME=`date '+%H:%M:%S'`         # current time
declare TMP=                            # temporary results
declare TMP2=
declare TMP3=
declare -i CPU=                         # current CPU busy (percent)
declare -i MEM=                         # current virtual memory (percent)
declare PAGE=                           # current context switches
declare NET=                            # current network speed (mseconds)
declare LEN=                            # length of a string
declare OLD=                            # for fixing vmstat results
declare -i DSK=                         # disk activity (interrupts)
declare -i MEM_TOTAL=0                  # Total virtual memory

# Functions


# VERTICAL BAR
```

```
#
# Draw a vertical bar graph 10 characters high.  The bar is drawn with '#'
# and the blank areas with '.'.
#
# Parameter 1 - the value of the graph , a percent
# Parameter 2 - the old value of the bar, to speed drawing
# ─────────────────────────────────────

function vertical_bar {

  declare -i DOTCNT  # number of periods to draw
  declare -i CNT     # number of number signs to draw

  # If the new bar is equal to the old one in this spot, don't bother
  # redrawing since it hasn't changed—unless it's zero since we may be
  # drawing this column for the first time.

  if [ $1 -ne 0 ] ; then
     if [ $1 -eq $2 ] ; then
        printf "%s" "$RIGHT""$RIGHT"
        return
     fi
  fi

  # Convert the magnitude of the bar to a number between 0 and 10
  # Round to the nearest integer
  # Constrain the percent to 0..10 if it is out of range

  if [ $1 -gt 100 ] ; then
     CNT=10
  elif [ $1 -lt 0 ]; then
     CNT=0
  else
     CNT=\($1+5\)/10          # 0..100 rounded to 0..10
  fi

  # Draw the vertical bar.  DOTCNT is the number of periods to draw
  # to fill in the graph.

  DOTCNT=10-CNT
  while [ $((DOTCNT--)) -gt 0 ] ; do
    printf "%s" "."""$DOWN""$LEFT"
  done
  while [ $((CNT--)) -gt 0 ] ; do
    printf "%s" "#""$DOWN""$LEFT"
  done
```

Listing A.1   **Continued**

```
  printf "%s" "$UP10""$RIGHT""$RIGHT"


}
readonly -f vertical_bar
declare -t vertical_bar


# CPU GRAPH
#
# Update the vertical bar CPU usage graph.
# Parmaeter 1 - the new bar height to add to the graph
# ─────────────────────────────────────

function cpu_graph {

  if [ -z "$1" ] ; then # debug
      alarm "$FUNCNAME received a null string"
      return
  fi
  LAST="$CPU8"
  CPU8="$CPU7"
  CPU7="$CPU6"
  CPU6="$CPU5"
  CPU5="$CPU4"
  CPU4="$CPU3"
  CPU3="$CPU2"
  CPU2="$CPU1"
  CPU1="$1"

  vertical_bar "$CPU8" "$LAST"
  vertical_bar "$CPU7" "$CPU8"
  vertical_bar "$CPU6" "$CPU7"
  vertical_bar "$CPU5" "$CPU6"
  vertical_bar "$CPU4" "$CPU5"
  vertical_bar "$CPU3" "$CPU4"
  vertical_bar "$CPU2" "$CPU3"
  vertical_bar "$CPU1" "$CPU2"

  printf "%s" "$RIGHT""$RIGHT"

}
readonly -f cpu_graph
declare -t cpu_graph
```

```
# MEM GRAPH
#
# Update the vertical bar memory graph
# Parmaeter 1 - the new bar height to add to the graph
# ─────────────────────────────────────

function mem_graph {

  # Sanity check

  if [ -z "$1" ] ; then # debug
     alarm "$FUNCNAME received a null string"
     return
  fi

  # Insert new value into the graph

  LAST="$MEM8"
  MEM8="$MEM7"
  MEM7="$MEM6"
  MEM6="$MEM5"
  MEM5="$MEM4"
  MEM4="$MEM3"
  MEM3="$MEM2"
  MEM2="$MEM1"
  MEM1="$1"

  # Draw the bars

  vertical_bar "$MEM8" "$LAST"
  vertical_bar "$MEM7" "$MEM8"
  vertical_bar "$MEM6" "$MEM7"
  vertical_bar "$MEM5" "$MEM6"
  vertical_bar "$MEM4" "$MEM5"
  vertical_bar "$MEM3" "$MEM4"
  vertical_bar "$MEM2" "$MEM3"
  vertical_bar "$MEM1" "$MEM2"

  printf "%s" "$RIGHT""$RIGHT"

}
readonly -f mem_graph
declare -t mem_graph


# PAGE GRAPH
```

Listing A.1   **Continued**

```
#
# Update the vertical bar page fault graph
# Parmaeter 1 - the new bar height to add to the graph
# ─────────────────────────────────────

function page_graph {

  # Sanity check

  if [ -z "$1" ] ; then # debug
     alarm "$FUNCNAME received a null string"
     return
  fi

  # Insert new value into the graph

  LAST="$PAG8"
  PAG8="$PAG7"
  PAG7="$PAG6"
  PAG6="$PAG5"
  PAG5="$PAG4"
  PAG4="$PAG3"
  PAG3="$PAG2"
  PAG2="$PAG1"
  PAG1="$1"

  # Draw the bars

  vertical_bar "$PAG8" "$LAST"
  vertical_bar "$PAG7" "$PAG8"
  vertical_bar "$PAG6" "$PAG7"
  vertical_bar "$PAG5" "$PAG6"
  vertical_bar "$PAG4" "$PAG5"
  vertical_bar "$PAG3" "$PAG4"
  vertical_bar "$PAG2" "$PAG3"
  vertical_bar "$PAG1" "$PAG2"
  printf "%s" "$RIGHT""$RIGHT"

}
readonly -f page_graph
declare -t page_graph


# NET GRAPH
```

```
#
# Update the vertical bar page network traffic
# Parmaeter 1 - the new bar height to add to the graph
# ————————————————————————————

function net_graph {

  # Sanity check

  if [ -z "$1" ] ; then # debug
     alarm "$FUNCNAME received a null string"
     return
  fi

  # Insert new value into the graph

  LAST="$NET8"
  NET8="$NET7"
  NET7="$NET6"
  NET6="$NET5"
  NET5="$NET4"
  NET4="$NET3"
  NET3="$NET2"
  NET2="$NET1"
  NET1="$1"

  # Draw the bars

  vertical_bar "$NET8" "$LAST"
  vertical_bar "$NET7" "$NET8"
  vertical_bar "$NET6" "$NET7"
  vertical_bar "$NET5" "$NET6"
  vertical_bar "$NET4" "$NET5"
  vertical_bar "$NET3" "$NET4"
  vertical_bar "$NET2" "$NET3"
  vertical_bar "$NET1" "$NET2"

  printf "%s" "$RIGHT""$RIGHT"

}
readonly -f net_graph
declare -t net_graph


# DISK GRAPH
#
```

Listing A.1 **Continued**

```
# Update the vertical bar page disk interrupts
# Parmaeter 1 - the new bar height to add to the graph
# ─────────────────────────────────────────

function disk_graph {

  # Sanity check

  if [ -z "$1" ] ; then # debug
     alarm "$FUNCNAME received a null string"
     return
  fi

  # Insert new value into the graph

  LAST="$DSK8"
  DSK8="$DSK7"
  DSK7="$DSK6"
  DSK6="$DSK5"
  DSK5="$DSK4"
  DSK4="$DSK3"
  DSK3="$DSK2"
  DSK2="$DSK1"
  DSK1="$1"

  # Draw the bars

  vertical_bar "$DSK8" "$LAST"
  vertical_bar "$DSK7" "$DSK8"
  vertical_bar "$DSK6" "$DSK7"
  vertical_bar "$DSK5" "$DSK6"
  vertical_bar "$DSK4" "$DSK5"
  vertical_bar "$DSK3" "$DSK4"
  vertical_bar "$DSK2" "$DSK3"
  vertical_bar "$DSK1" "$DSK2"
  printf "%s" "$RIGHT""$RIGHT"

}
readonly -f disk_graph
declare -t disk_graph


# ALARM
#
```

```
# Add a message to the alarm log.  Duplicate messages are discarded.
# Parameter 1 = the message to add
# ————————————————————————————————

function alarm {

  # Anything logged this time around means system isn't OK, even if it was
  # a repeated message that was suppressed

  SYSTEM_OK=

  # Ignore repeated alarms

  [ "$1" = "$LASTLOG" ] && return
  LASTLOG="$1"

  # Add the log message to the list of alarms

  LOG8="$LOG7"
  LOG7="$LOG6"
  LOG6="$LOG5"
  LOG5="$LOG4"
  LOG4="$LOG3"
  LOG3="$LOG2"
  LOG2="$LOG1"
  LOG1="$TIME - ""$1"

  LOG_UPDATED=1
}
readonly -f alarm
declare -t alarm



# ————————————————————————————————
# Main Script Begins Here
# ————————————————————————————————


# Usage/Help
# ————————————————————————————————

if [ $# -gt 0 ] ; then
    if [ "$1" = "-h" -o "$1" = "—help" ] ; then
        printf "%s\n" "$SCRIPT:$LINENO: Show system resource usage graphs"
        printf "%s\n" "There are no parameters for this script"
        printf "\n"
```

Listing A.1   **Continued**

```
      exit 0
   else
      printf "%s\n" "$SCRIPT:$LINENO: Unexpected options/parameters"
      exit 192
   fi
fi


# Sanity checks
# ─────────────────────────────

if [ ! -x "$ping" ] ; then
   printf "%s\n" "$SCRIPT:$LINENO: Can't find/execute $ping" >&2
   exit 192
fi
if [ ! -x "$vmstat" ] ; then
   printf "%s\n" "$SCRIPT:$LINENO: Can't find/execute $vmstat" >&2
   exit 192
fi
if [ ! -x "$df" ] ; then
   printf "%s\n" "$SCRIPT:$LINENO: Can't find/execute $df" >&2
   exit 192
fi
if [ ! -x "$free" ] ; then
   printf "%s\n" "$SCRIPT:$LINENO: Can't find/execute $free" >&2
   exit 192
fi
if [ -z "$LINES" ] ; then
   printf "%s\n" "$SCRIPT:$LINENO: LINES is not declared.  Export LINES" >&2
   exit 192
fi
if [ $LINES -lt 35 ] ; then
   printf "%s\n" "$SCRIPT:$LINENO: Your display must be >= 35 lines high" >&2
   exit 192
fi
if [ -z "$COLUMNS" ] ; then
   printf "%s\n" "$SCRIPT:$LINENO: COLUMNS is not declare.  Export COLUMNS" >&2
   exit 192
fi
if [ $COLUMNS -lt 80 ] ; then
   printf "%s\n" "$SCRIPT:$LINENO: Your display must be >= 80 columns wide" >&2
   exit 192
fi
if [ -z "$HOME_CURSOR" ] ; then
```

```
    printf "%s\n" "$SCRIPT:$LINENO: cannot HOME the cursor" >&2
    printf "%s\n" "on this $TERM display" >&2
    exit 192
fi
if [ -z "$UP" ] ; then
    printf "%s\n" "$SCRIPT:$LINENO: cannot move the cursor UP" >&2
    printf "%s\n" "on this $TERM display" >&2
    exit 192
fi
if [ -z "$DOWN" ] ; then
    printf "%s\n" "$SCRIPT:$LINENO: cannot move the cursor DOWN" >&2
    printf "%s" " (Some terminfo/termcap databases have cud1/do set" >&2
    printf "%s\n" " improperly)" >&2
    printf "%s\n" " (Try declaring down as DOWN=\$'\e[B')" >&2
    exit 192
fi
if [ -z "$LEFT" ] ; then
    printf "%s\n" "$SCRIPT:$LINENO: cannot move the cursor LEFT" >&2
    printf "%s\n" "on this $TERM display" >&2
    exit 192
fi
if [ -z "$RIGHT" ] ; then
    printf "%s\n" "$SCRIPT:$LINENO: cannot move the cursor RIGHT" >&2
    printf "%s\n" "on this $TERM display" >&2
    exit 192
fi
if [ -z "$CEOL" ] ; then
    printf "%s\n" "$SCRIPT:$LINENO: cannot clear to end of line" >&2
    printf "%s\n" "on this $TERM display" >&2
    exit 192
fi
if [ ! -x "$hostname" ] ; then
    printf "%s\n" "$SCRIPT:$LINENO: cannot find or execute $hostname" >&2
    exit 192
fi
declare -rx HOST=`uname -n`                    # name of computer


# Get the total amount of physical memory

MEM_TOTAL=`free | grep "^Mem" | tr -s ' ' | cut -d\  -f2`

# Clear the screen

tput reset
tput clear
```

Listing A.1 **Continued**

```
printf "%s - system monitor script    Please wait...\n" "$0"


# ─────────────────────────────────────────
# Main Loop
# ─────────────────────────────────────────


while true ; do

  # Get the system statistics with vmstat

  TMP=`nice -20 $vmstat $INTERVAL 2 2>&1`
  if [ $? -ne 0 ] ; then
      alarm `printf "vmstat error: %s" "$TMP" | tail -1`
      VMSTAT=
  else
      VMSTAT=`printf "%s\n" "$TMP" | tail -1`
  fi
  LEN=${#VMSTAT}   # length of VMSTAT
  OLD=0


  # Reduce all spaces to single spaces.  Trim leading spaces

  while [ $LEN -ne $OLD ] ; do
      OLD=$LEN
      VMSTAT="${VMSTAT//  / }"
      VMSTAT=`printf "%s\n" "$VMSTAT" | sed 's/^\ //g'`
      LEN=${#VMSTAT}
  done


  # Extract the vmstat columns into variables
  # Use only what we need

  #PROC_R=`printf "%s\n" "$VMSTAT" | cut -d\  -f1`
  #PROC_B=`printf "%s\n" "$VMSTAT" | cut -d\  -f2`
  PROC_W=`printf "%s\n" "$VMSTAT" | cut -d\  -f3`
  #MEM_SWPD=`printf "%s\n" "$VMSTAT" | cut -d\  -f4`
  MEM_FREE=`printf "%s\n" "$VMSTAT" | cut -d\  -f5`
  MEM_BUF=`printf "%s\n" "$VMSTAT" | cut -d\  -f6`
  MEM_CACHE=`printf "%s\n" "$VMSTAT" | cut -d\  -f7`
  #SWAP_SI=`printf "%s\n" "$VMSTAT" | cut -d\  -f8`
```

```
#SWAP_SO=`printf "%s\n" "$VMSTAT" | cut -d\  -f9`
#IO_BLKI=`printf "%s\n" "$VMSTAT" | cut -d\  -f10`
#IO_BLKO=`printf "%s\n" "$VMSTAT" | cut -d\  -f11`
SYS_SI=`printf "%s\n" "$VMSTAT" | cut -d\  -f12`
SYS_CS=`printf "%s\n" "$VMSTAT" | cut -d\  -f13`
CPU_US=`printf "%s\n" "$VMSTAT" | cut -d\  -f14`
CPU_SY=`printf "%s\n" "$VMSTAT" | cut -d\  -f15`
IDLE=`printf "%s\n" "$VMSTAT" | cut -d\  -f16`


# Get ready to update the screen

TIME=`date '+%H:%M:%S'`
SYSTEM_OK=1
LOG_UPDATED=

# Perform the network test
#
# (some ping's won't return an error if it fails so we'll double check by
# making sure "trip" is in the # result.  No "trip" means probably an error
# message.)

TMP=`$ping $LAN_HOST -c 1 2>&1`
TMP2="$?"
TMP3=`printf "%s" "$TMP" | grep trip`
if [ $TMP2 -ne 0 -o -z "$TMP3" ] ; then
   alarm "Ping to LAN host $LAN_HOST failed: network load unknown"
   NET=99
else
   NET=`printf "%s\n" "$TMP3" | cut -d\/  -f4 | cut -d\. -f1`
   if [ ${NET:0:4} = "mdev" ] ; then
      NET=`printf "%s\n" "$TMP3" | cut -d\/  -f5 | cut -d\. -f1`
   fi
fi


# Draw stats bar at the top of the screen

printf "%s" "$HOME_CURSOR""$INVERSE""$TIME""   "
printf "%s" "CPU: $CPU_US""%"" usr, $CPU_SY""%"" sys, $IDLE""%"" idle    "
printf "%s\n" "MEM: $MEM_TOTAL total, $MEM_FREE free $CEOL""$INVERSE_OFF"


# Compute values for the vertical bar graphs & Alarm tests

# CPU busy is the 100% minus the idle percent
```

Listing A.1   **Continued**

```
# Show an alarm if the CPU limit is exceeded three times
# or if the kernel usage exceeds 50%

CPU=100-IDLE
if [ $CPU_SY -gt 50 ] ; then
    alarm "Kernel bottleneck - system CPU usage $CPU_SY""%"
fi
if [ $CPU -gt $CPU_LIMIT ] ; then
    if [ $CPU1 -gt $CPU_LIMIT ] ; then
        if [ $CPU2 -gt $CPU_LIMIT ] ; then
            alarm "CPU bottleneck - $CPU""% busy"
        fi
    fi
fi

# Signs of heavy system loads

if [ $SYS_CS -gt $THRASHING ] ; then
    alarm "System Thrashing - $SYS_CS context switches"
elif [ "$PROC_W" -gt 0 ] ; then
    alarm "Swapped out $PROC_W processes"
fi

# Show an alarm if the net limit is exceeded three times

if [ $NET -gt $NET_LIMIT ] ; then
    if [ $NET1 -gt $NET_LIMIT ] ; then
        if [ $NET2 -gt $NET_LIMIT ] ; then
            alarm "Network bottleneck - $NET ms"
        fi
    fi
fi
if [ $SYS_SI -gt $DISK_LIMIT ] ; then
    alarm "Disk bottleneck - $SYS_SI device interrupts"
fi

# Physical memory is used memory / total memory
# Show an alarm if the limit is exceeded three times

MEM=100*\(MEM_TOTAL-MEM_FREE\)/MEM_TOTAL
if [ $MEM2 -gt $MEM_LIMIT ] ; then
    if [ $MEM1 -gt $MEM_LIMIT ] ; then
        if [ $MEM -gt $MEM_LIMIT ] ; then
            alarm "virtual memory shortage - memory $MEM""% in use"
```

```
      fi
   fi
fi

# Check temp directory space

TMP=`$df 2>&1`
if [ $? -ne 0 ] ; then
   alarm "`printf "%s" "$TMP" | tail -1`"
else
   TMP=`printf "%s" "$TMP" | grep " /tmp"`
   if [ -n "$TMP" ] ; then                      # if on a partition
      TMP=`printf "%s" "$TMP" | grep "100%"`
      if [ -n "$TMP" ] ; then
         alarm "$0: /tmp appears to be full"
      fi
   fi
fi

PAGE=SYS_CS/80                                   # top of Faults graph is 8000


# Draw vertical bar graphs

printf "\n"
cpu_graph  "$CPU"
mem_graph  "$MEM"
page_graph "$PAGE"
net_graph "$((10*NET))"                          # 100% = 10 nanoseconds

printf "%s\n" "$DOWN10"
printf "%s" "CPU Used          Memory           Thrashing (CS)"
printf "%s\n\n" "    LAN Traffic"

DSK=SYS_SI/DISK_GRAPH_TOP
disk_graph "$DSK"

printf "%s\n" "$DOWN10"
printf "%s\n" "Disk Traffic"


# Nothing new logged?  Then show all is well in log
# (SYSTEM_OK is cleared in the alarm function)

[ -n "$SYSTEM_OK" ] && alarm "System OK"
```

```
# Show alarm history, but only if it has changed

if [ -n "$LOG_UPDATED" ] ; then
   printf "%s\n"
   printf "%s\n" "$LOG1" "$CEOL"
   printf "%s\n" "$LOG2" "$CEOL"
   printf "%s\n" "$LOG3" "$CEOL"
   printf "%s\n" "$LOG4" "$CEOL"
   printf "%s\n" "$LOG5" "$CEOL"
   printf "%s\n" "$LOG6" "$CEOL"
   printf "%s\n" "$LOG7" "$CEOL"
   printf "%s\n" "$LOG8" "$CEOL"
fi

# sit quietly for a while before generating next screen

nice sleep $SLEEP

done

exit 0
```

B

Summary of Bash Built-In Commands

alias—Manages aliases.

bg—Starts a suspended task in the background.

bind—Manages keyboard mappings.

builtin—Runs a built-in shell command.

cd—Changes the directory.

command—Runs a Linux command.

declare—Declares variables.

dirs—Displays cd directory stack.

disown—Stops monitoring a background job.

echo—Prints to standard output.

enable—Turns the built-in shell commands on or off.

eval—Runs a command after performing shell substitutions/expansions.

exec—Leaves the shell and switches to a new program.

exit—Exits Bash and returns a status code.

export—Manages exported variables.

false—Returns a non-zero status code.

fc—Finds and edits command history lines.

fg—Runs a suspended job in the foreground.

function—Declares a function.

hash—Manages a Bash command table.

history—Manages the command history.

jobs—Manages your background jobs.

let—Evaluates expressions.

local—Declares a local function variable.

logout—Exits the shell when in interactive mode.

popd—Discards a cd directory stack entry.

printf—Prints with formatting to standard output.

pushd—Adds a change directory stack entry.

pwd—Shows the current directory's pathname.

read—Reads from standard input or a file.

readonly—Manages read-only variables.

return—Returns from a function.

set—Turns a Bash option on or off, or assigns new parameter values.

shift—Shifts the parameters.

shopt—Shows or changes shell options.

source—Runs another script and returns.

suspend—Puts a script to sleep until a signal is received.

test—Evaluates an expression.

time—Shows execution statistics for a command.

times—Shows the accumulated execution statistics for the shell.

trap—Manages signal handlers or catch signals.

true—Returns a success status code (that is, 0).

type—Determines the type of command (that is, whether it's built in or an external command).

typeset—(obsolete) Declares variables.

ulimit—Manages the user's resources.

umask—Manages the default file-creation permissions.

unalias—Discards an alias.

unset—Discards a variable.

C

Bash Options

Table C.1   shopt **Options**

Option	Default	Description
-o allexport	Off	All variables that are modified or created are exported.
-o braceexapnd	On	The shell performs curly brace expansion.
cdable_vars	Off	The built-in cd command assumes that unrecognized directories are variables containing a directory path.
cdspell	Off	Spell-checks the directory component in a cd path.
checkhash	Off	Verifies that commands in the command lookup table still exist before trying a path search for the command to run.
checkwinsize	Off	Determines whether the display window has been resized after every command.
cmdhist	On	Allows multiple line history command editing.
dotglob	Off	Allows . files in a pathname expansion.
-o emacs	Off	Use emacs-style line-editing keys.
-o errexit	Off	Exits immediately if a command exits with a non-zero status.
execfail	Off	Script fails when built-in exec command can't execute a command.
expand_aliases	On	Allows aliases.
extglob	Off	Enables extended pattern-matching features for file-names.
-o hashall	On	Remembers the location of commands as they are looked up.
histappend	Off	Command history appends the history file instead of overwriting it.

Table C.1 **Continued**

Option	Default	Description
histreedit	Off	Enables user to edit failed history substitutions.
-o histexpand	On	Enables ! style history substitution.
-o history	on	Enables command history.
histverify	Off	History substitutions can be further edited.
hostcomplete	On	Completes hostnames containing an @.
huponexit	Off	Sends a hang-up signal to all jobs still running when this script exits.
-o ignoreeof	Off	Ensures that an interactive shell will not exit upon reading end-of-file.
interactive-comments	On	Allows comments to appear in interactive commands.
-o keyword	Off	All assignment arguments are placed in the environment for a command, not just those that precede the command name.
lithist	Off	A line with multiple commands is split up and stored as separate commands in the command history.
mailwarn	Off	Informs the user when new mail arrives when at the shell prompt.
-o monitor	On	Enables job control.
no_empty_cmd_completion	Off	Doesn't allow command completion on an empty line.
nocaseglob	Off	Ignores case when pattern-matching pathnames.
-o noclobber	Off	If set, does not allow existing regular files to be overwritten by redirection of output.
-o noexec	Off	Reads commands but does not execute them.
-o noglob	Off	Disables filename generation (*globbing*).
-o notify	Off	Notifies users of job termination immediately.
-o nounset	Off	Treats unset variables as errors when substituting.
nullglob	Off	Patterns that do not match anything return an empty string instead of themselves.
-o onecmd	Off	Exits after reading and executing one command.
-o physical	Off	If set, does not follow symbolic links when executing commands, such as cd, that change the current directory.
-o posix	Off	Conforms to the POSIX 1003.2 standard.
-o privileged	Off	Turned on whenever the real and effective user IDs do not match. Disables processing of the $ENV file and -o importing of shell functions. Turning this option off causes the effective uid and gid to be set to the real uid and gid.

Table C.1 **Continued**

Option	Default	Description
progcomp	On	Enables programmable completion.
promptvars	On	Process prompts strings for variables and parameters.
restricted_shell	–	On if the shell is a restricted shell. This option is read-only.
shift_verbose	Off	Returns an error when no parameters are left to shift.
sourcepath	On	Finds scripts for . or source commands using the PATH variable.
-o verbose	Off	Prints shell input lines as they are read.
-o vi	Off	Uses vi-style line-editing keys.
xpg_echo	Off	Built-in command echo processes escape sequences by default.
-o xtrace	Off	Prints commands and their arguments as they are executed.

Table C.2 **Bash set Switches**

Switch	Description
-a	Same as allexport
-b	Same as notify
-e	Same as errexit
-f	Same as noglob
-h	Same as hashall
-I	Forces the shell to be an "interactive" one. Interactive shells always read ~/.bashrc on startup
-k	Same as keyword
-m	Same as monitor
-n	Same as noexec
-o option	Changes a shopt option (same as shopt -o)
-p	Same as privileged
-t	Same as oncmd
-u	Same as nounset
-v	Same as verbose
-x	Same as xtrace
-B	Same as braceexpand
-C	Same as noclobber
-H	Same as histexpand
-P	Same as physical

D

Error Codes

THE FOLLOWING LIST CONTAINS THE C language short form for an error code, the error code numeric value, and a short description of the error.

C Name	Value	Description
EPERM	1	Operation not permitted
ENOENT	2	No such file or directory
ESRCH	3	No such process
EINTR	4	Interrupted system call
EIO	5	I/O error
ENXIO	6	No such device or address
E2BIG	7	Arg list too long
ENOEXEC	8	Exec format error
EBADF	9	Bad file number
ECHILD	10	No child processes
EAGAIN	11	Try again
ENOMEM	12	Out of memory
EACCES	13	Permission denied
EFAULT	14	Bad address
ENOTBLK	15	Block device required
EBUSY	16	Device or resource busy
EEXIST	17	File exists
EXDEV	18	Cross-device link
ENODEV	19	No such device
ENOTDIR	20	Not a directory
EISDIR	21	Is a directory
EINVAL	22	Invalid argument
ENFILE	23	File table overflow

C Name	Value	Description
EMFILE	24	Too many open files
ENOTTY	25	Not a tty device
ETXTBSY	26	Text file busy
EFBIG	27	File too large
ENOSPC	28	No space left on device
ESPIPE	29	Illegal seek
EROFS	30	Read-only file system
EMLINK	31	Too many links
EPIPE	32	Broken pipe
EDOM	33	Math argument out of domain
ERANGE	34	Math result not representable
EDEADLK	35	Resource deadlock would occur
ENAMETOOLONG	36	Filename too long
ENOLCK	37	No record locks available
ENOSYS	38	Function not implemented
ENOTEMPTY	39	Directory not empty
ELOOP	40	Too many symbolic links encountered
EWOULDBLOCK	–	Same as EAGAIN
ENOMSG	42	No message of desired type
EIDRM	43	Identifier removed
ECHRNG	44	Channel number out of range
EL2NSYNC	45	Level 2 not synchronized
EL3HLT	46	Level 3 halted
EL3RST	47	Level 3 reset
ELNRNG	48	Link number out of range
EUNATCH	49	Protocol driver not attached
ENOCSI	50	No CSI structure available
EL2HLT	51	Level 2 halted
EBADE	52	Invalid exchange
EBADR	53	Invalid request descriptor
EXFULL	54	Exchange full
ENOANO	55	No anode
EBADRQC	56	Invalid request code
EBADSLT	57	Invalid slot
EDEADLOCK	–	Same as EDEADLK
EBFONT	59	Bad font file format
ENOSTR	60	Device not a stream
ENODATA	61	No data available

C Name	Value	Description
ETIME	62	Timer expired
ENOSR	63	Out of streams resources
ENONET	64	Machine is not on the network
ENOPKG	65	Package not installed
EREMOTE	66	Object is remote
ENOLINK	67	Link has been severed
EADV	68	Advertise error
ESRMNT	69	Srmount error
ECOMM	70	Communication error on send
EPROTO	71	Protocol error
EMULTIHOP	72	Multihop attempted
EDOTDOT	73	RFS specific error
EBADMSG	74	Not a data message
EOVERFLOW	75	Value too large for defined data type
ENOTUNIQ	76	Name not unique on network
EBADFD	77	File descriptor in bad state
EREMCHG	78	Remote address changed
ELIBACC	79	Cannot access a needed shared library
ELIBBAD	80	Accessing a corrupted shared library
ELIBSCN	81	A .lib section in an .out is corrupted
ELIBMAX	82	Linking in too many shared libraries
ELIBEXEC	83	Cannot exec a shared library directly
EILSEQ	84	Illegal byte sequence
ERESTART	85	Interrupted system call should be restarted
ESTRPIPE	86	Streams pipe error
EUSERS	87	Too many users
ENOTSOCK	88	Socket operation on non-socket
EDESTADDRREQ	89	Destination address required
EMSGSIZE	90	Message too long
EPROTOTYPE	91	Protocol wrong type for socket
ENOPROTOOPT	92	Protocol not available
EPROTONOSUPPORT	93	Protocol not supported
ESOCKTNOSUPPORT	94	Socket type not supported
EOPNOTSUPP	95	Operation not supported on transport endpoint
EPFNOSUPPORT	96	Protocol family not supported
EAFNOSUPPORT	97	Address family not supported by protocol
EADDRINUSE	98	Address already in use
EADDRNOTAVAIL	99	Cannot assign requested address

C Name	Value	Description
ENETDOWN	100	Network is down
ENETUNREACH	101	Network is unreachable
ENETRESET	102	Network dropped connection because of reset
ECONNABORTED	103	Software caused connection abort
ECONNRESET	104	Connection reset by peer
ENOBUFS	105	No buffer space available
EISCONN	106	Transport endpoint is already connected
ENOTCONN	107	Transport endpoint is not connected
ESHUTDOWN	108	Cannot send after transport endpoint shutdown
ETOOMANYREFS	109	Too many references; cannot splice
ETIMEDOUT	110	Connection timed out
ECONNREFUSED	111	Connection refused
EHOSTDOWN	112	Host is down
EHOSTUNREACH	113	No route to host
EALREADY	114	Operation already in progress
EINPROGRESS	115	Operation now in progress
ESTALE	116	Stale NFS file handle
EUCLEAN	117	Structure needs cleaning
ENOTNAM	118	Not a XENIX-named type file
ENAVAIL	119	No XENIX semaphores available
EISNAM	120	Is a named type file
EREMOTEIO	121	Remote I/O error
EDQUOT	122	Quota exceeded
ENOMEDIUM	123	No medium found
EMEDIUMTYPE	124	Wrong medium type

E

Signals

THE FOLLOWING LIST CONTAINS THE C LANGUAGE short form for a signal, the signal numeric value, and a short description of the purpose of the signal.

Value	C Name	Description
1	SIGHUP	Connection hang up
2	SIGINT	Interrupt
3	SIGQUIT	Quit
4	SIGILL	Illegal instruction (not reset)
5	SIGTRAP	Trace trap (not reset)
6	SIGABRT	Used by abort
7	SIGBUS	Bus error
8	SIGFPE	Floating-point exception
9	SIGKILL	Kill (cannot be caught or ignored)
10	SIGUSR1	User defined
11	SIGSEGV	Segmentation violation
12	SIGUSR2	User defined
13	SIGPIPE	Write on a pipe with no one to read it
14	SIGALRM	Alarm clock
15	SIGTERM	Terminate (kill default)
17	SIGCHLD	Child status change
18	SIGCONT	Stopped process has been continued
19	SIGSTOP	Stop (cannot be caught or ignored)
20	SIGTSTP	User stop requested from tty
21	SIGTTIN	Background tty read attempted
22	SIGTTOU	Background tty write attempted

Value	C Name	Description
23	SIGURG	Urgent condition on I/O channel
24	SIGXCPU	CPU time limit exceeded
25	SIGXFSZ	File size limit exceeded
26	SIGVTALRM	Virtual timer expired
27	SIGPROF	Profiling timer expired
28	SIGWINCH	Window size change
29	SIGIO	Input/output possible
30	SIGPWR	Power failure
31	SIGSYS	Bad system call

ASCII Table

THE FOLLOWING IS A LIST OF ASCII CODES, their official name, the console keys for those codes, and any special HTML or `printf` characters used to represent them.

Decimal	Octal	Hexadecimal	Name	Keyboard	HTML/`printf` Equivalent
0	0	0	NUL	Control-@	-
1	1	1	SOH	Control-A	-
2	2	2	STX	Control-B	-
3	3	3	ETX	Control-C	-
4	4	4	EOT	Control-D	-
5	5	5	ENQ	Control-E	-
6	6	6	ACK	Control-F	-
7	7	7	BEL	Control-G	-
8	10	8	BS	Control-H	\b
9	11	9	TAB	Control-I	\t
10	12	A	LF	Control-J	\n
11	13	B	VT	Control-K	\v
12	14	C	FF	Control-L	\f
13	15	D	CR	Control-K	\r
14	16	E	SO	Control-L	-
15	17	F	SI	Control-M	-
16	20	10	DLE	Control-N	-
17	21	11	DC1	Control-O	-
18	22	12	DC2	Control-P	-
19	23	13	DC3	Control-Q	-
20	24	14	DC4	Control-R	-
21	25	15	NAK	Control-S	-
22	26	16	SYN	Control-T	-

Decimal	Octal	Hexadecimal	Name	Keyboard	HTML/printf Equivalent
23	27	17	ETB	Control-U	-
24	30	18	CAN	Control-V	-
25	31	19	EM	Control-W	-
26	32	1A	SUB	Control-X	-
27	33	1B	EASC	Control-Y	-
28	34	1C	FS	Control-Z	-
29	35	1D	GS	-	-
30	36	1E	RS	-	-
31	37	1F	US	-	-
32	40	20	Space	Spacebar	-
33	41	21	!	!	-
34	42	22	"	"	&quot;
35	43	23	#	#	-
36	44	24	$	$	-
37	45	25	%	%	-
38	46	26	&	&	&amp;
39	47	27	'	'	-
40	50	28	(	(	-
41	51	29	)	)	-
42	52	2A	★	★	-
43	53	2B	+	+	-
44	54	2C	'	'	-
45	55	2D	-	-	-
46	56	2E	.	.	-
47	57	2F	/	/	-
48	60	30	0	0	-
49	61	31	1	1	-
50	62	32	2	2	-
51	63	33	3	3	-
52	64	34	4	4	-
53	65	35	5	5	-
54	66	36	6	6	-
55	67	37	7	7	-
56	70	38	8	8	-
57	71	39	9	9	-
58	72	3A	:	:	-
59	73	3B	;	;	-
60	74	3C	<	<	&lt;

Decimal	Octal	Hexadecimal	Name	Keyboard	HTML/printf Equivalent
61	75	3D	=	=	-
62	76	3E	>	>	&gt;
63	77	3F	?	?	-
64	100	40	@	@	-
65	101	41	A	A	-
66	102	42	B	B	-
67	103	43	C	C	-
68	104	44	D	D	-
69	105	45	E	E	-
70	106	46	F	F	-
71	107	47	G	G	-
72	110	48	H	H	-
73	111	49	I	I	-
74	112	4A	J	J	-
75	113	4B	K	K	-
76	114	4C	L	L	-
77	115	4D	M	M	-
78	116	4E	N	N	-
79	117	4F	O	O	-
80	120	50	P	P	-
81	121	51	Q	Q	-
82	122	52	R	R	-
83	123	53	S	S	-
84	124	54	T	T	-
85	125	55	U	U	-
86	126	56	V	V	-
87	127	57	W	W	-
88	130	58	X	X	-
89	131	59	Y	Y	-
90	132	5A	Z	Z	-
91	133	5B	[	[	-
92	134	5C	\	\	-
93	135	5D	]	]	-
94	136	5E	^	^	-
95	137	5F	_	_	-
96	140	60	`	`	-
97	141	61	a	a	-

Decimal	Octal	Hexadecimal	Name	Keyboard	HTML/printf Equivalent
98	142	62	b	b	-
99	143	63	c	c	-
100	144	64	d	d	-
101	145	65	e	e	-
102	146	66	f	f	-
103	147	67	g	g	-
104	150	68	h	h	-
105	151	69	i	i	-
106	152	6A	j	j	-
107	153	6B	k	k	-
108	154	6C	l	l	-
109	155	6D	m	m	-
110	156	6E	n	n	-
111	157	6F	o	o	-
112	160	70	p	p	-
113	161	71	q	q	-
114	162	72	r	r	-
115	163	73	s	s	-
116	164	74	t	t	-
117	165	75	u	u	-
118	166	76	v	v	-
119	167	77	w	w	-
120	170	78	x	x	-
121	171	79	y	y	-
122	172	7A	z	z	-
123	173	7B	{	{	-
124	174	7C	|	|	-
125	175	7D	}	}	-
126	176	7E	~	~	-
127	177	7F	DEL	Delete	-

Glossary

Absolute paths are pathnames leading to a file from the root directory.

Aliases are the short forms for commands.

Arguments are additional information supplied to a command to change its behavior.

Arrays, in Bash programming, are variables containing open-ended lists of values.

Archiving is the storage of a number of files into a single file.

Attributes are variable options that can be turned on or off with the `declare` command.

Bindings are the association of particular keys to a Bash editing feature.

Blocking is the stopping of a script while it waits for more information to read on a pipe or socket, or while it waits for information to be read because the pipe or socket is full.

A **built-in** is a command that is a part of Bash and not a Linux command stored externally on a disk.

CGI stands for Common Gateway Interface, a method of running scripts from a Web server.

Command history is a list of the most recently typed commands.

Compression is a reduction of file size by encoding the file.

Conflicts are changes involving the same part of the script that CVS is unable to combine automatically.

Consoles are administration terminals attached to a system.

Constants are variables declared with the read-only attribute.

A **crontab** is a list of jobs for the cron command to execute.

The **current directory** is the default directory for a file, denoted by . in Linux.

CVS is the Concurrent Version System, a popular version control system.

Daemons are programs that run independently of a shell session, continually performing some task.

Dangling links are symbolic links that point to a deleted file.

Distributions are complete Linux systems, usually assembled on CD-ROMs or DVD-ROMs.

efs2 is the second extended file system, the standard Linux disk storage standard.

efs3 is the third extended file system, a variation that uses a technique called "journaling" to prevent data loss due to an equipment failure.

emacs mode involves command editing in an interactive session using keys similar to the emacs editor.

Environment is a Linux term for the collection of variables and open files exported from one program to another.

Environment variables are the variables Linux shares between programs via its environment.

The **epoch** is the start of the Linux calendar, January 1, 1970.

Expansion is the replacement of variables and expressions embedded in an executable line.

Exporting variables is the process of providing the variables to programs run from the script.

Expressions are formulas that calculate values.

FIFOs (First-In, First-Out) are named pipes.

Filename completion is when Bash, in an interactive session, searches for a suitable filename matching specified characters.

Filters are commands that take the results of one command and modify them in some way in order to supply them to another command or file.

Flags are string variables that indicate a given condition if the value is not an empty string.

Globbing is pattern matching by the shell's wildcard filename matching conventions.

Hard links are links that act identically to the files they represent.

Here files are the lines of data associated with the << redirection operator.

A home directory is the directory a user is given when he or she logs in, specified with ~ in Bash.

Hostnames are computer names used to reference specific machines on a network.

Indexes are the positions of items in an array.

Inode density represents the number of inodes per storage capacity.

Inodes are the unique identification numbers for Linux files.

Job control is the capability to manage background tasks using built-in shell commands.

Jobs are background tasks started from the shell.

Keywords are words or symbols with special meaning to Bash.

Links are shortcuts referring to a file.

Lock files are files that indicate a certain condition, typically that a resource or another file is in use.

Named pipes are special files that can be read by one script while being written to by another.

Open source refers to software that is released with the source code to the general public so that programmers can rebuild or alter the software to suit their needs.

A parameter is a switch or an argument.

The **parent directory** is a directory immediately containing the current directory, specified by .. in Linux.

Patch files contain lists of changes to upgrade one set of files to another set.

Pathnames (or **paths**) are strings that describe the location of a file.

Permissions are the access rights to a file.

PIDs are process identification numbers.

Pipe files are named pipes.

A **pipeline** is a series of commands joined by the pipe symbol (|).

Polling is the act of continually checking to see whether a daemon has new work to do.

Process substitution is the redirection of the input or output of a command through a temporary pipe file to be read or written by another command.

Regular files contain data that can be read or instructions that can be executed, as opposed to files such as directories or pipes.

Relative paths are pathnames leading to a file from the current directory.

A **repository** is the database maintained by a version control system where all master copies are kept.

The **root directory** is the top-most directory in the directory hierarchy, the / directory.

Sanity checks are tests at the beginning of a script that verify the existence of files and variables.

A **shar file** is a shell archive created by the shar command.

A **shell** is a program that runs operating system commands.

Shell archives are collections of text files or scripts encoded as single shell scripts.

A **shell option** is a flag that enables or disables a particular Bash feature.

Sparse files are files that contain a large amount of zeros that, under efs2, don't consume any disk space.

Standard error is the default file to which error messages are written. The symbol is &2 and the path is /dev/stderr.

Standard input is the default file from which input is read for commands. The symbol is &0 and the path is /dev/stdin.

Standard output is the default file to which output is written. The symbol is &1 and the path is /dev/stdout.

Status codes are numbers between 0 and 255 that indicate what problems occurred when the previous command was executed.

Switches (also called "options" or "flags") are characters proceeded by a minus sign that enable command features.

Symbolic links are links that are sometimes treated as different files than the ones they represent.

Text streams are text files in a shell pipeline.

TCP/IP stands for Transport Control Protocol/Internet Protocol, the communications standard of the Internet.

Traps are signal handlers.

UDP stands for User Datagram Protocol.

Utilities are commands that provide a general-purpose function useful in many applications, such as returning the date or counting the number of lines in a file.

Version control systems are programs that maintain a master copy of data files, scripts, and source programs to track changes and share scripts among several programmers.

vi mode is command editing in an interactive way using keys similar to the vi editor.

Word designators are the ! history recall command's syntax for selecting or modifying specific line items.

Word splitting is the act of Bash dividing up the parameters of a command into individual words.

Words consist of a shell command and each of its parameters after quotation marks and backslashes are interpreted.

Index

B

C

H

I

How can we make this index more useful? Email us at indexes@samspublishing.com

O

Q - R

via . (source) command, 251

via exec command, 252-253

via Linux, 249-250

runtime error checking, 54-55

S

-s (all) switches, help command, 31

-s (--only-delimited) switches, cut command, 192

-s (--serial) switches, paste command, 194

-s (set) switches, shopt command, 64

-s (--silent) switches, csplit command, 181

-s (--spaces) switches, fold command, 195

-s (--squeeze-repeats) switches, tr command, 218

-s (stopped) switches, jobs command, 159

-s (substitute) switches, fc command, 327

-s (symbolic-link) switches, cp command, 34

-s switches

bind command, 42

columns command, 194

enable command, 63

history command, 21

wipe command, 278

-S switches

compgen command, 323

umask command, 273

sanity checks (scripts), 54-55, 90-91

saving

command histories, 20-21

file descriptors, 188

scancode mode (console input modes), 234

--scancodes switches, showkey command, 235

script fragments, parameters, 252

script shells, restricted, 277

scripts

~/.bashrc (Bash resources), 44

aliases, turning on/off, 36

CGI, 284

displaying form variables, 290-293

error messages, 285-287

form input tags, 289

cleanup sections, 55-57

comments, 52

console, 233

console input modes, switching between, 235

continually executing, writing, 256-259

daemon, 256-259

debugging

-n (no execution) switches, 125

-o errexit option, 125, 143

-o nounset option, 126, 143

-o xtrace option, 126-127, 143

debug traps, 128

design principles, 52

exit handlers, 163

global declarations, 54

headers, 53

hello.sh, 51

here files, 60

keyboard input, reading, 57-58

mixer.bash example, 109-112

parameters, 148-154

peek shell script example, 337-354

positional parameters, 145-148

profile files, 44

recurring, writing, 254-256

redirections, 58-59

combining, 61

standard errors, 61

standard input, 61

standard outputs, 60

report.bash report formatter example script, 122-124

repositories, deleting from, 132

resource limits, 275-276

running, 52

. (source) command, 251

cron programs, 253-256

exec command, 252-253

in C programs, 330

Linux, 249-250

superuser logins, 270

runtime error checking, 54-55

sanity checks, 54-55, 90-91

shell functions, 260-261

signals, 159

How can we make this index more useful? Email us at indexes@samspublishing.com

V